100 TUESDAY TIPS

by GRIZ and NORM

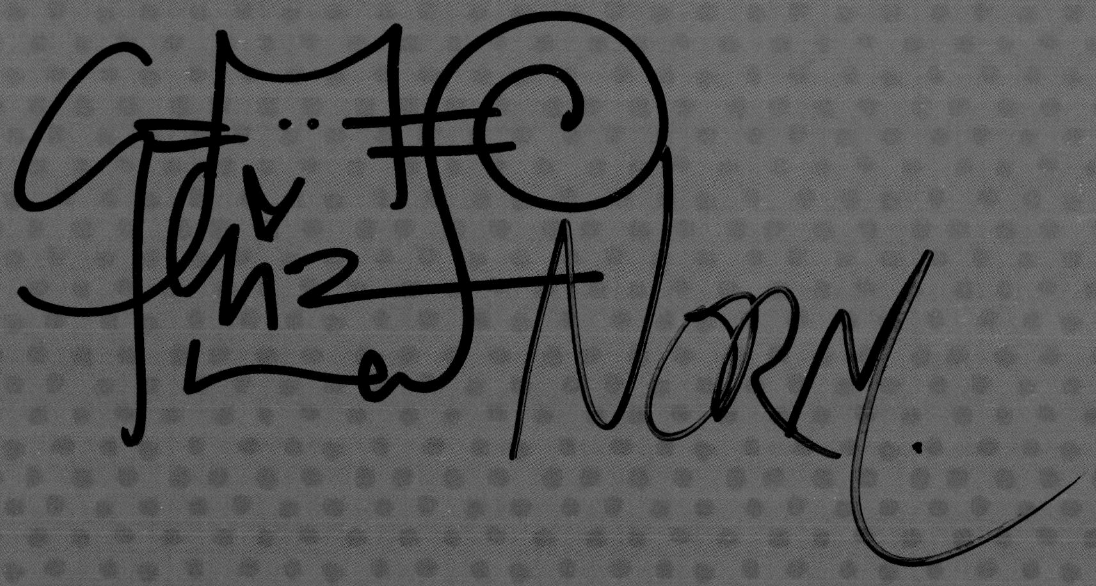

ISBN-13 : 978-0-9908750-0-0

www.GRIZandNORM.com

This book is dedicated to
Teachers and Students

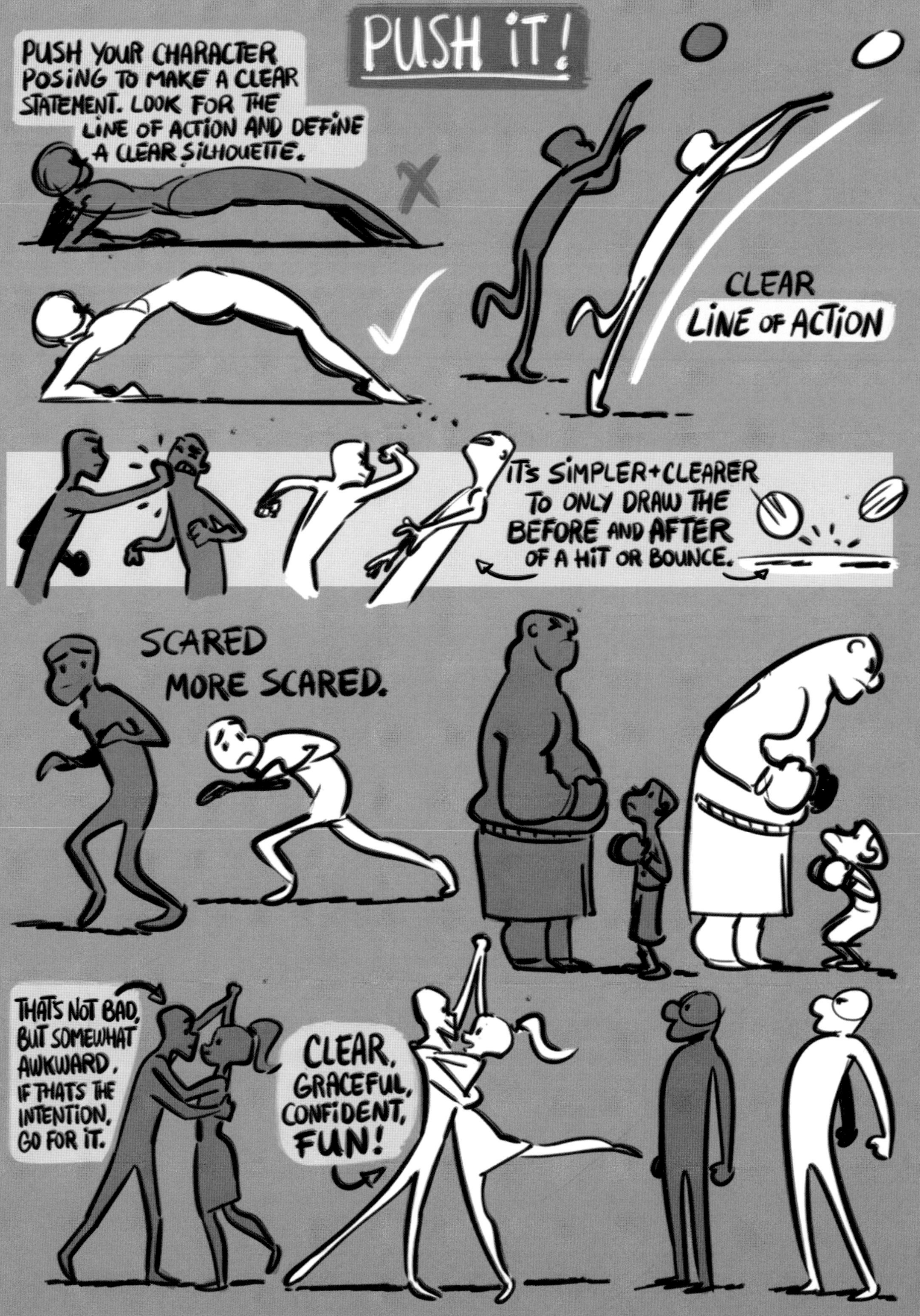
PUSH IT!
PUSH YOUR CHARACTER POSING TO MAKE A CLEAR STATEMENT. LOOK FOR THE LINE OF ACTION AND DEFINE A CLEAR SILHOUETTE.
CLEAR LINE OF ACTION
IT'S SIMPLER+CLEARER TO ONLY DRAW THE BEFORE AND AFTER OF A HIT OR BOUNCE.
SCARED
MORE SCARED.
THAT'S NOT BAD, BUT SOMEWHAT AWKWARD, IF THATS THE INTENTION, GO FOR IT.
CLEAR, GRACEFUL, CONFIDENT, FUN!

THE 3 STEPS

THE MOST ABBREVIATED OVERVIEW OF MY CHARACTER DRAWING/POSING PROCESS.

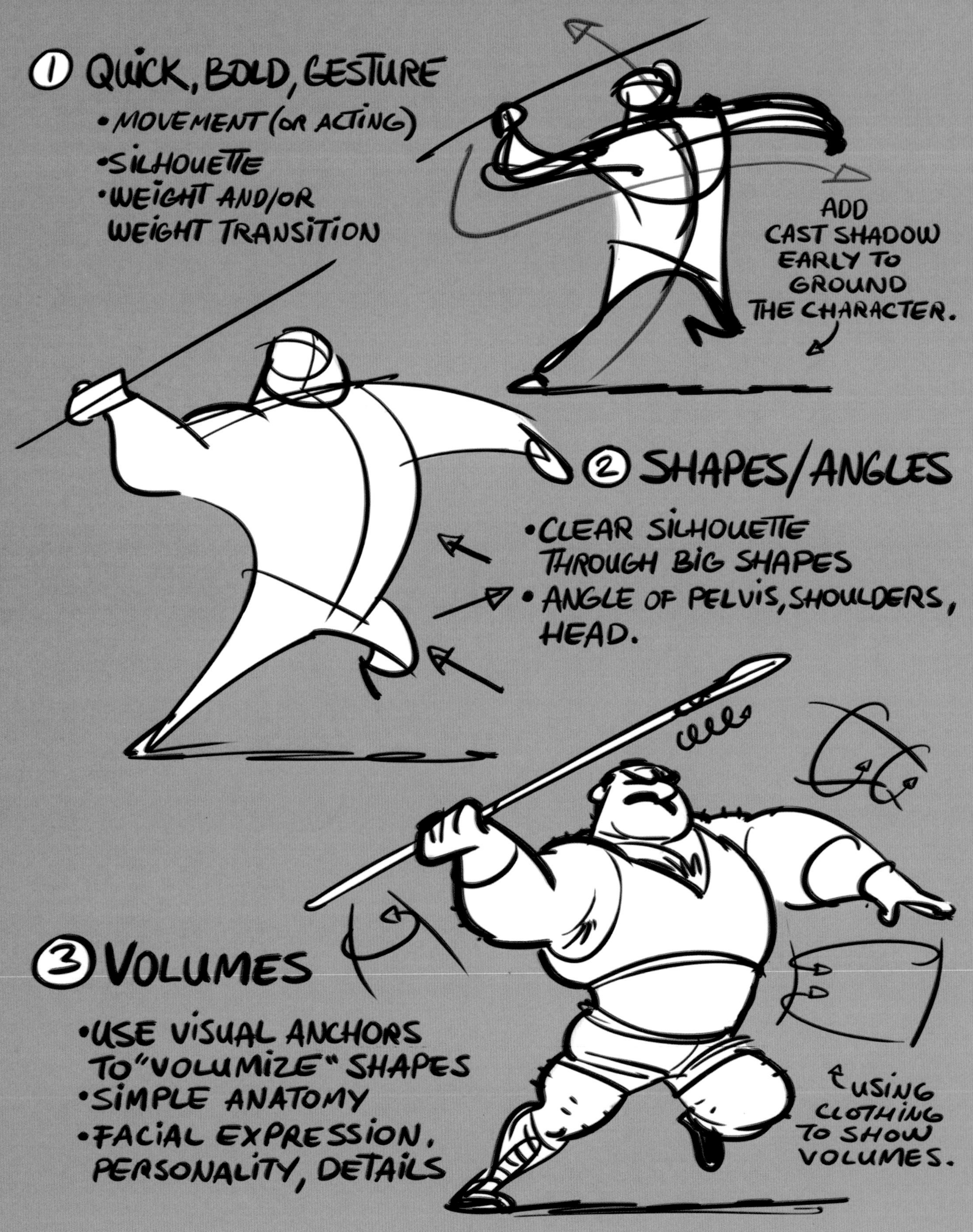

SIMPLE VOLUMES

THE IDEA:
SUGGEST VOLUME AND PERSPECTIVE THROUGH RECEDING CURVED LINES.

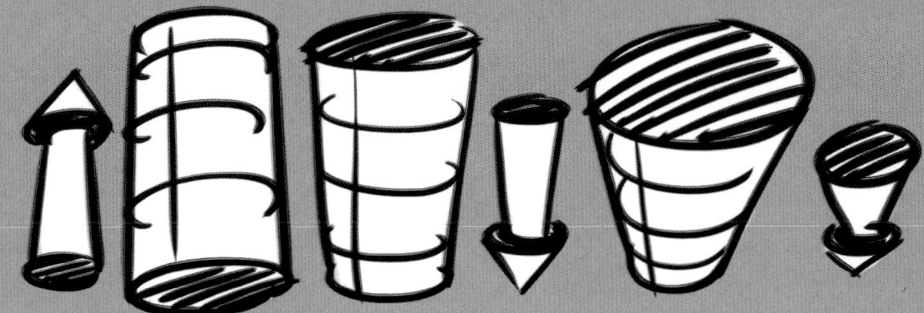

SHOW COMPRESSION

THE CHALLENGE IS APPLYING THE IDEA ON ORGANIC SHAPES OF THE BODY.

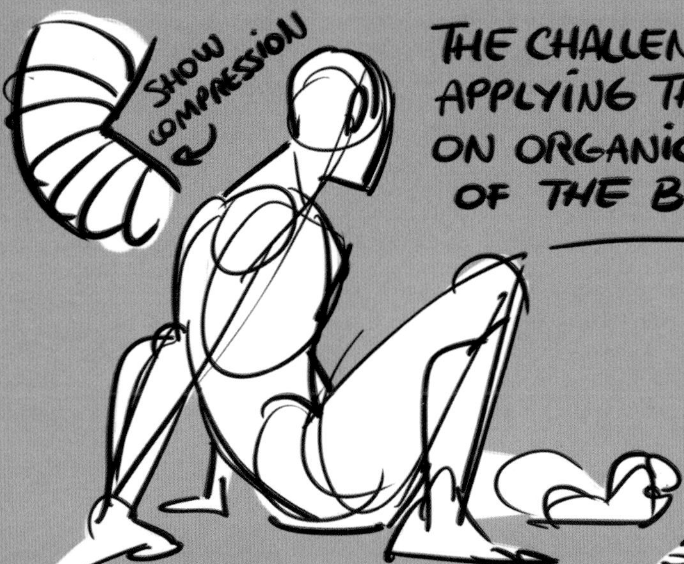

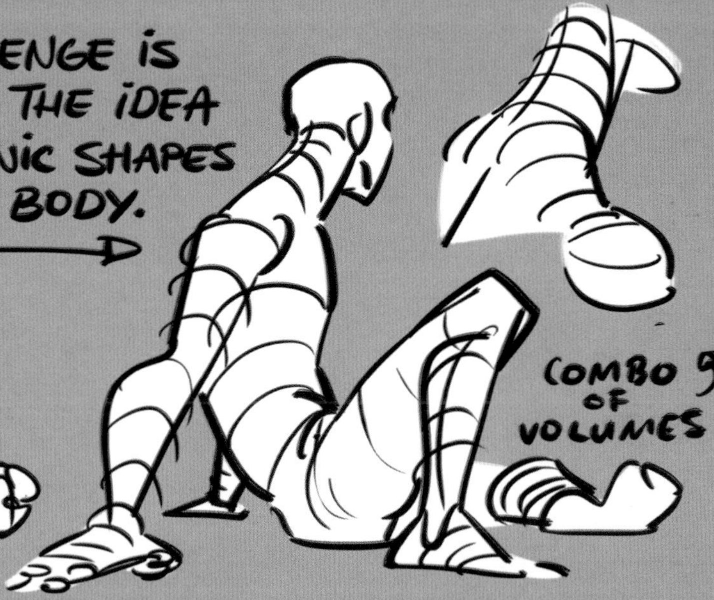

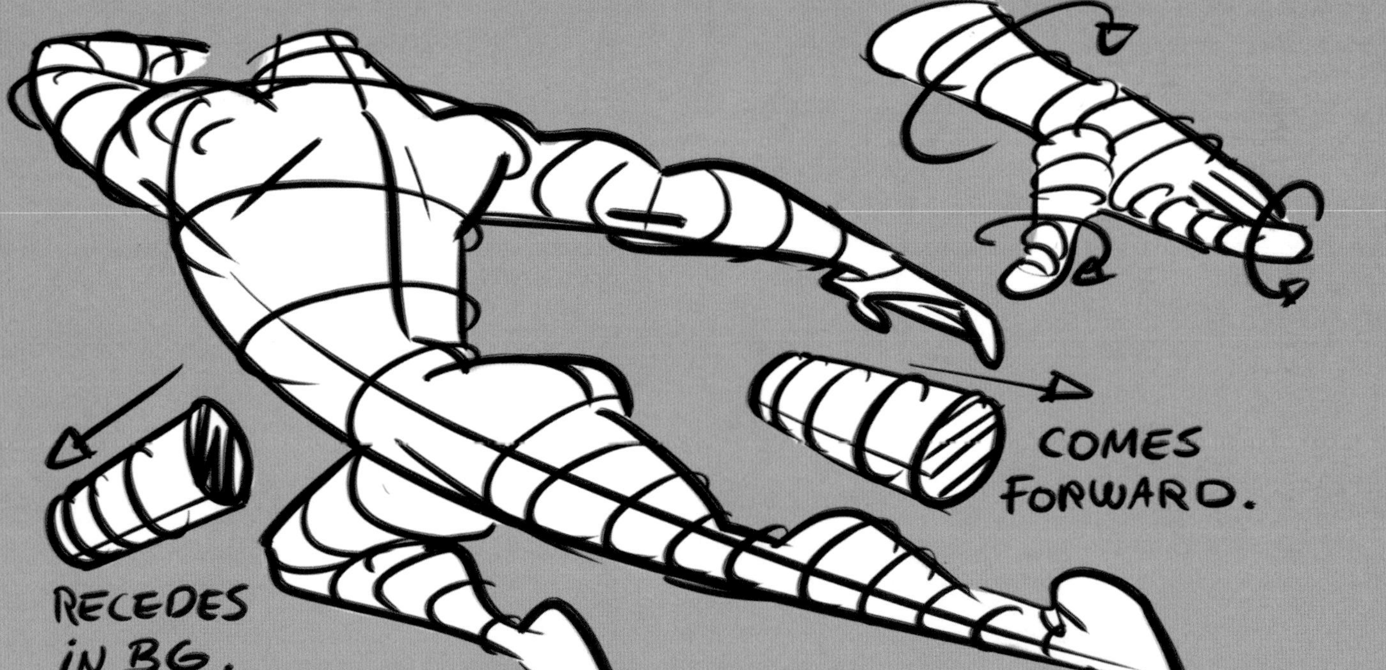

COMBO OF VOLUMES

COMES FORWARD.

RECEDES IN BG.

THE NEXT STEP IS TO SUGGEST VOLUMES BY RELYING ON VISIBLE ITEMS INSTEAD. (SEE VISUAL ANCHORS.)

90 - 10 Rule

The 90-10 Rule is also known as the 'Rule of Contrast'.

- ⊛ Your eyes will always go to the area of highest contrast / difference.
- ⊛ Meaning 90 % of something & 10% of the opposite.

There are 3 different kinds of contrast :

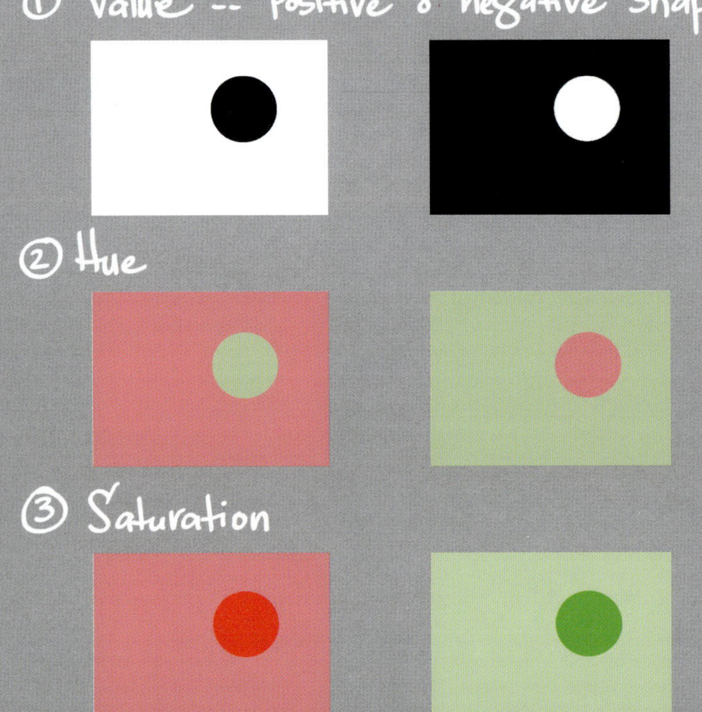

[TIPS] = Put the 10 % on the most important part of your piece.

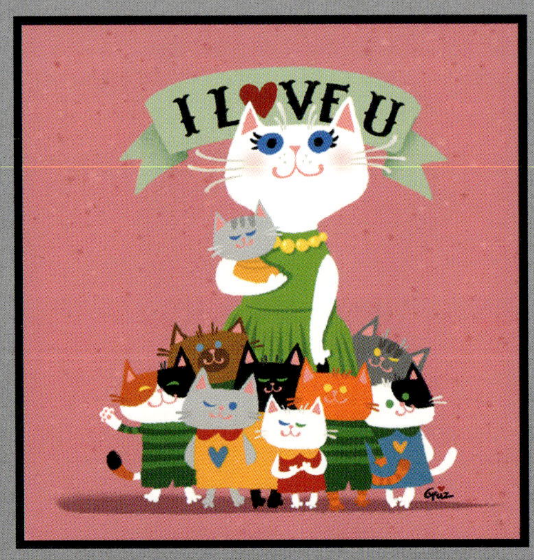

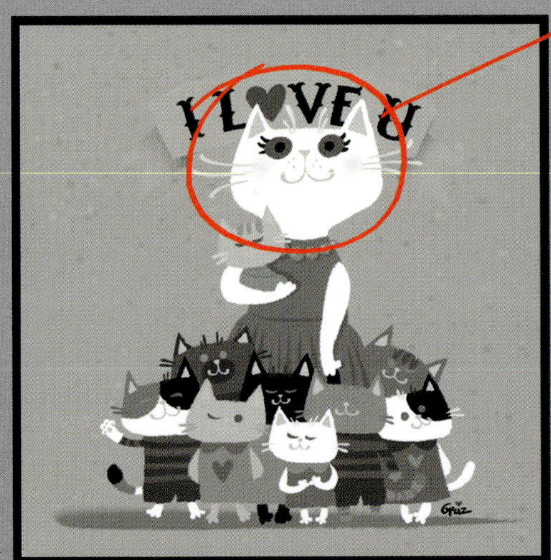

highest contrast

70-20-10 Rule

This is basically the rule of contrast with an accent ⇒ 90 + 10

70 + 20

70% of one general color ; 20% of a different color & 10% accent

⊛ You can also break each section of your composition to have its own 70-20-10

example :

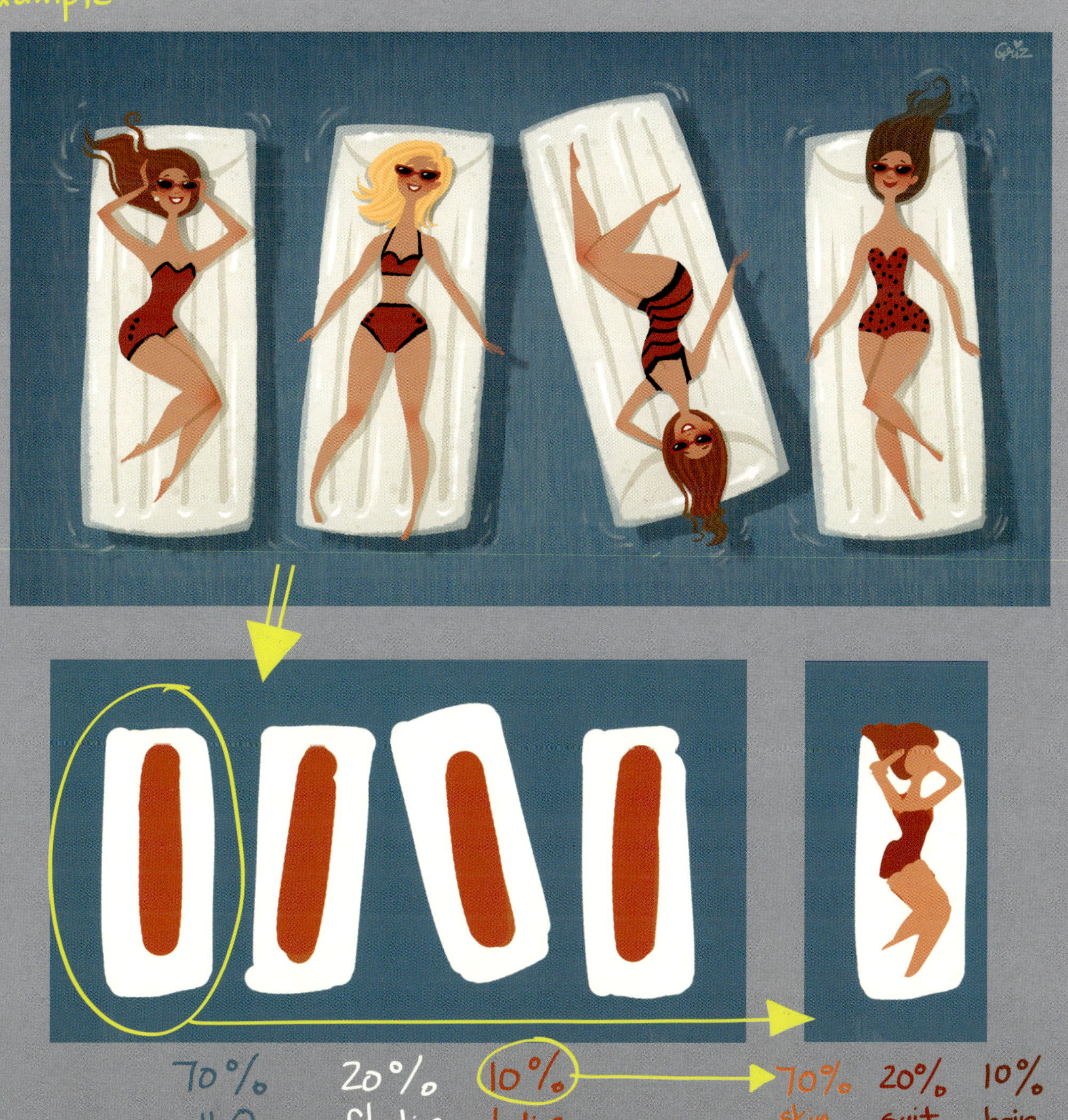

LINE OF ACTION (LOA)

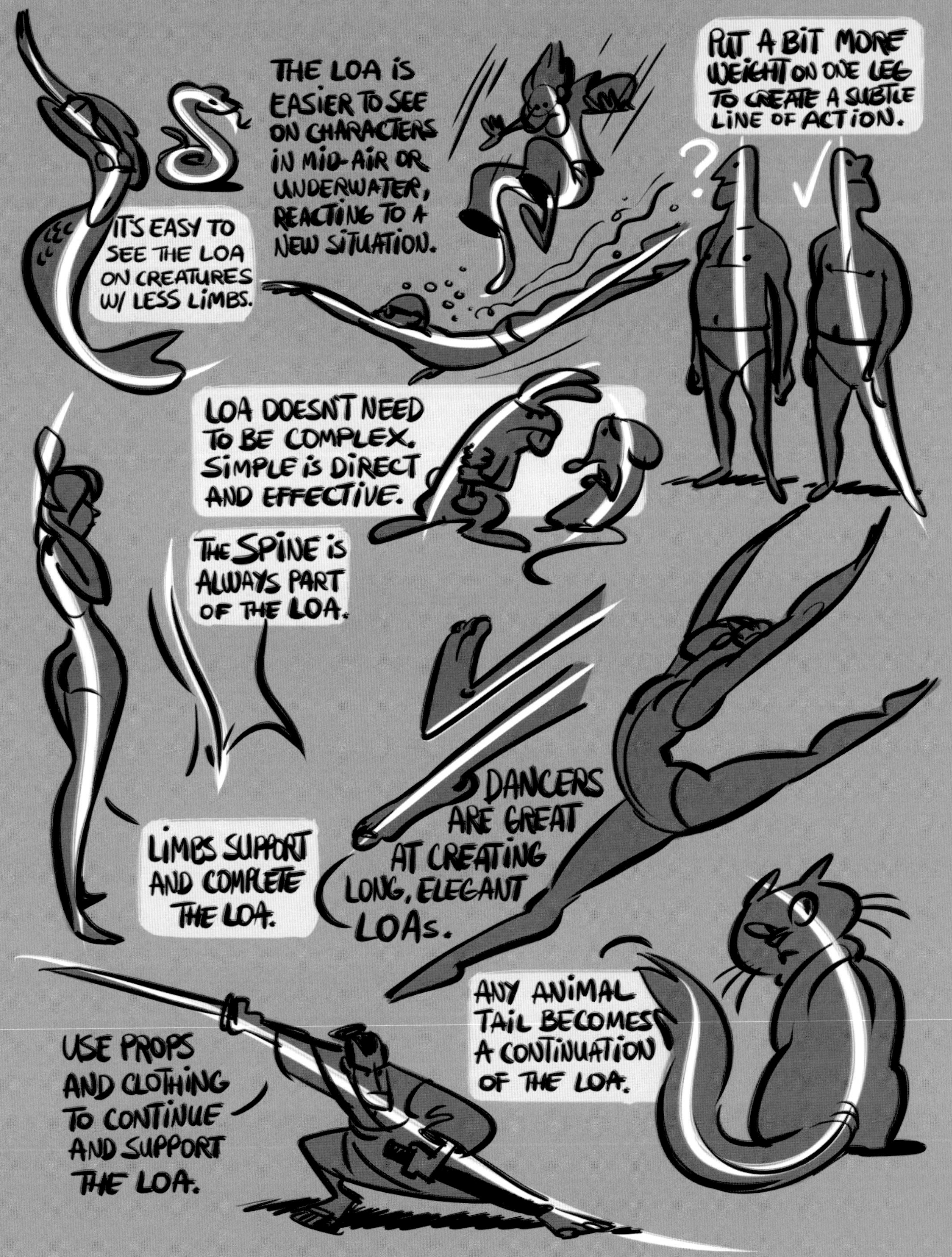

CLEAR SILHOUETTE

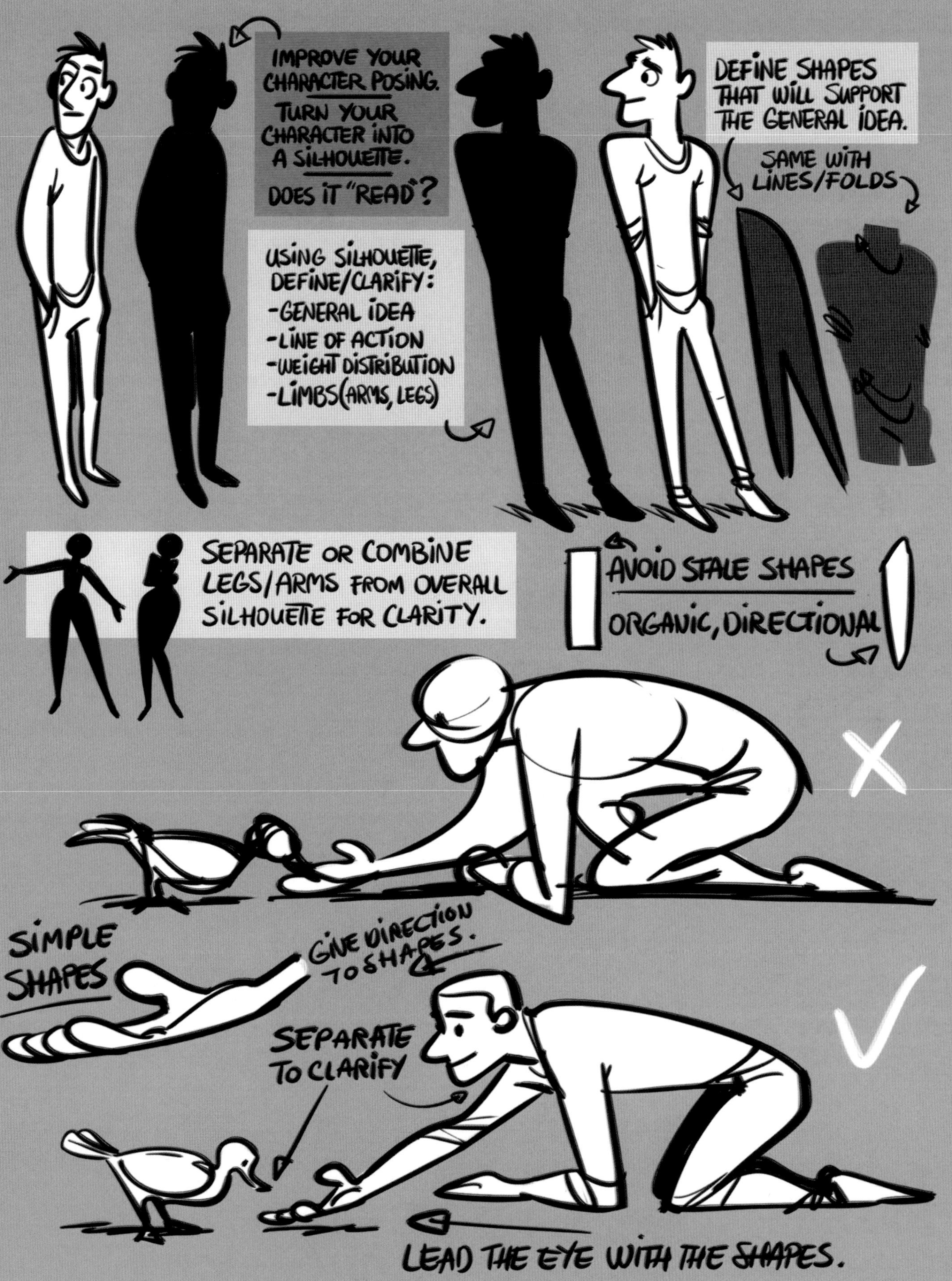

Color Palette: Split Complementary

Complementary colors are colors that are opposite of each other.

① Direct complementary -- directly the opposite

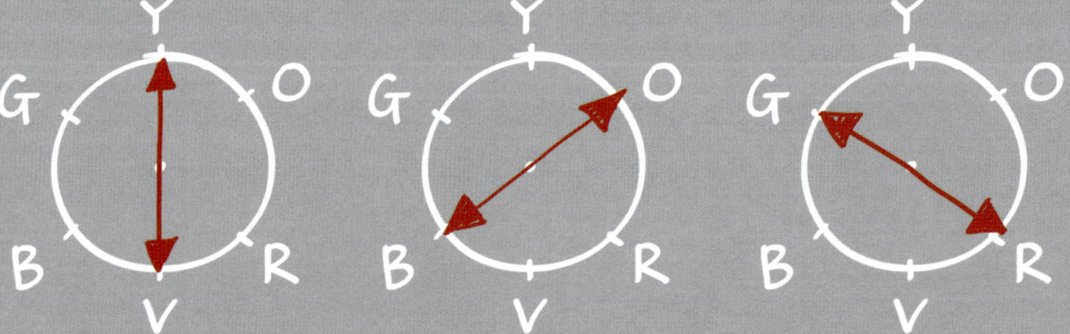

② Split complementary -- the opposite color is split

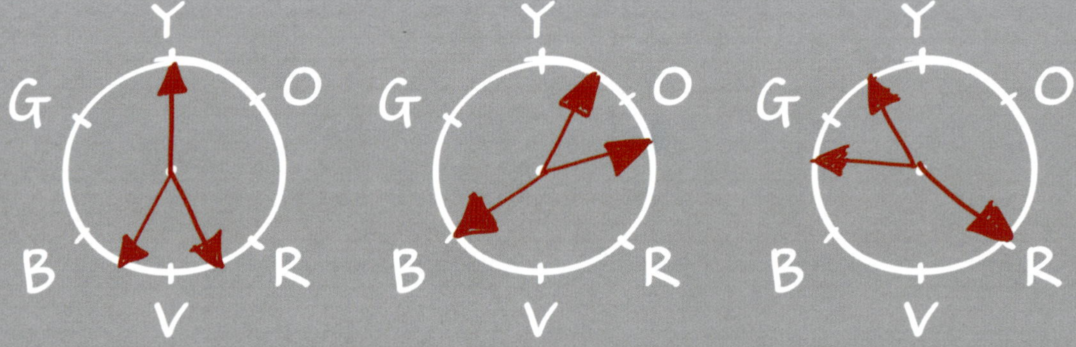

⊛ Split Complementary is my favorite color theme. I like to shift the wheel a bit to find my color.

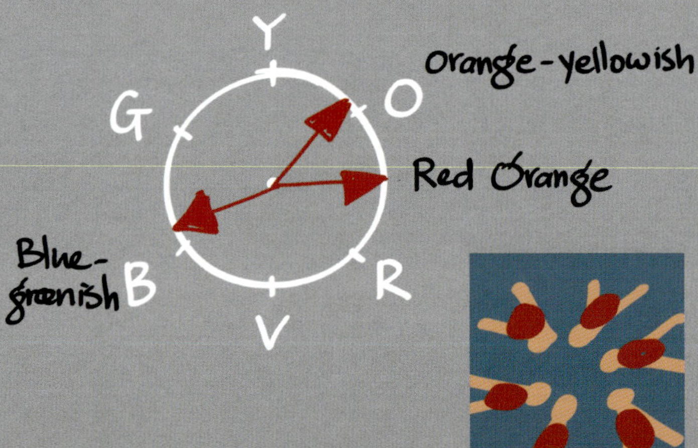

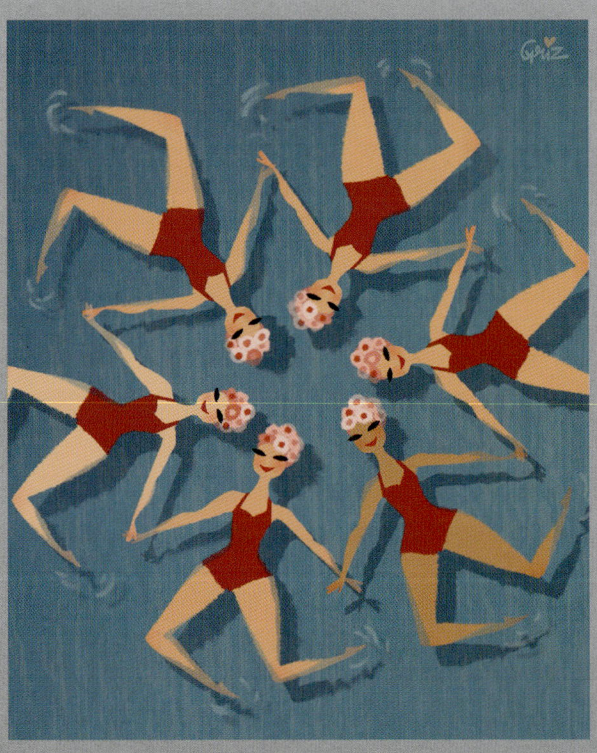

Creating Easy Color Palette

① Find an image

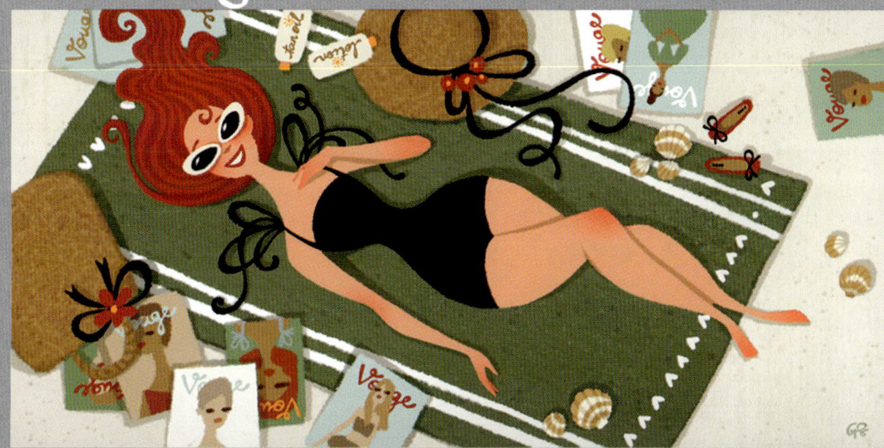

② Filter → Pixelate → Mosaic

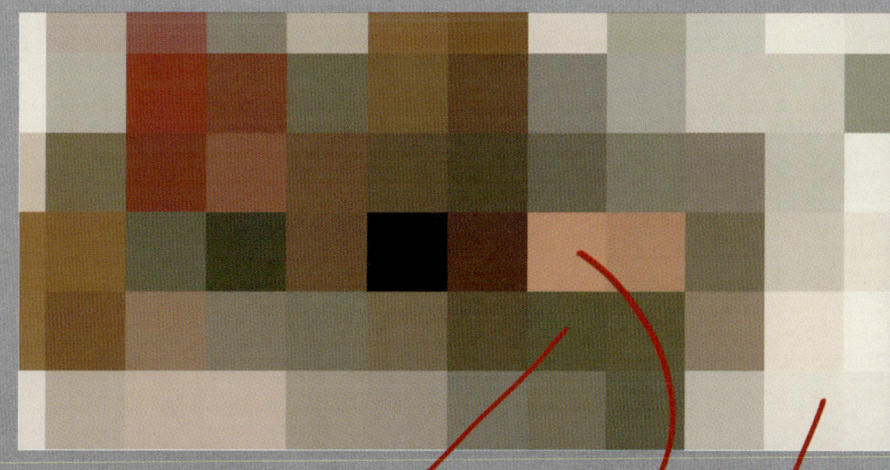

③ Color Pick a general color

④ Increase the saturation of the color so it's closer to the original painting. If you don't do this step, your painting will be desaturated.

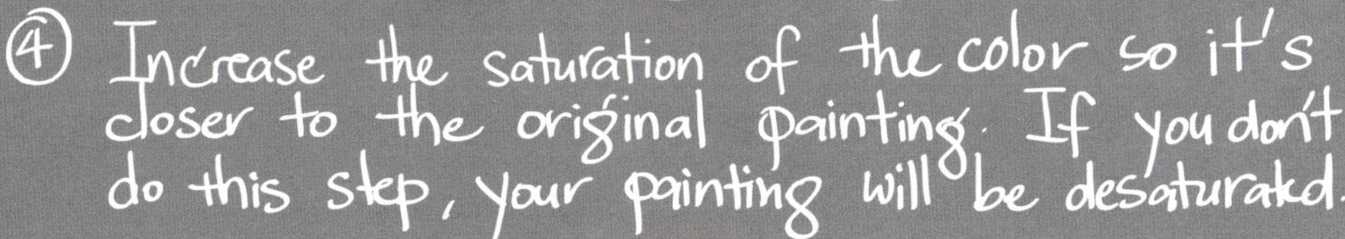

STRAIGHT AGAINST CURVES

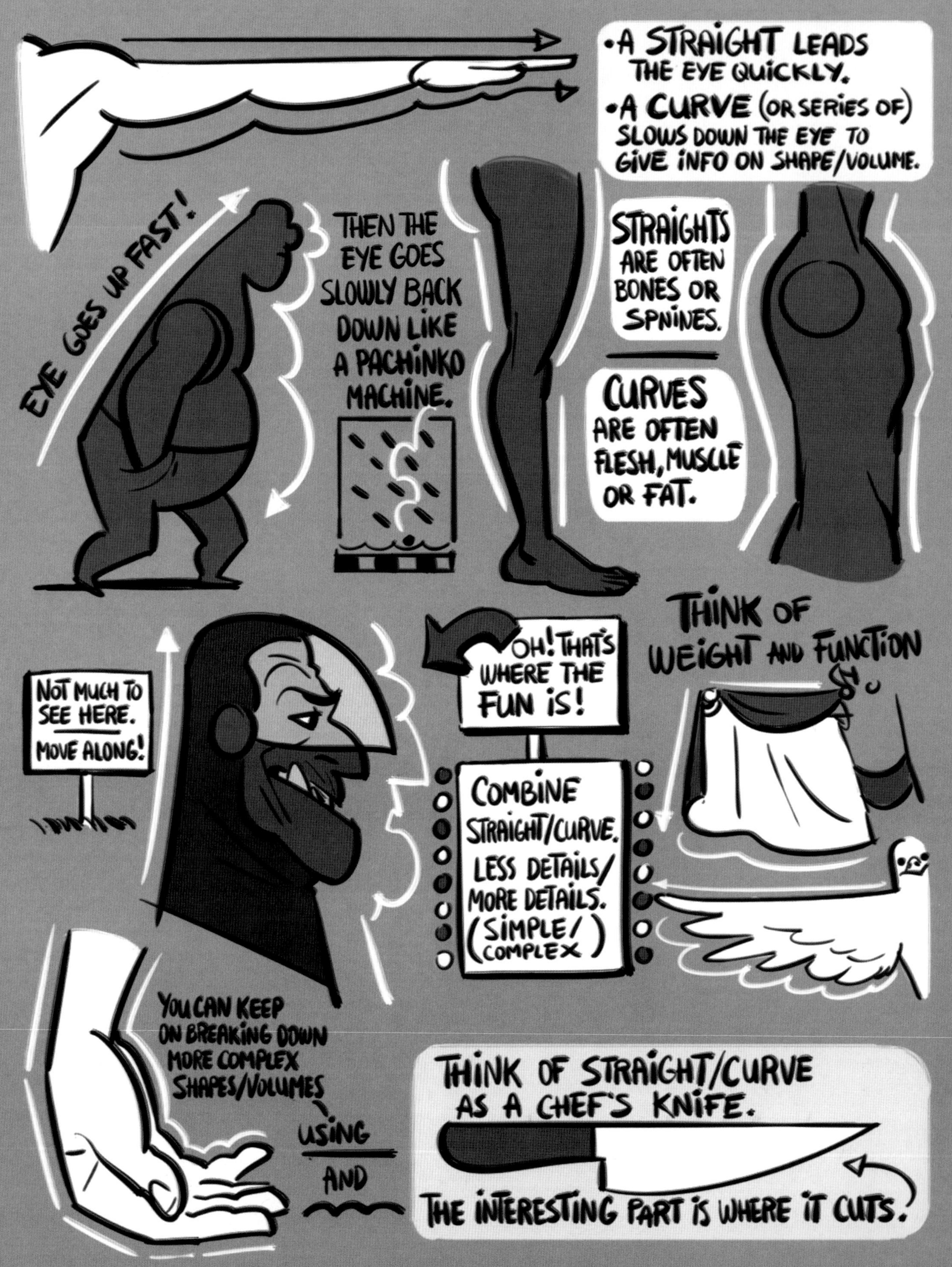

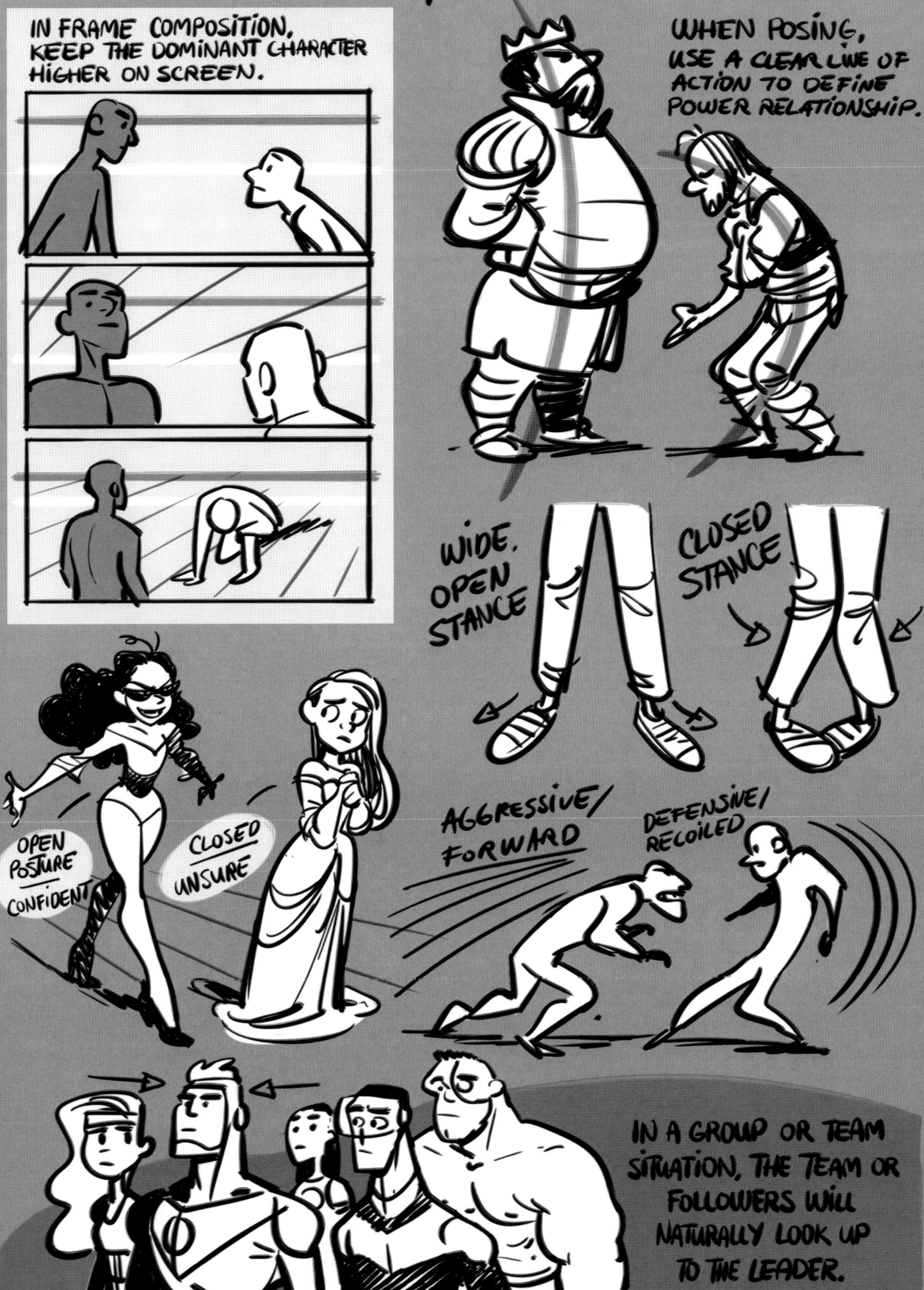
POWER/DOMINANCE
IN FRAME COMPOSITION, KEEP THE DOMINANT CHARACTER HIGHER ON SCREEN.
WHEN POSING, USE A CLEAR LINE OF ACTION TO DEFINE POWER RELATIONSHIP.
WIDE, OPEN STANCE
CLOSED STANCE
OPEN POSTURE
CONFIDENT
CLOSED
UNSURE
AGGRESSIVE/ FORWARD
DEFENSIVE/ RECOILED
IN A GROUP OR TEAM SITUATION, THE TEAM OR FOLLOWERS WILL NATURALLY LOOK UP TO THE LEADER.

COLOR 101

① Basic Hue
PRIMARY
SECONDARY
TERTIARY
② Color is relative -- the temperature of warm or cool color depends on what you put next to it.
Same RED can be warm or cool.
example :
WARM Red
COOL Red
WARM Red
COOL Red
③ Basic color theme
ⓐ Triadic
Y
B
R
example using Red
ⓑ Monochromatic / Analogous
ⓒ Complementary
+ SPLIT Complementary

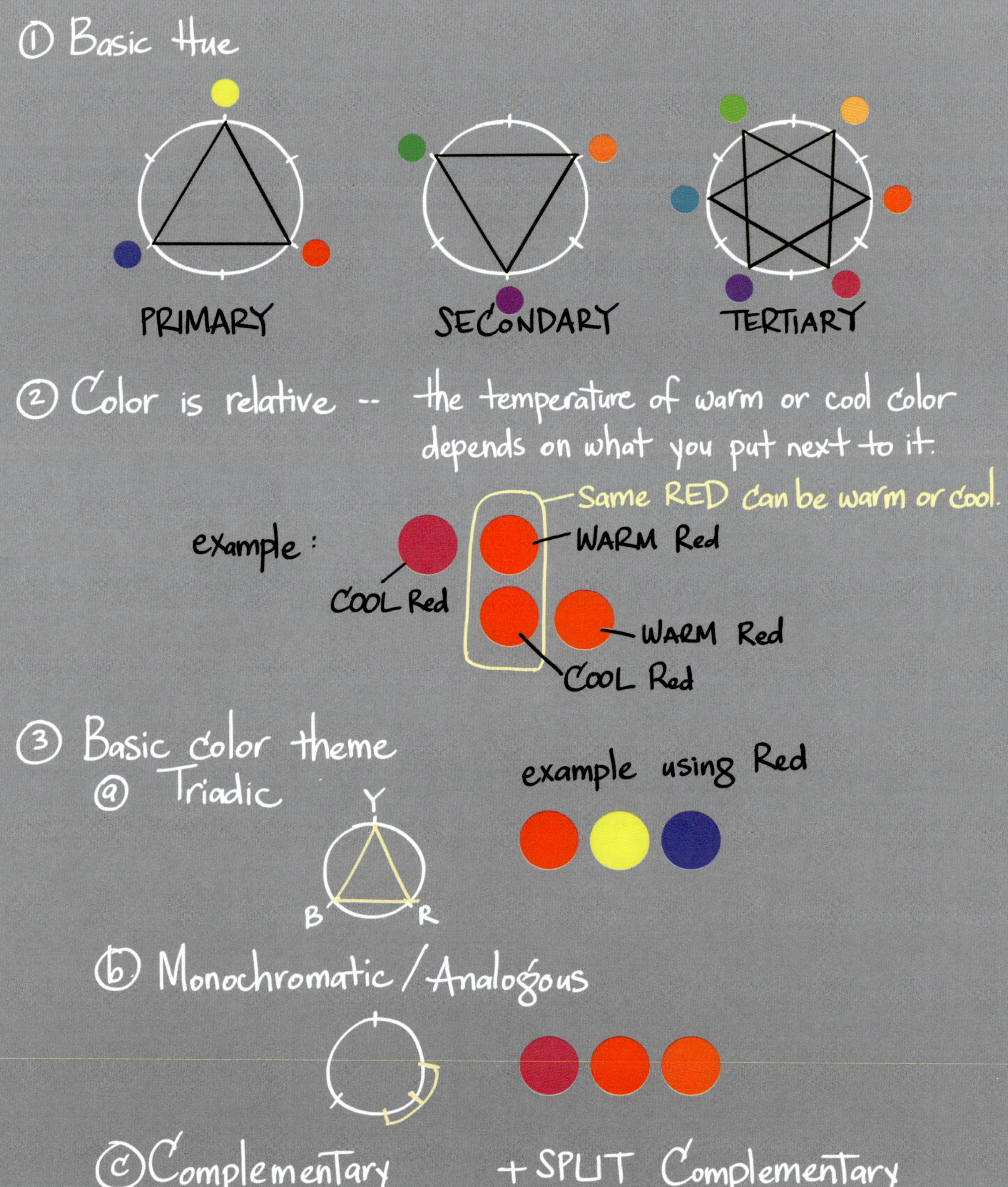

USE an ANCHOR COLOR

→ Pick one color to use as an anchor & apply basic COLOR THEORY to create a simple color palette.

ex: Boysenberry pie.

*. The pie filling color will be the anchor color which is a COOL RED or WARM VIOLET

*. The crust will be golden orange (WARM ORANGE)

⊛ Knowing these two basic color ideas, there's some basic possibilities

R O Y G B V

⊛ TRIAD → COOL RED, COOL YELLOW, COOL BLUE
→ WARM VIOLET, WARM ORANGE, WARM GREEN

⊛ COMPLEMENTARY → COOL RED, COOL GREEN
→ WARM VIOLET, WARM YELLOW

⊛ The 2nd TRIAD contains 2 of the basic color of the pie, therfore this will be good one to use, all we need is to add green.

⊛ Then add darker & lighter version of each color.

← warmer & lighter

← cooler & darker

⊛ Do combination

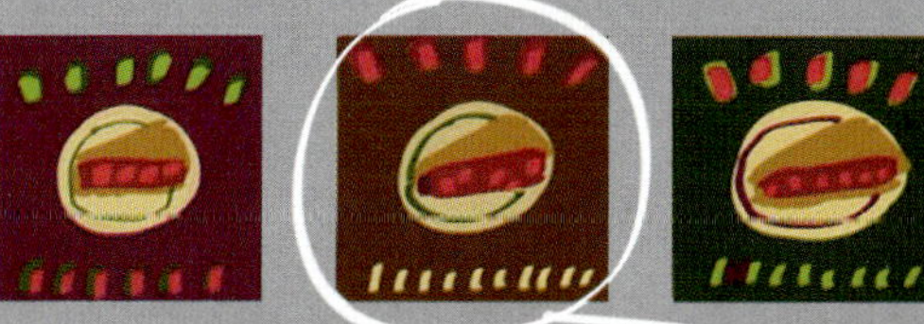

⊛ Pick one & elaborate more

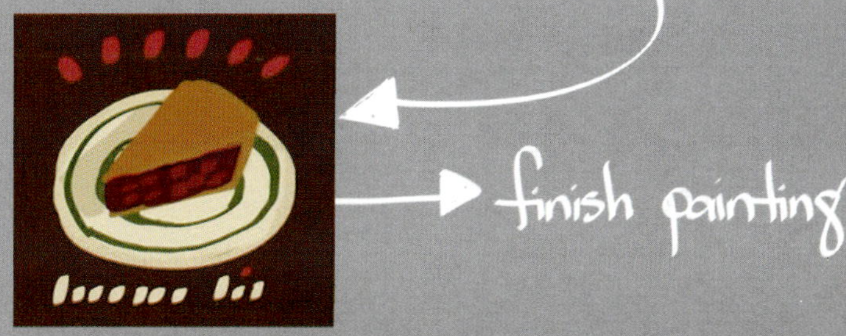

→ finish painting

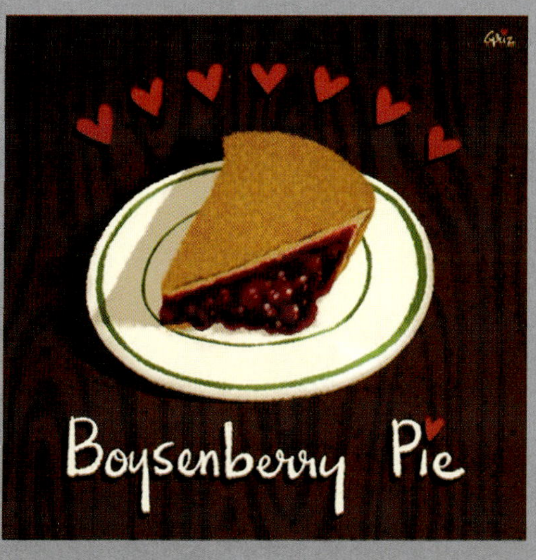

HANDS

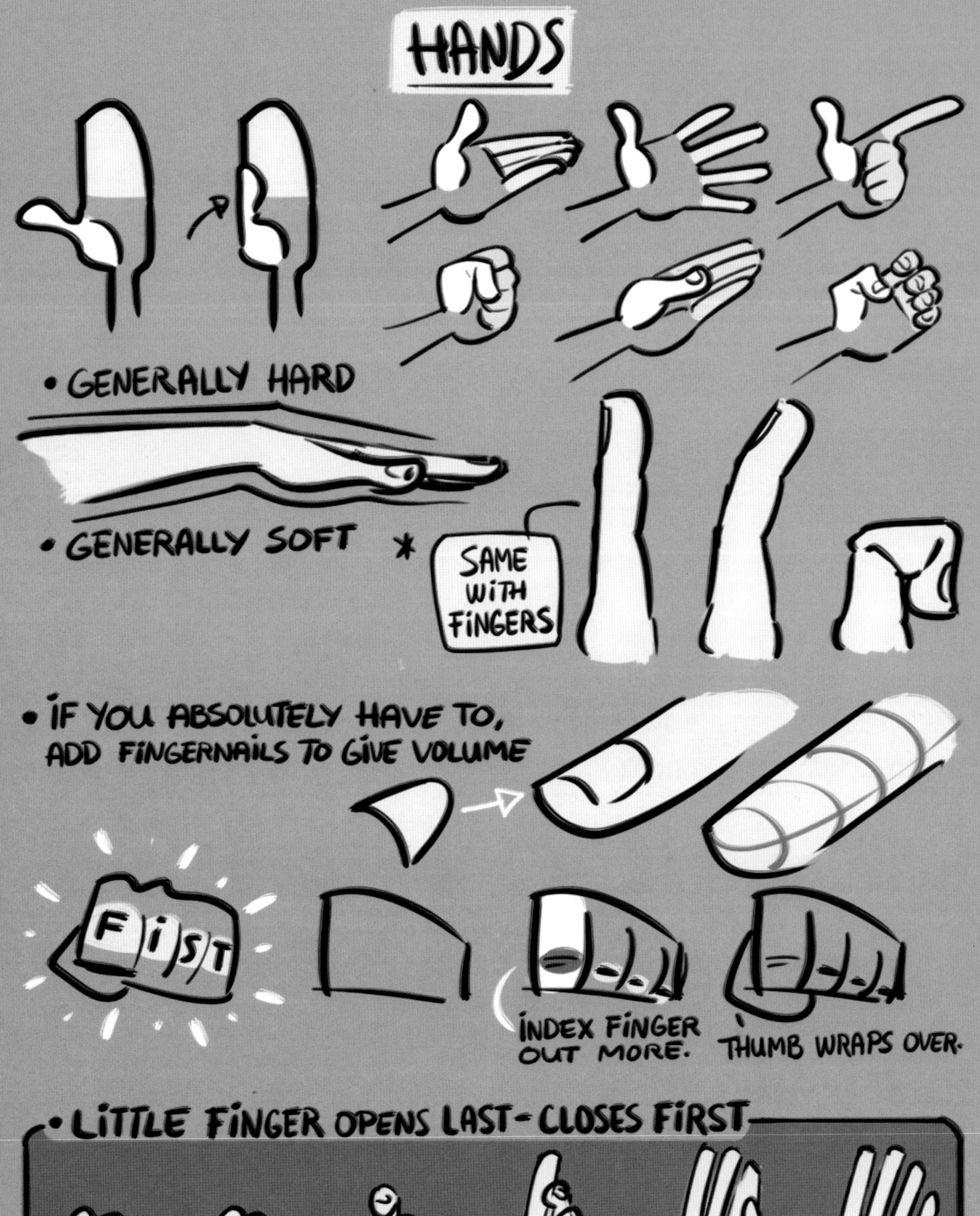

• LITTLE FINGER OPENS LAST - CLOSES FIRST

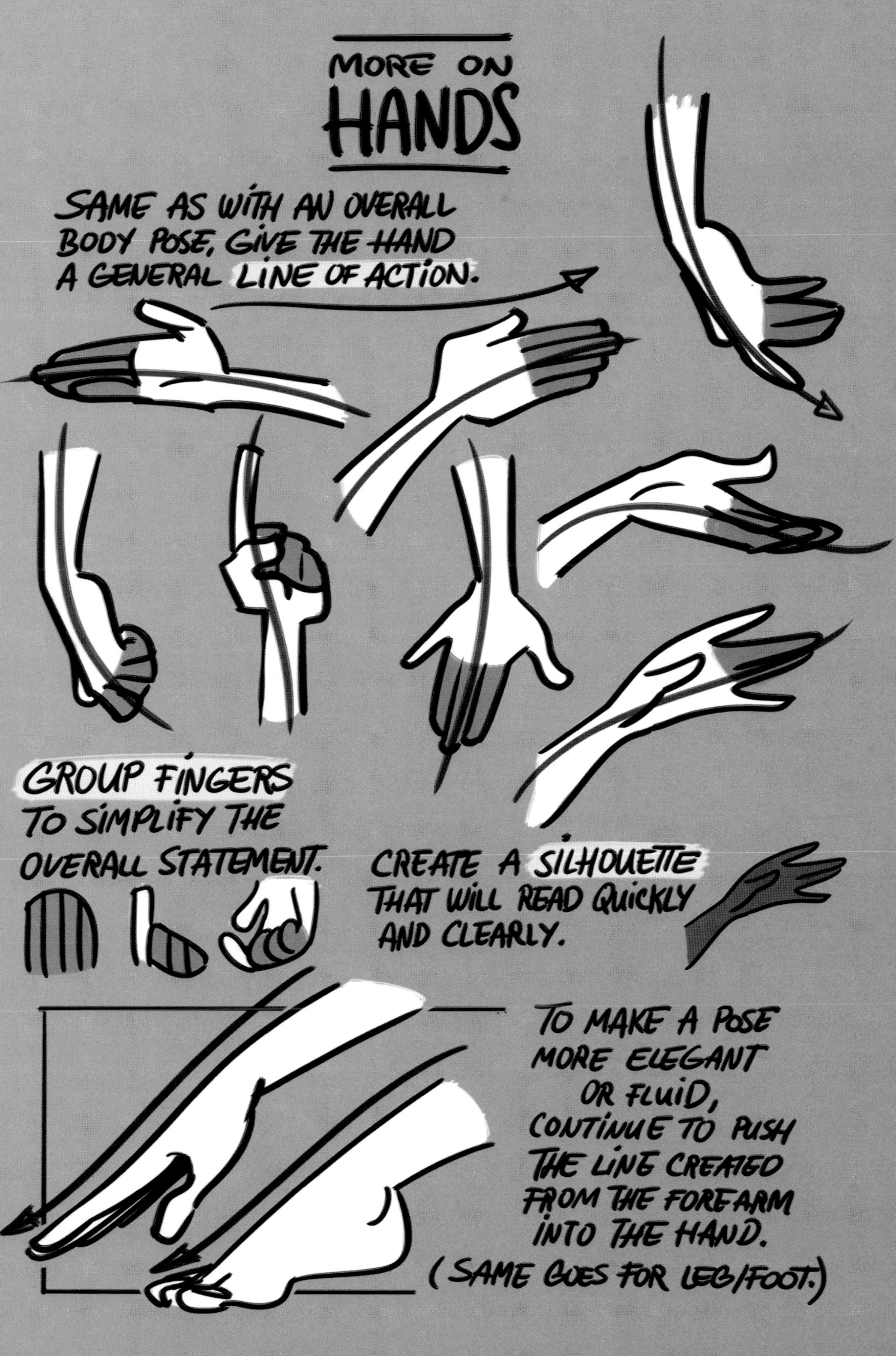

MORE ON
HANDS
SAME AS WITH AN OVERALL BODY POSE, GIVE THE HAND A GENERAL LINE OF ACTION.
GROUP FINGERS TO SIMPLIFY THE OVERALL STATEMENT.
CREATE A SILHOUETTE THAT WILL READ QUICKLY AND CLEARLY.
TO MAKE A POSE MORE ELEGANT OR FLUID, CONTINUE TO PUSH THE LINE CREATED FROM THE FOREARM INTO THE HAND.
(SAME GOES FOR LEG/FOOT.)

RED &/vs. GREEN

- A very popular Western Christmas color scheme

holly berries red   christmas pine tree green

- Fun fact: TRUE RED & TRUE GREEN at 100% intensity / saturation; both have 50% value ⟹ this complementary color scheme will HURT YOUR EYES the MOST !!!

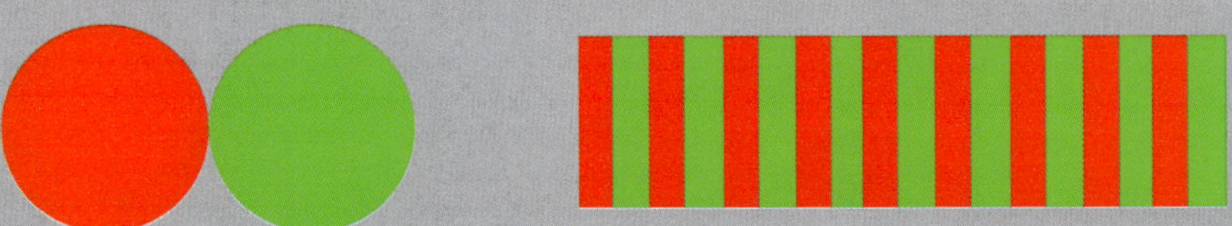

- Making RED & GREEN works:
Pick a star color & make the other one to support it by changing the value & saturation of the supporting color

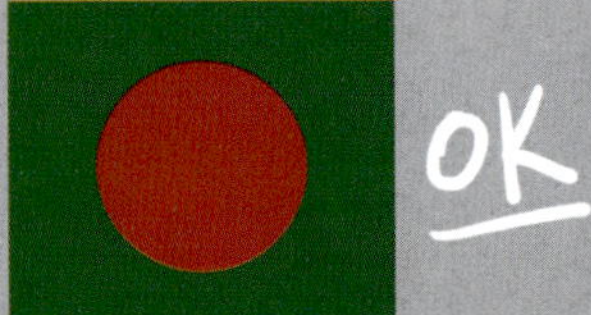

OK

the value difference helps, but both at 100% intensity, it still hurts your eyes

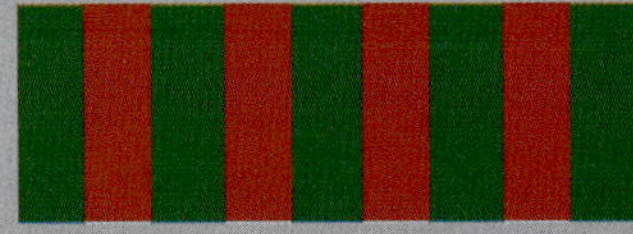

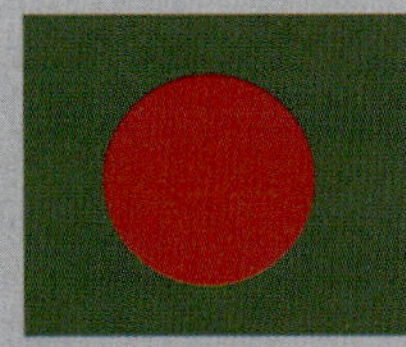

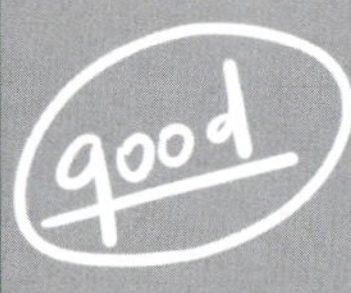

desaturing the green, help to make the RED seems more intense & doesn't hurt your eyes.

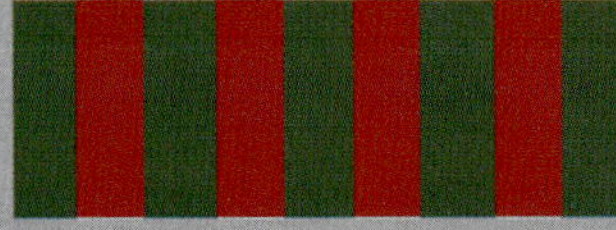

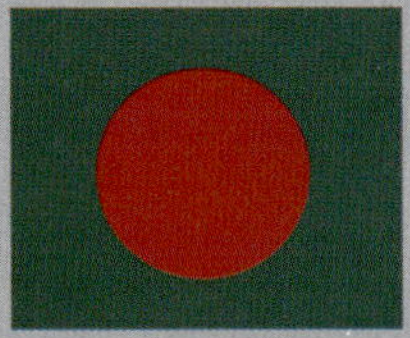

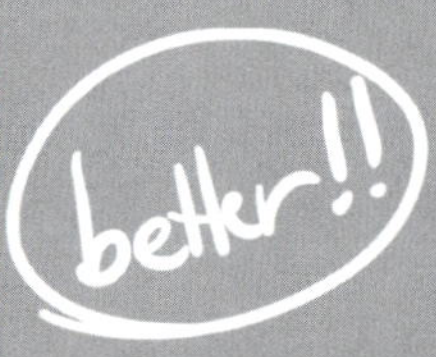

adding cool to the green, will make the RED more intense & warmer & easier on your eyes.

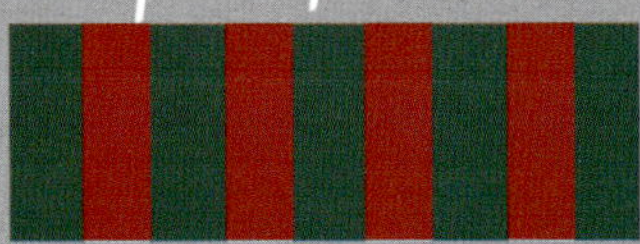

⊛ These examples use the same RED & changing the green ⊛

Making a series from one painting

① Make doodles from original painting

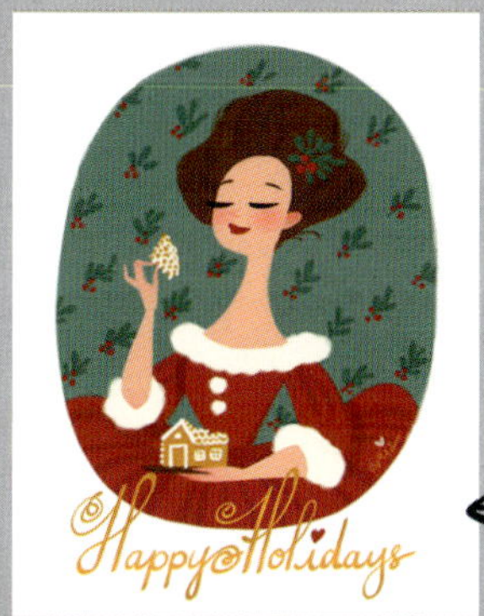

← original painting

original doodle

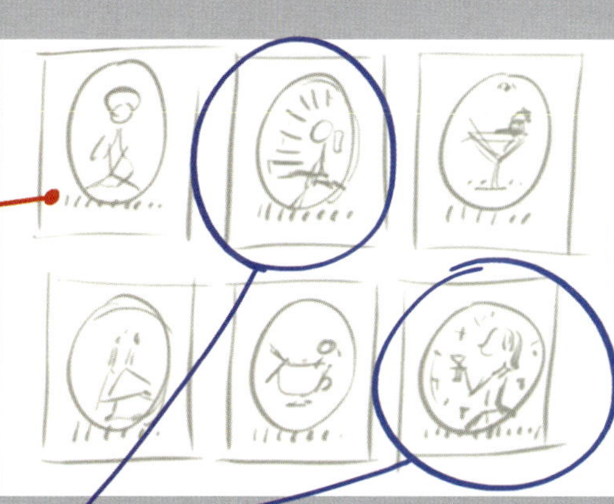

② Pick 2 (I like making a series in 3s)

③ See how they look together

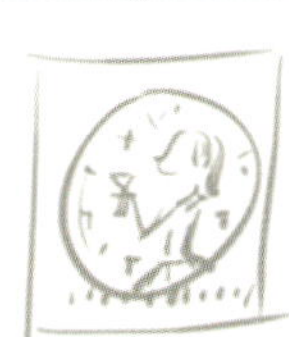
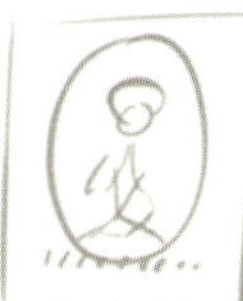
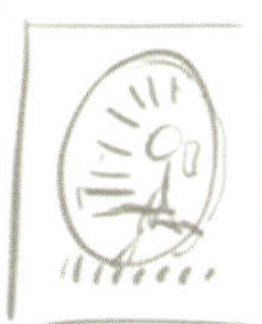

flip it, in case it looks better

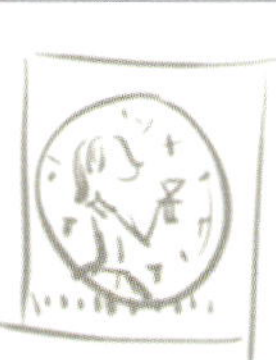
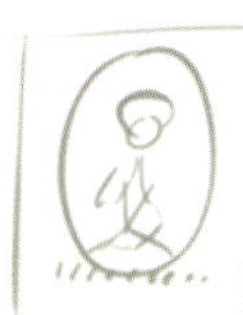
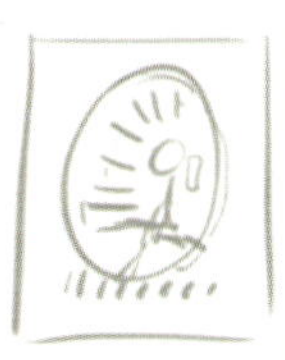

④ Make color comp using the same limited palette

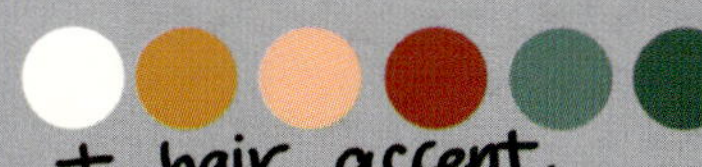

+ hair accent.

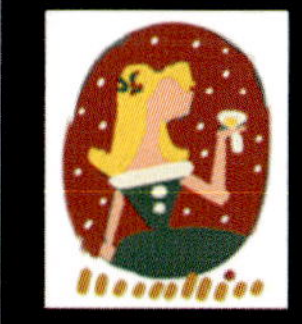
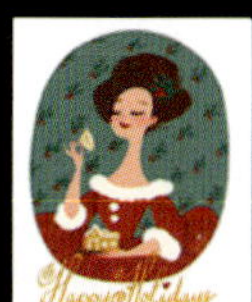
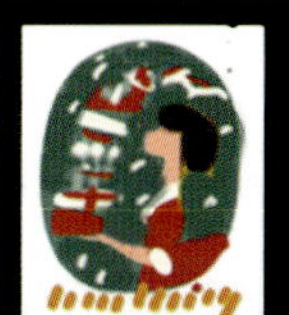
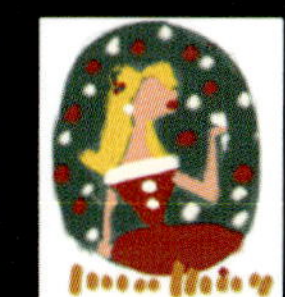
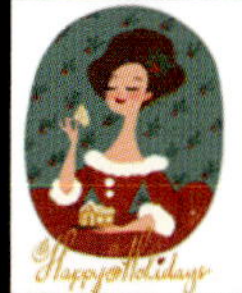
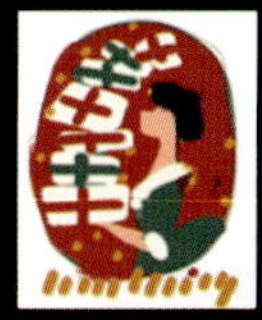
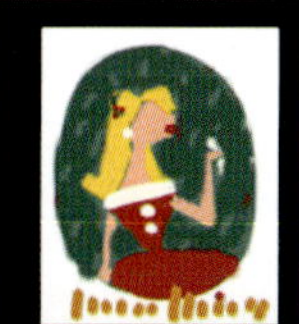
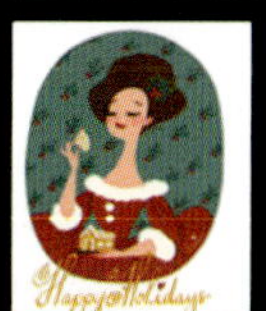
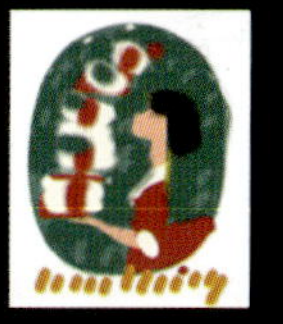

⑤ Pick one & Finish them

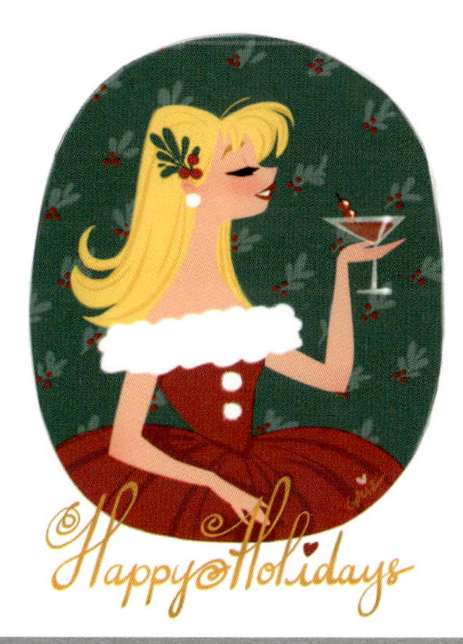

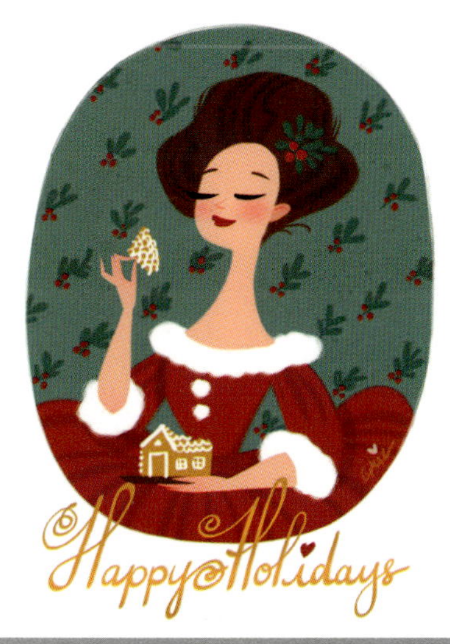

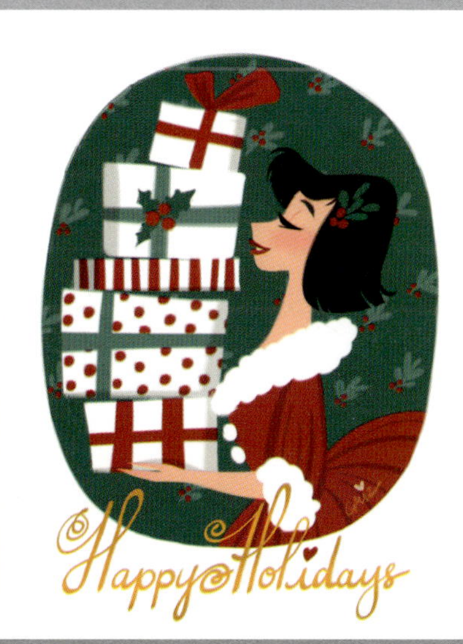

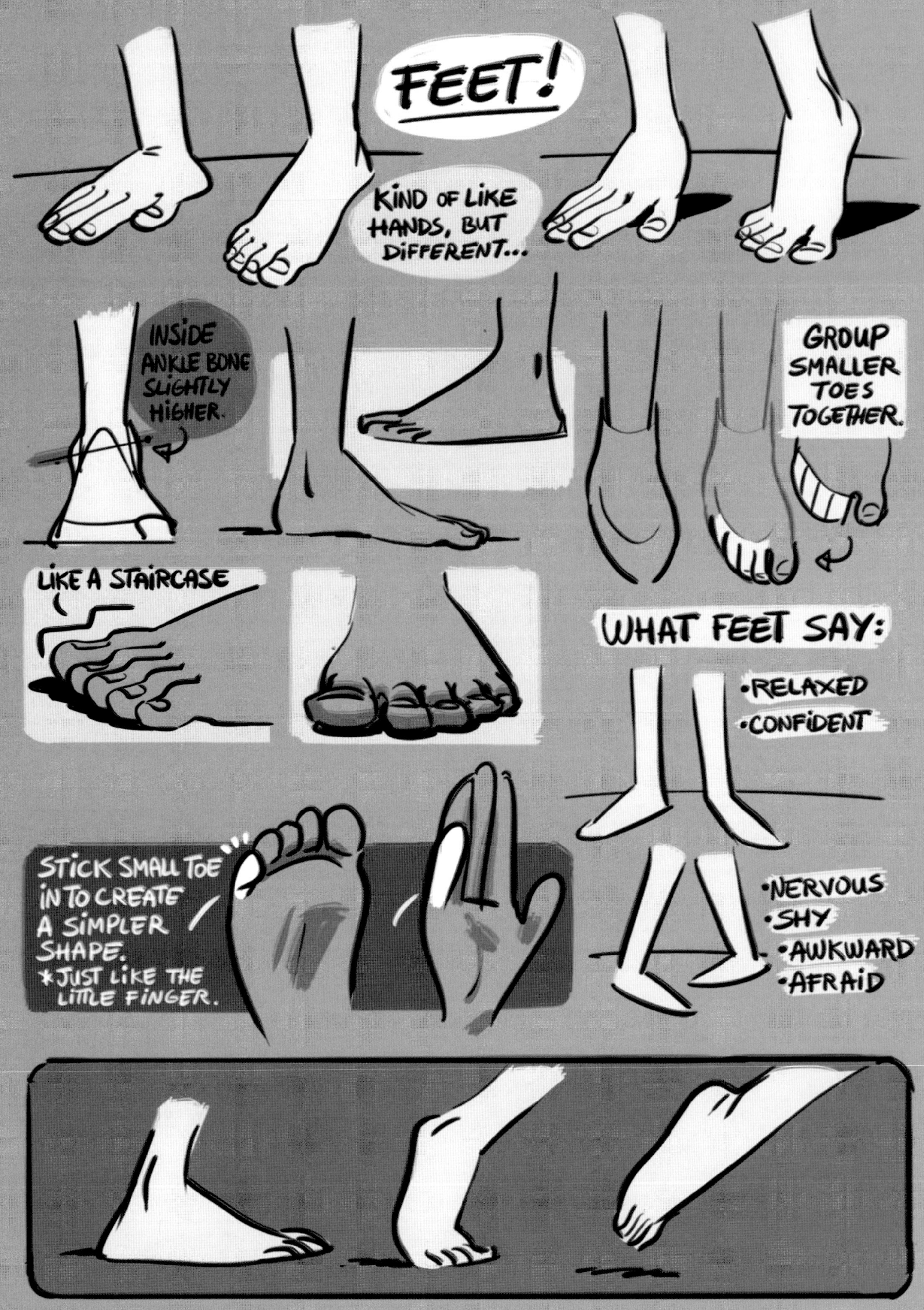
FEET!
KIND OF LIKE HANDS, BUT DIFFERENT...
INSIDE ANKLE BONE SLIGHTLY HIGHER.
GROUP SMALLER TOES TOGETHER.
LIKE A STAIRCASE
WHAT FEET SAY:
•RELAXED
•CONFIDENT
STICK SMALL TOE IN TO CREATE A SIMPLER SHAPE.
*JUST LIKE THE LITTLE FINGER.
•NERVOUS
•SHY
•AWKWARD
•AFRAID

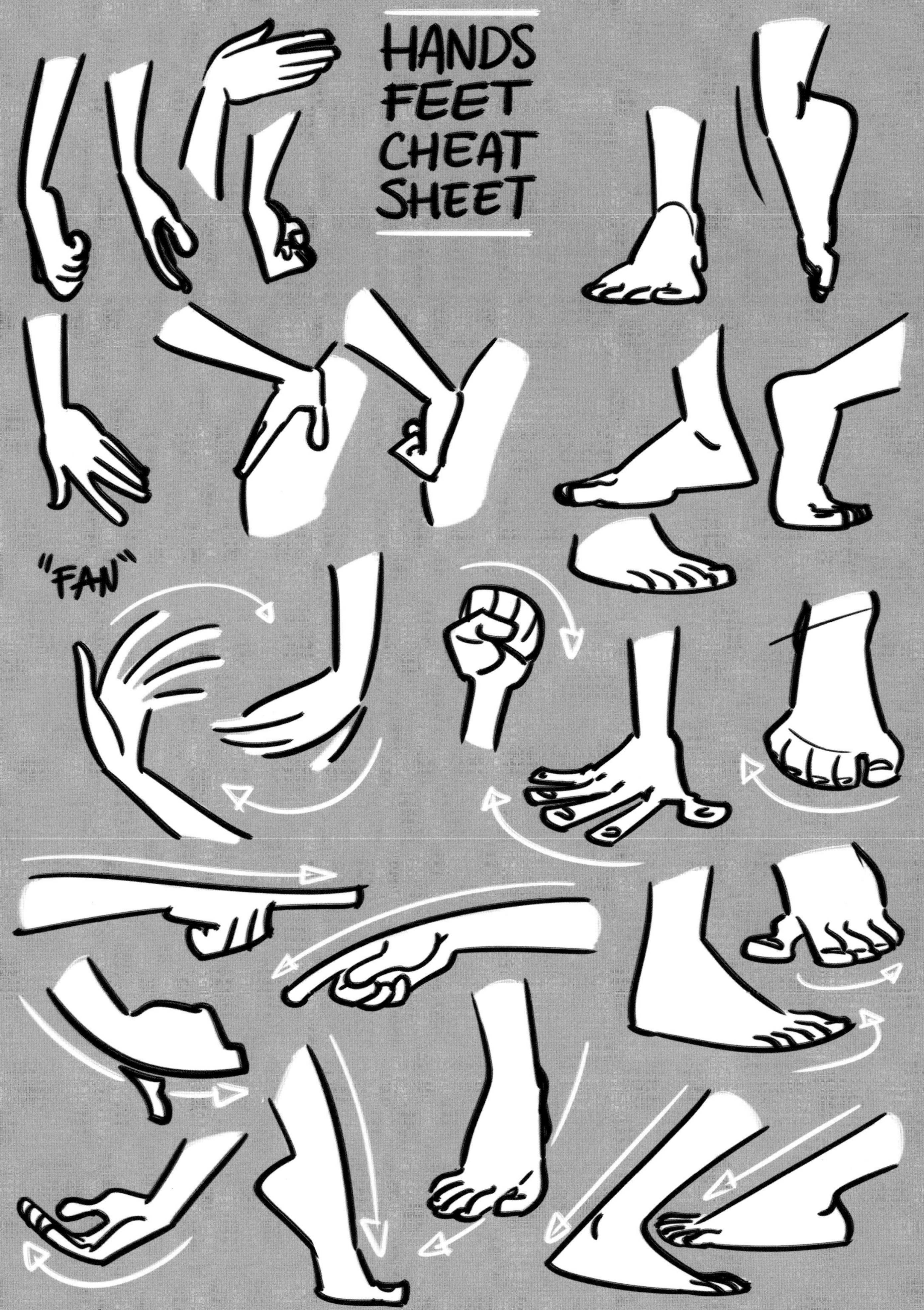
HANDS
FEET
CHEAT
SHEET
"FAN"

HIGHLIGHTS

- Warm object → Cool highlight
- Cool object → Warm highlight

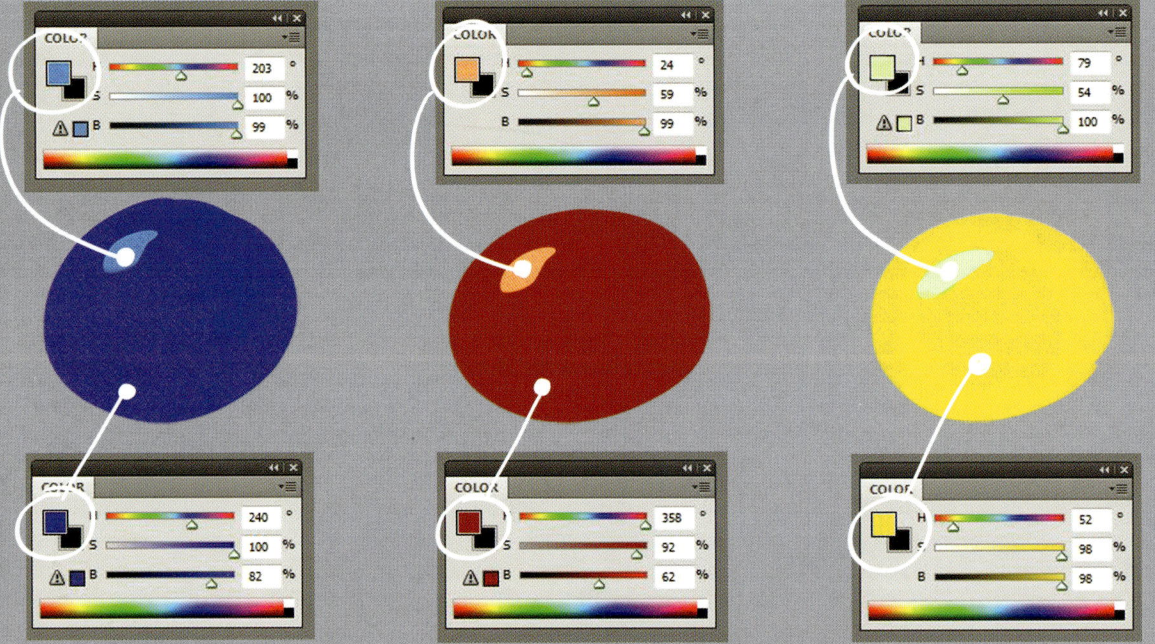

Example:

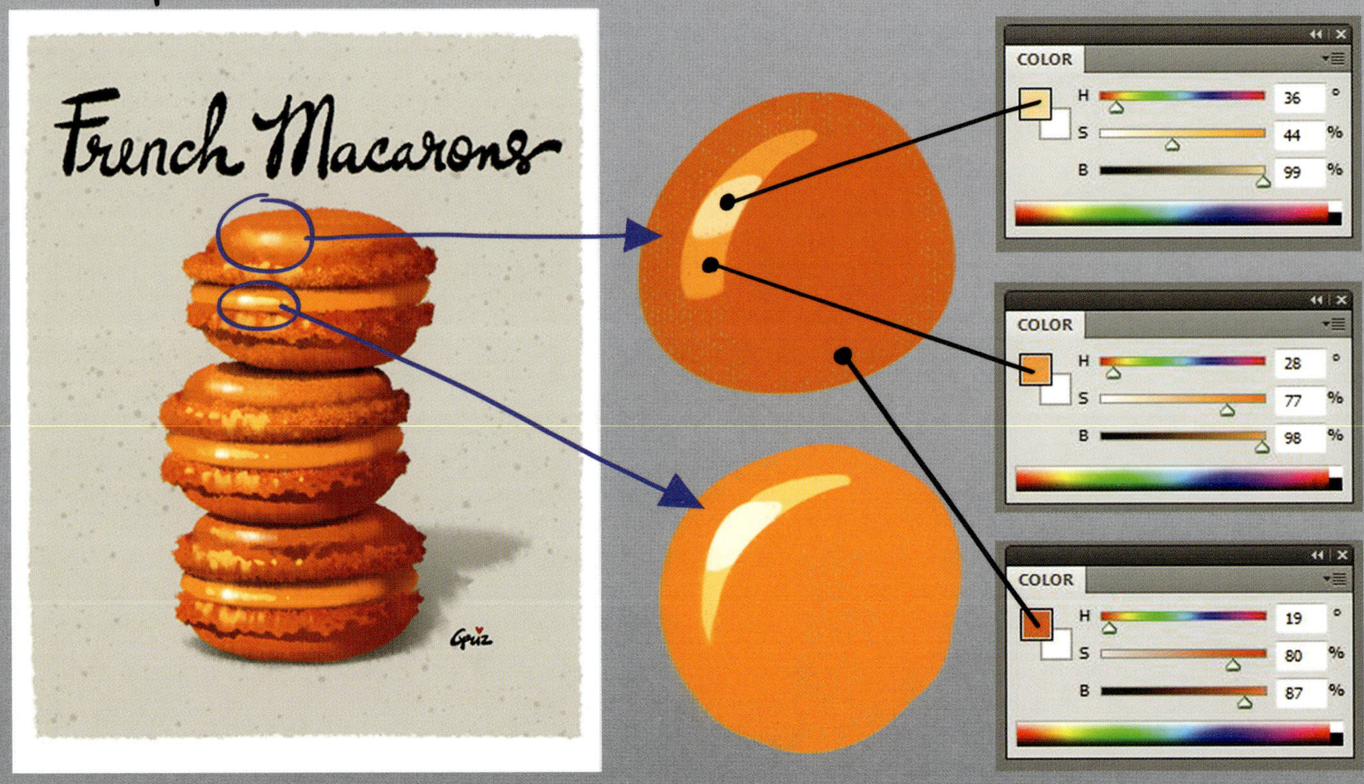

How to:

Paint a stylized SHINY object

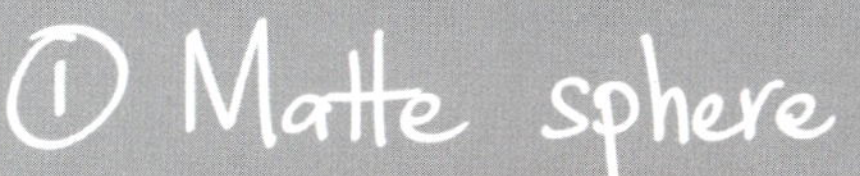

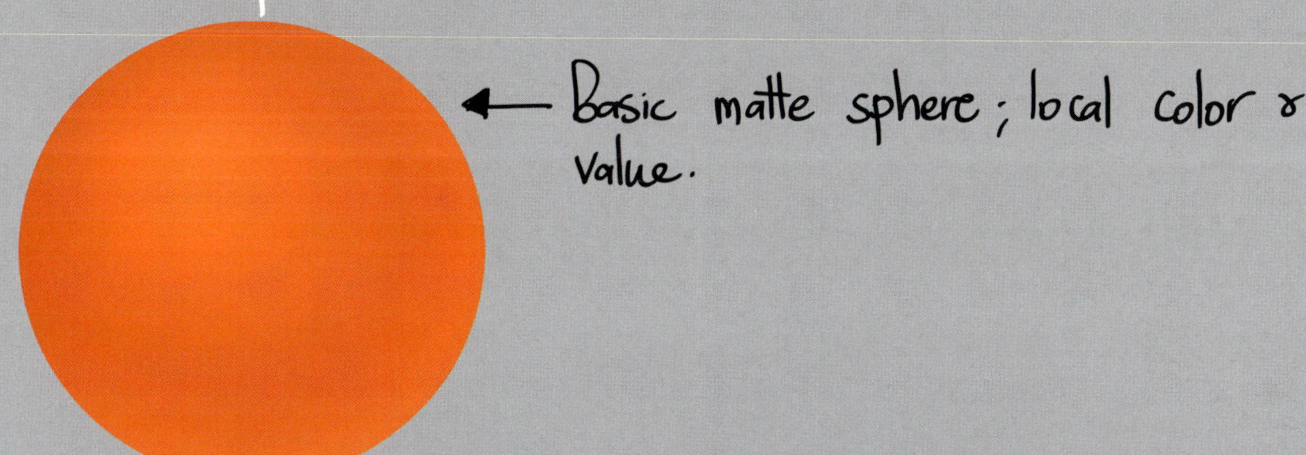

② Ceiling Reflection

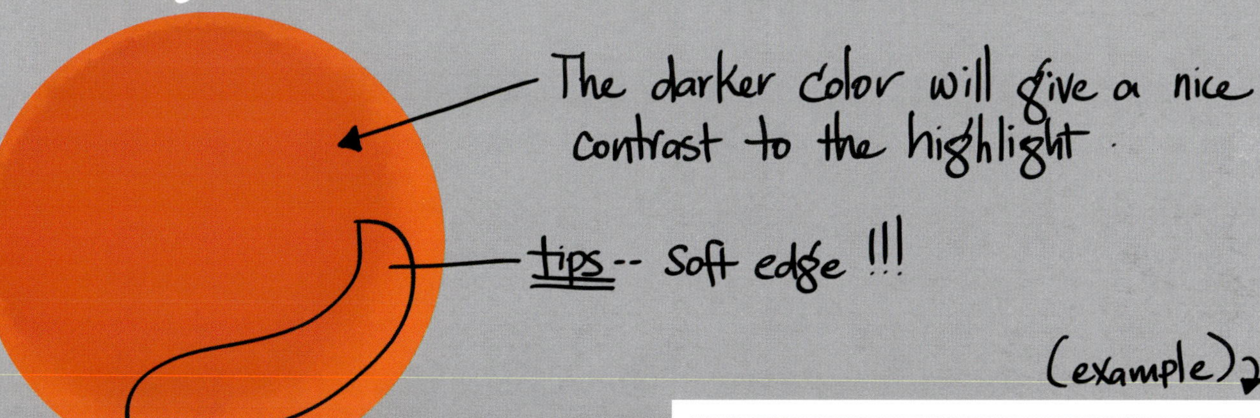

(example)

③ Highlight

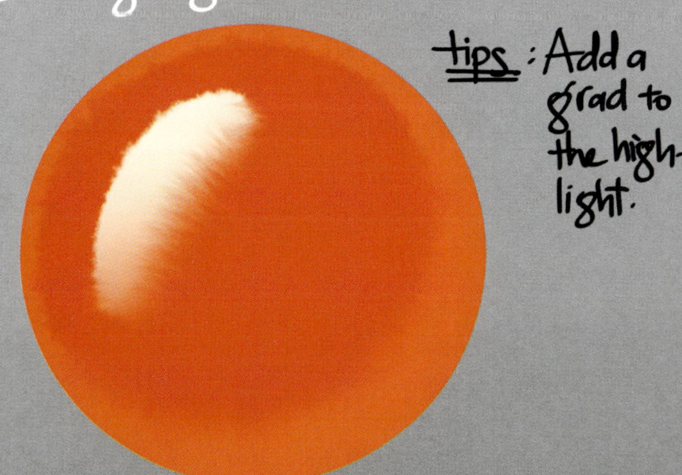

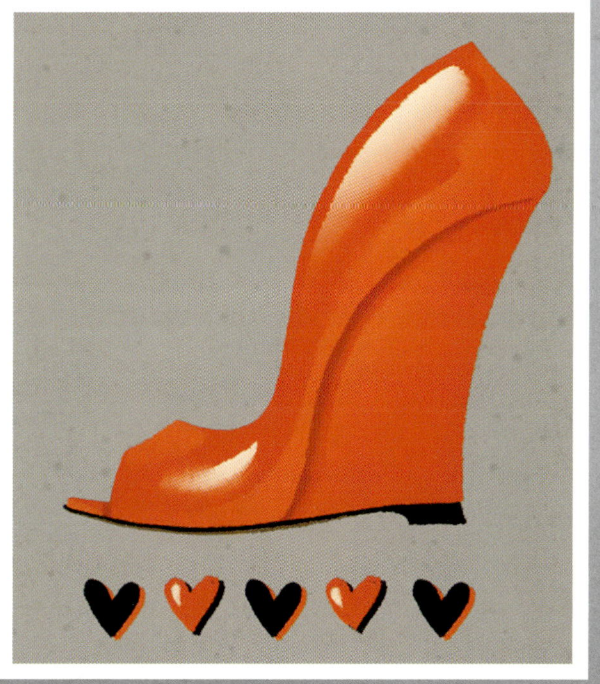

DRAWING EXERCISE

"100 FLOUR SACKS"

DRAW 100 DIFFERENT POSES OF A SIMPLE CHARACTER.

GOAL: IDENTIFYING AND USING BASIC ANIMATION PRINCIPLES TO GIVE LIFE TO A SIMPLE CHARACTER.

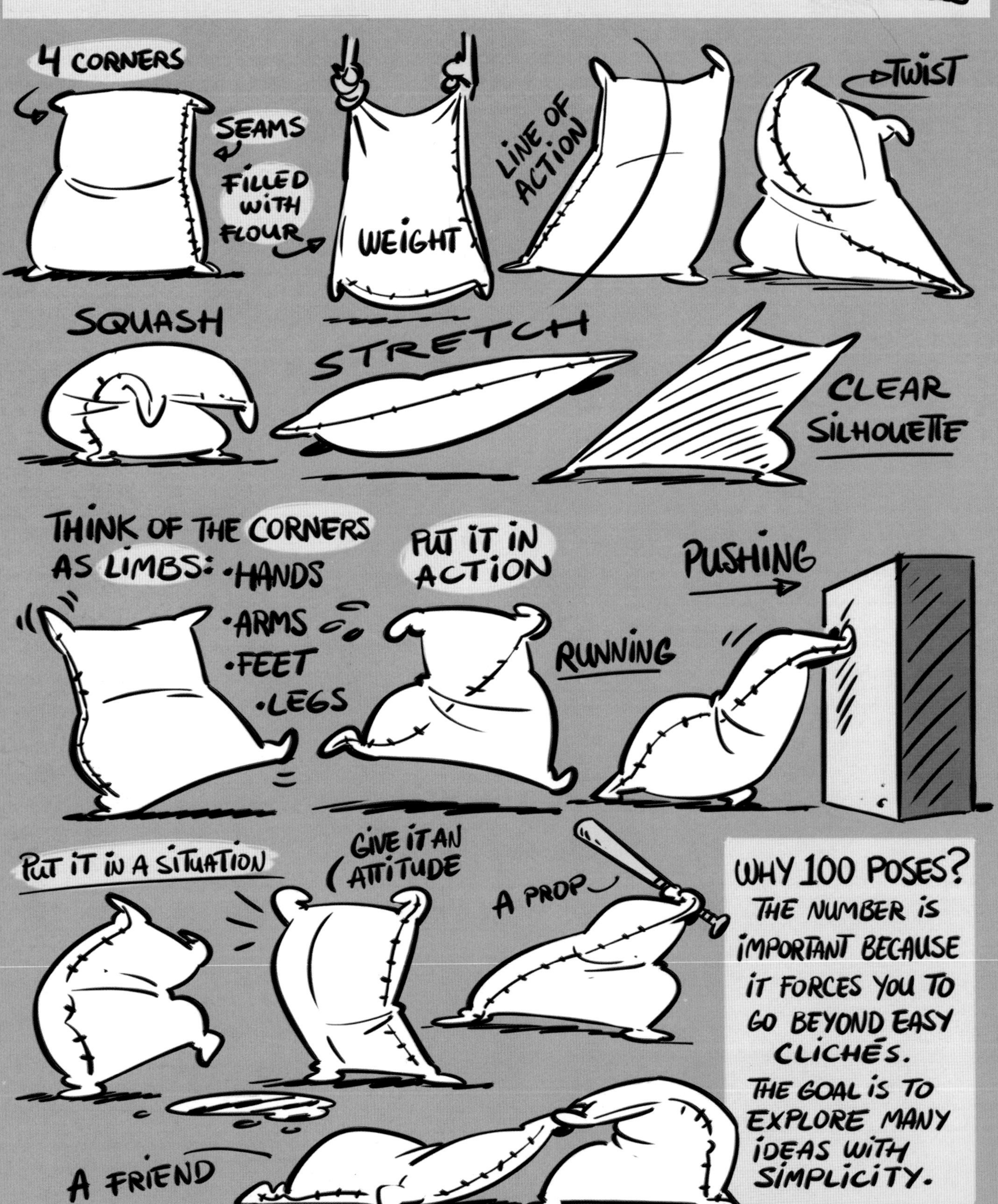

WHY 100 POSES?

THE NUMBER IS IMPORTANT BECAUSE IT FORCES YOU TO GO BEYOND EASY CLICHÉS.

THE GOAL IS TO EXPLORE MANY IDEAS WITH SIMPLICITY.

FROM THE FLOUR SACK TO GESTURE DRAWING

- SAME PRINCIPLES APPLY TO GESTURE DRAWING.
- A WAY TO AVOID GETTING STUCK ON ANATOMY.

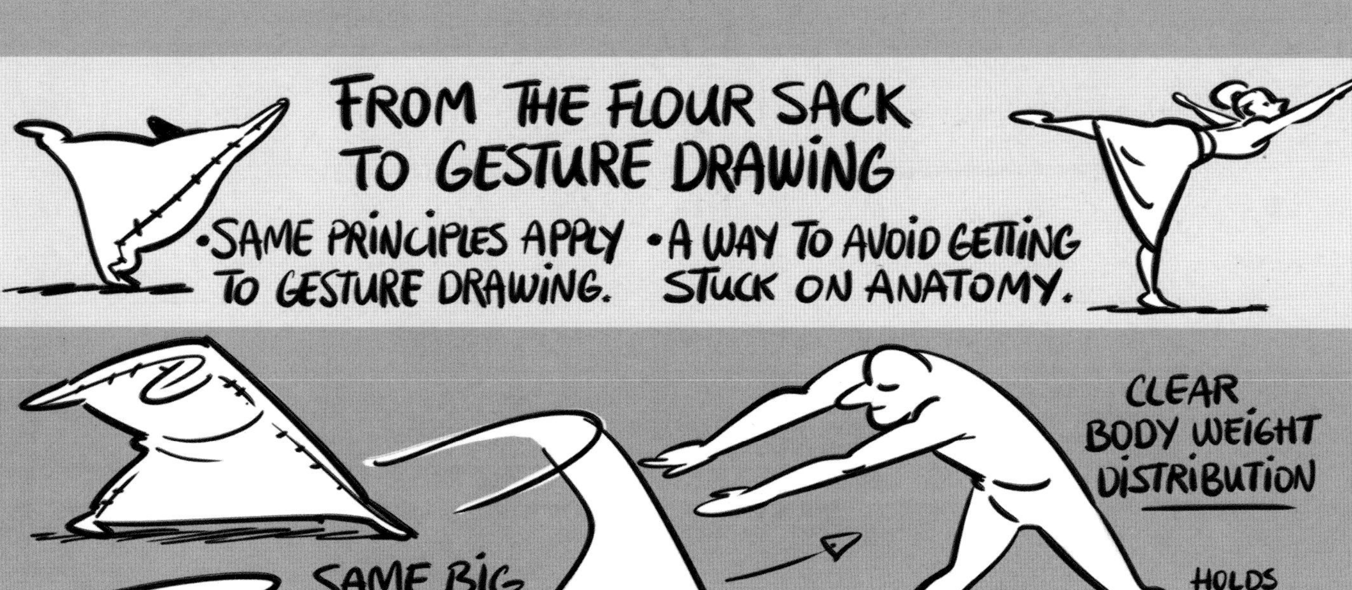

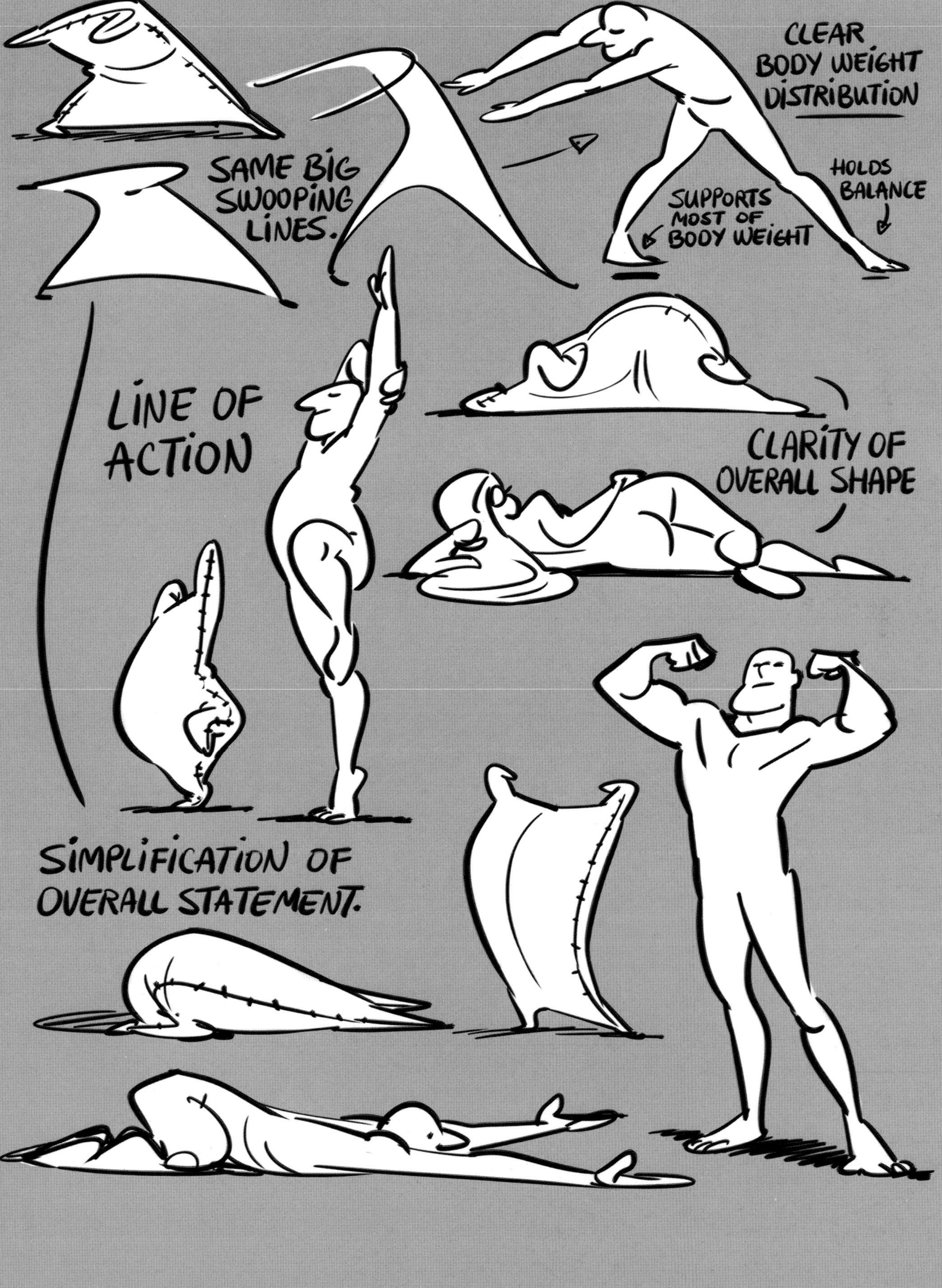

LINE OF ACTION

CLARITY OF OVERALL SHAPE

SIMPLIFICATION OF OVERALL STATEMENT.

Simple Palette Exercise

Use 1 (or 2) color w/ Black & White

example -- "Pumpkin Pie Kitty"

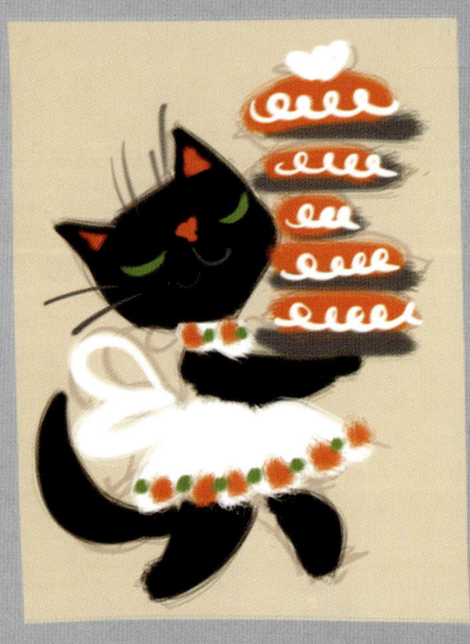

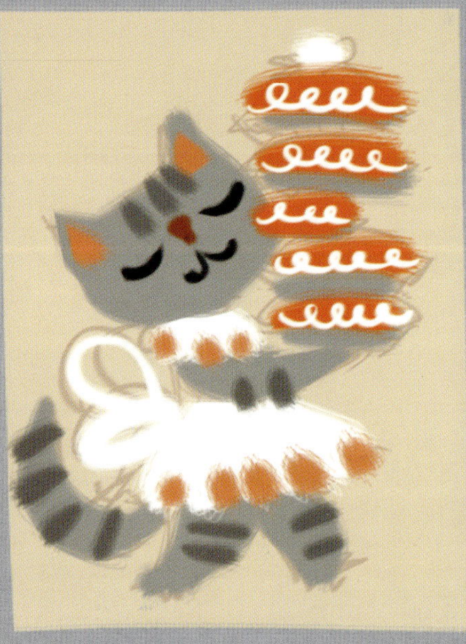

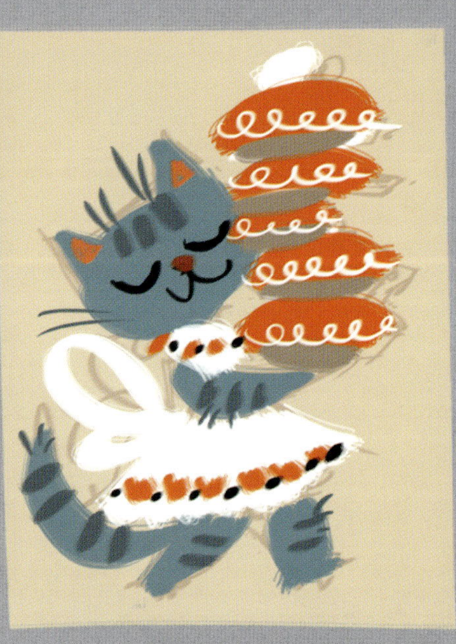

ⓐ

Orange
B & W
Green

↓

too Halloweeny

ⓑ

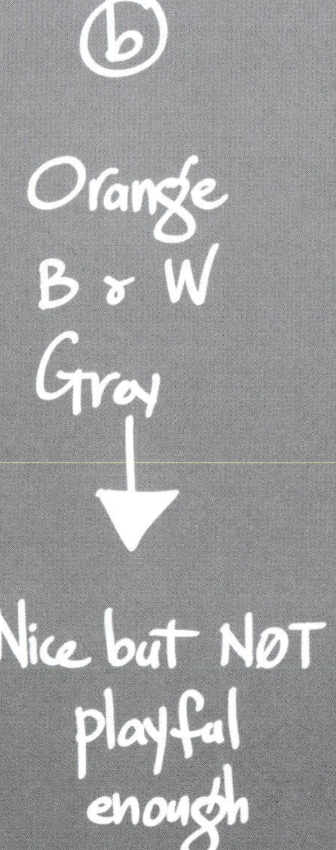

c

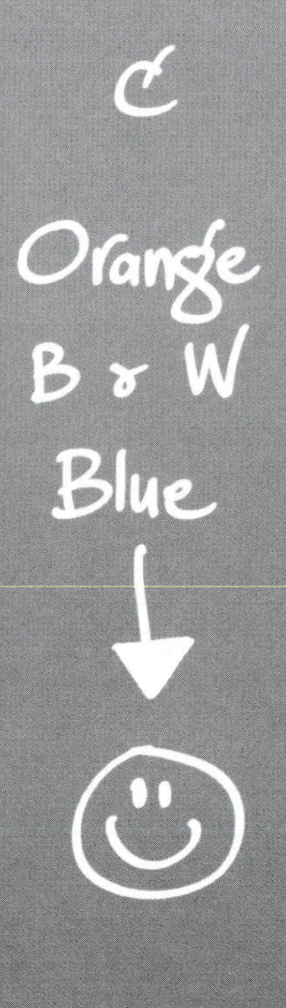

Process Painting

① Thumbnail sketch

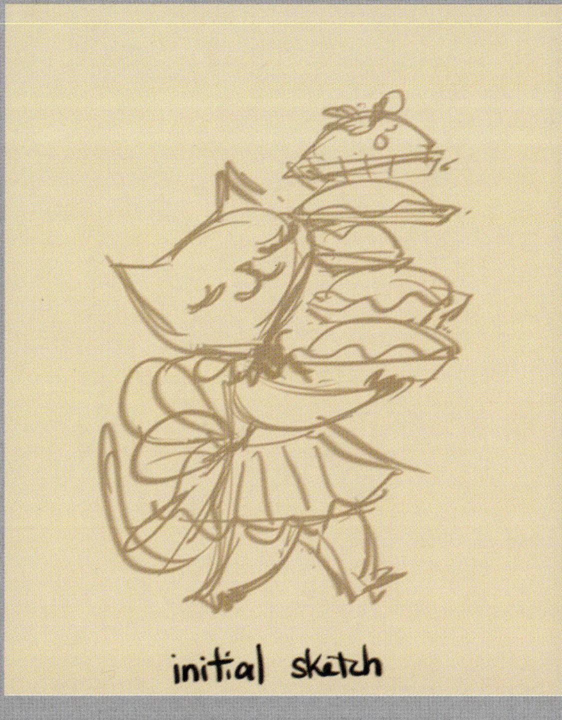

② Pick a color comp.

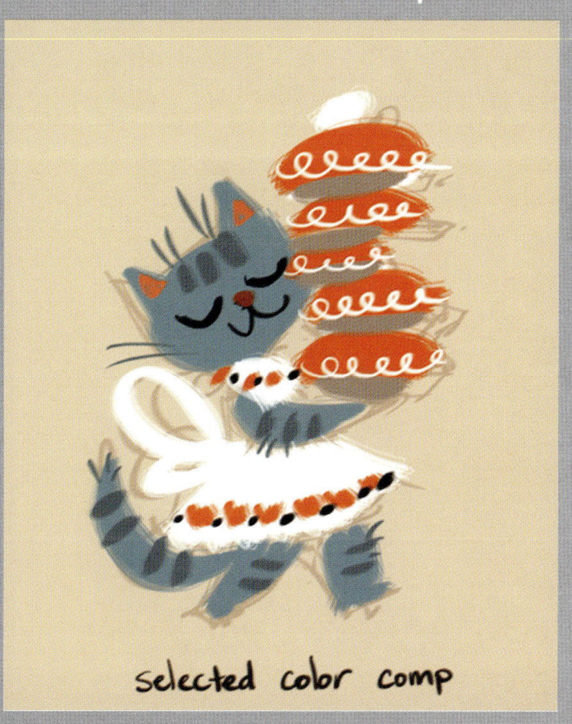

③ Clean up drawing from color comp.

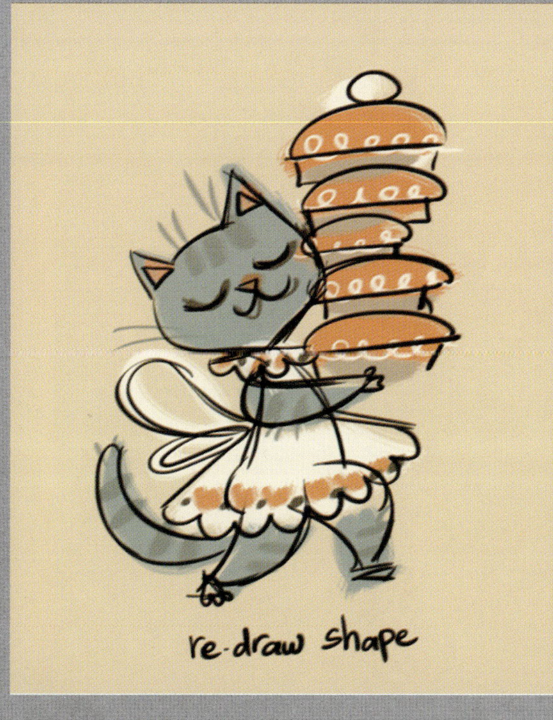

④ Final painting

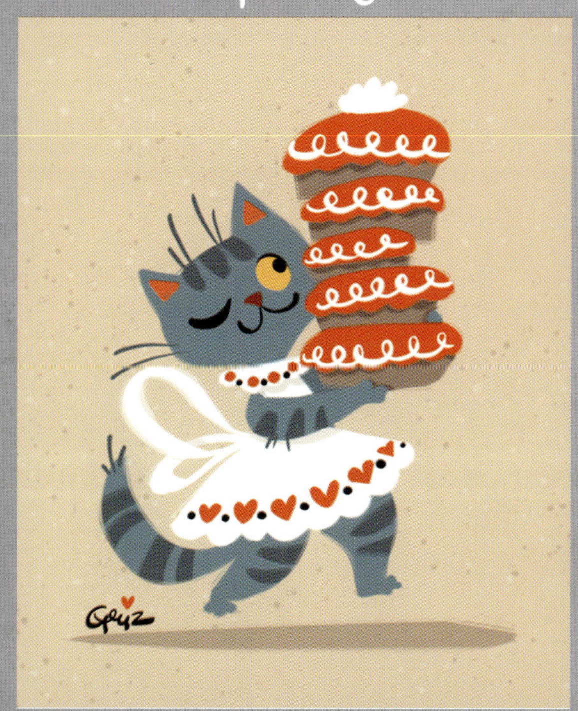

⊛ there's no right or wrong way to paint. This is one the way I paint.

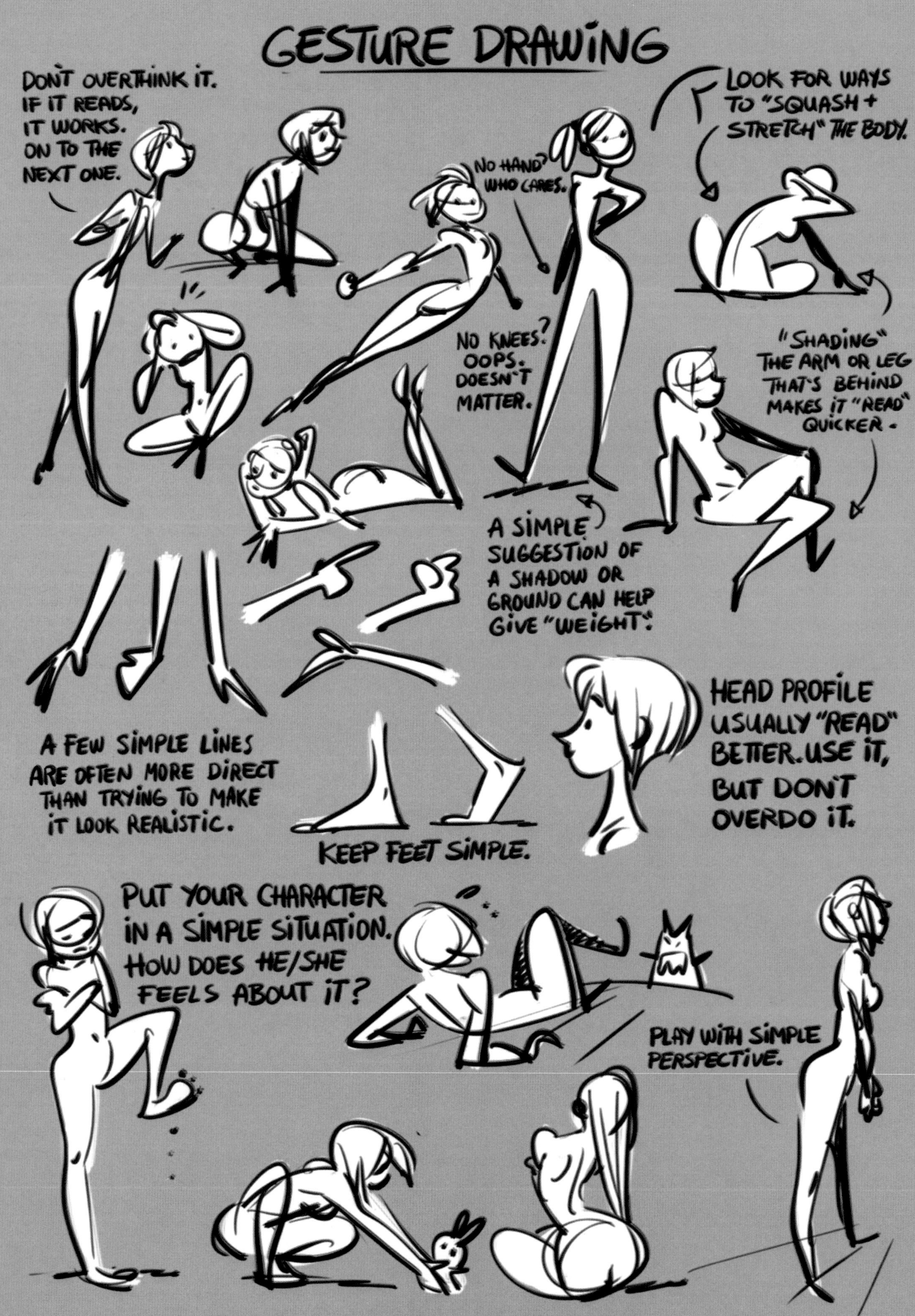
GESTURE DRAWING
DON'T OVERTHINK IT. IF IT READS, IT WORKS. ON TO THE NEXT ONE.
NO HAND? WHO CARES.
LOOK FOR WAYS TO "SQUASH + STRETCH" THE BODY.
NO KNEES? OOPS. DOESN'T MATTER.
"SHADING" THE ARM OR LEG THAT'S BEHIND MAKES IT "READ" QUICKER.
A SIMPLE SUGGESTION OF A SHADOW OR GROUND CAN HELP GIVE "WEIGHT".
A FEW SIMPLE LINES ARE OFTEN MORE DIRECT THAN TRYING TO MAKE IT LOOK REALISTIC.
KEEP FEET SIMPLE.
HEAD PROFILE USUALLY "READ" BETTER. USE IT, BUT DON'T OVERDO IT.
PUT YOUR CHARACTER IN A SIMPLE SITUATION. HOW DOES HE/SHE FEELS ABOUT IT?
PLAY WITH SIMPLE PERSPECTIVE.

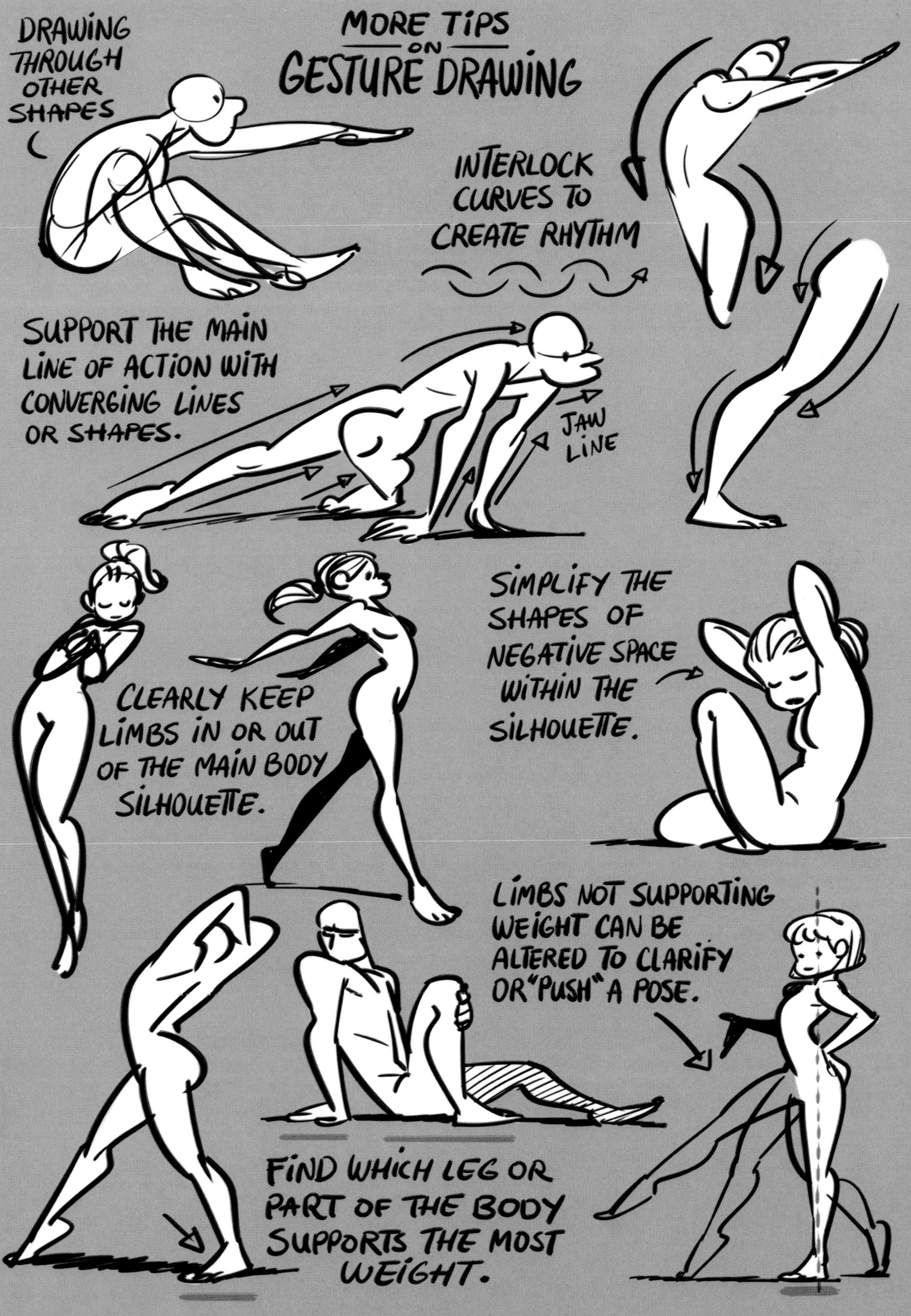
MORE TIPS ON GESTURE DRAWING
DRAWING THROUGH OTHER SHAPES
INTERLOCK CURVES TO CREATE RHYTHM
SUPPORT THE MAIN LINE OF ACTION WITH CONVERGING LINES OR SHAPES.
JAW LINE
CLEARLY KEEP LIMBS IN OR OUT OF THE MAIN BODY SILHOUETTE.
SIMPLIFY THE SHAPES OF NEGATIVE SPACE WITHIN THE SILHOUETTE.
LIMBS NOT SUPPORTING WEIGHT CAN BE ALTERED TO CLARIFY OR "PUSH" A POSE.
FIND WHICH LEG OR PART OF THE BODY SUPPORTS THE MOST WEIGHT.

Composition 101

Rule of 1/3

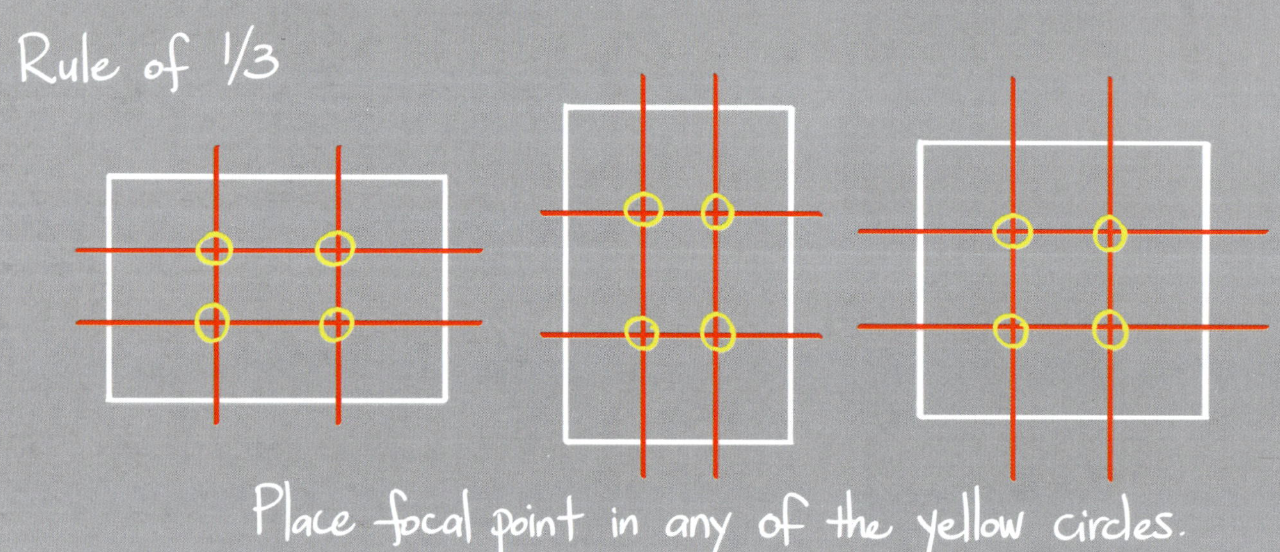

Place focal point in any of the yellow circles.

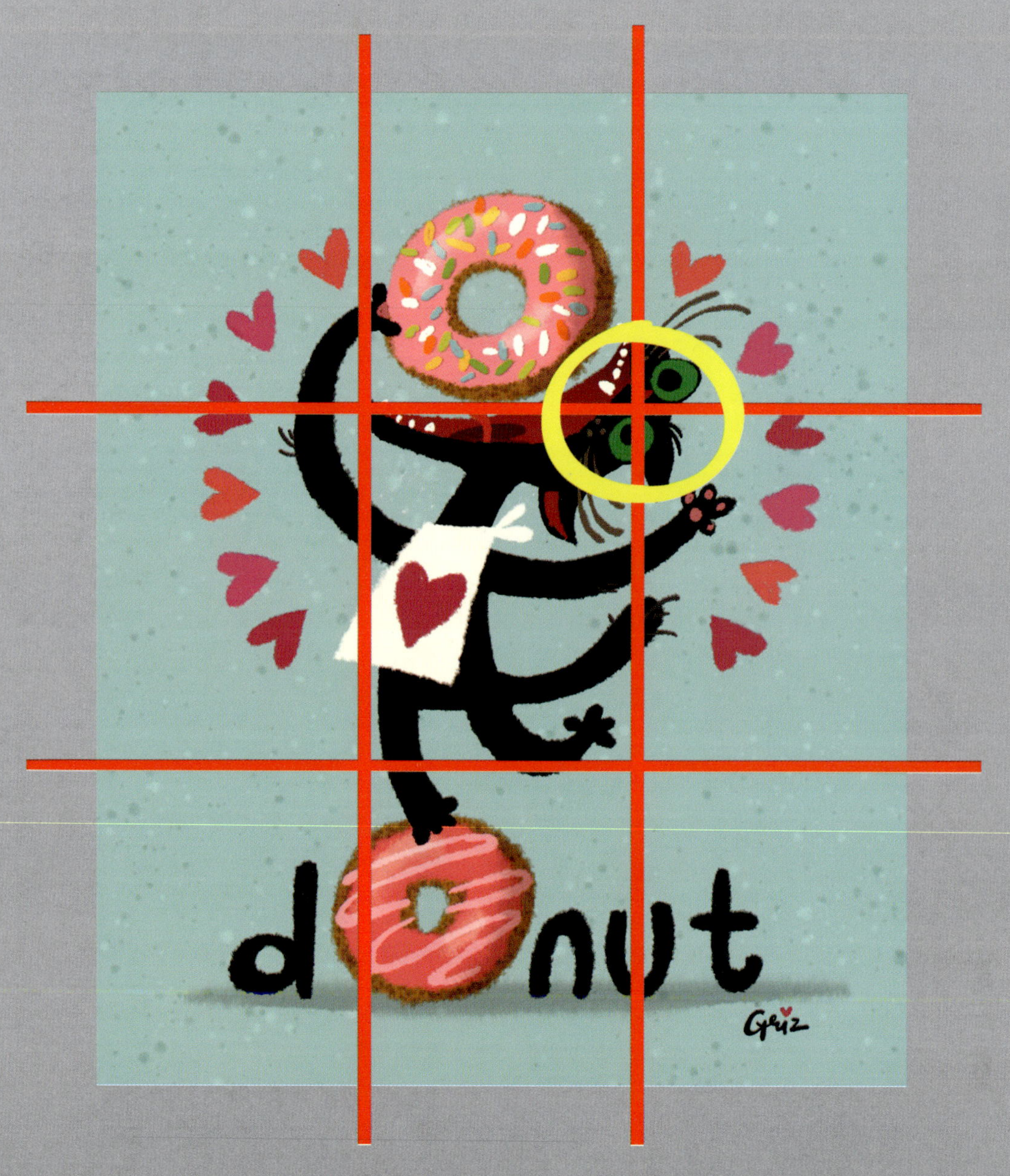

Good tangents

Yes, there is such a thing as a GOOD TANGENT
For example -- when it creates a new abstract shape

A line that would've been a bad tangent becomes good when there's a shape breaking it

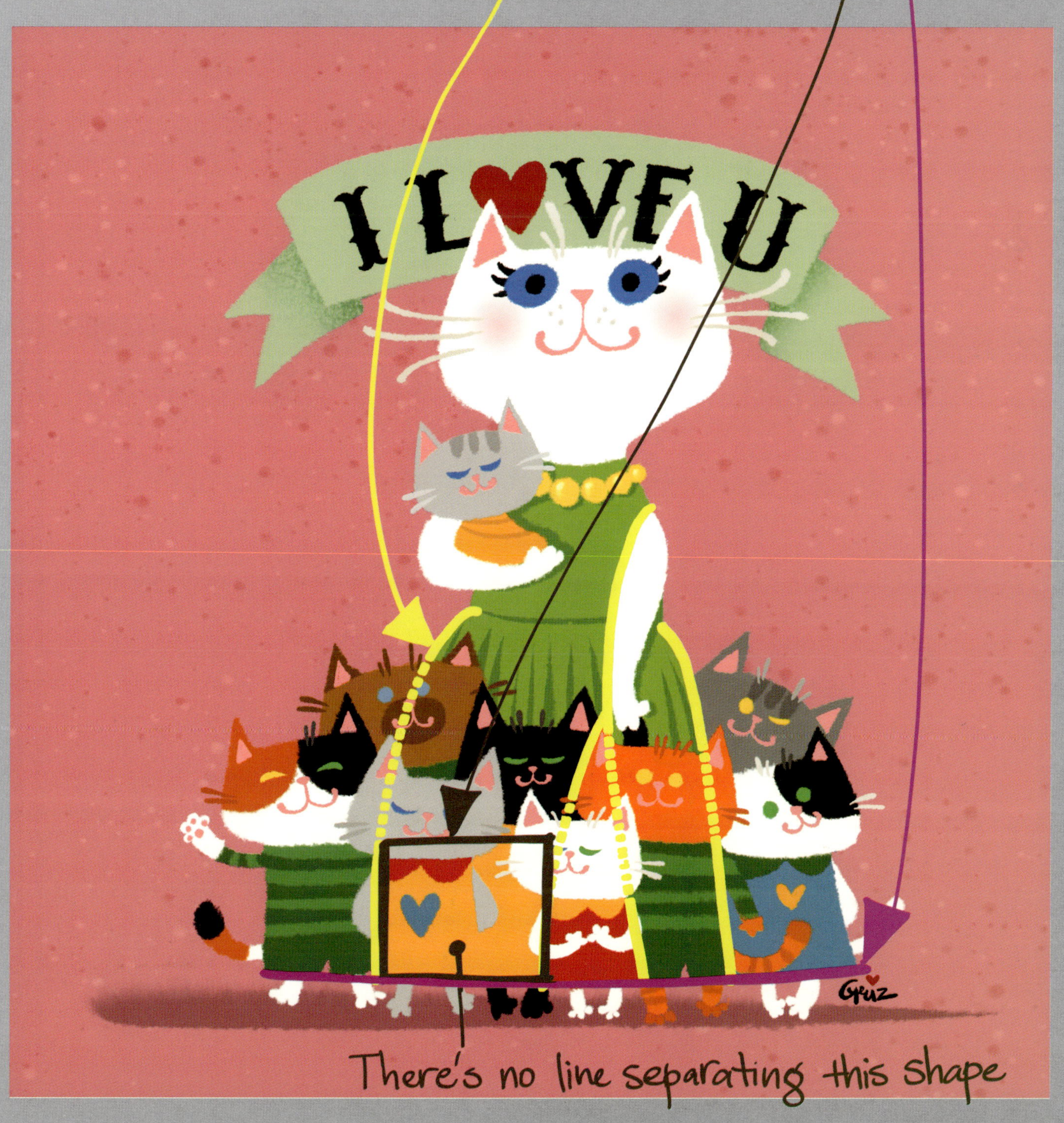

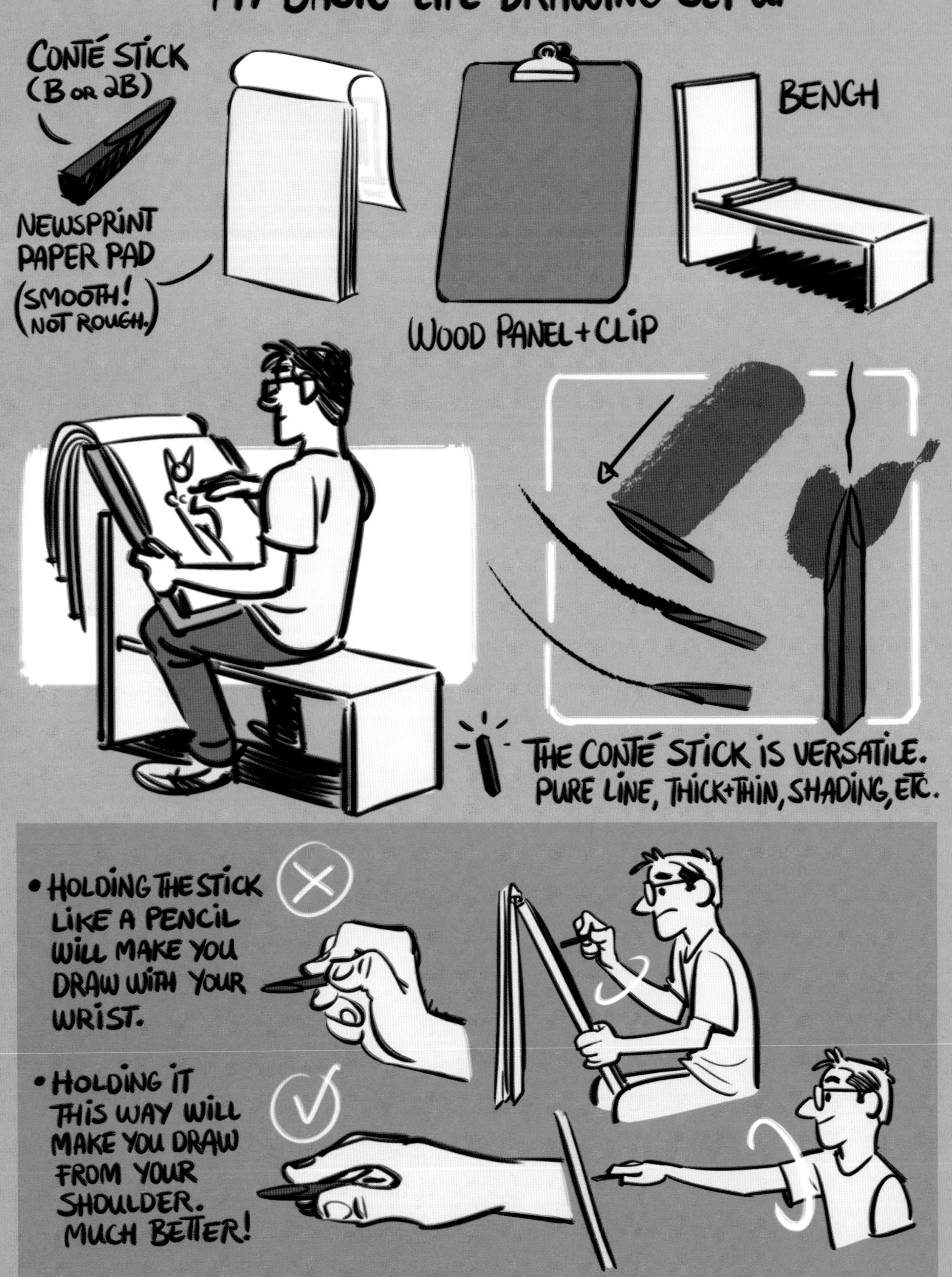
MY BASIC LIFE DRAWING SET-UP
CONTÉ STICK (B OR 2B)
NEWSPRINT PAPER PAD (SMOOTH! NOT ROUGH.)
WOOD PANEL + CLIP
BENCH
THE CONTÉ STICK IS VERSATILE. PURE LINE, THICK+THIN, SHADING, ETC.
• HOLDING THE STICK LIKE A PENCIL WILL MAKE YOU DRAW WITH YOUR WRIST.
• HOLDING IT THIS WAY WILL MAKE YOU DRAW FROM YOUR SHOULDER. MUCH BETTER!

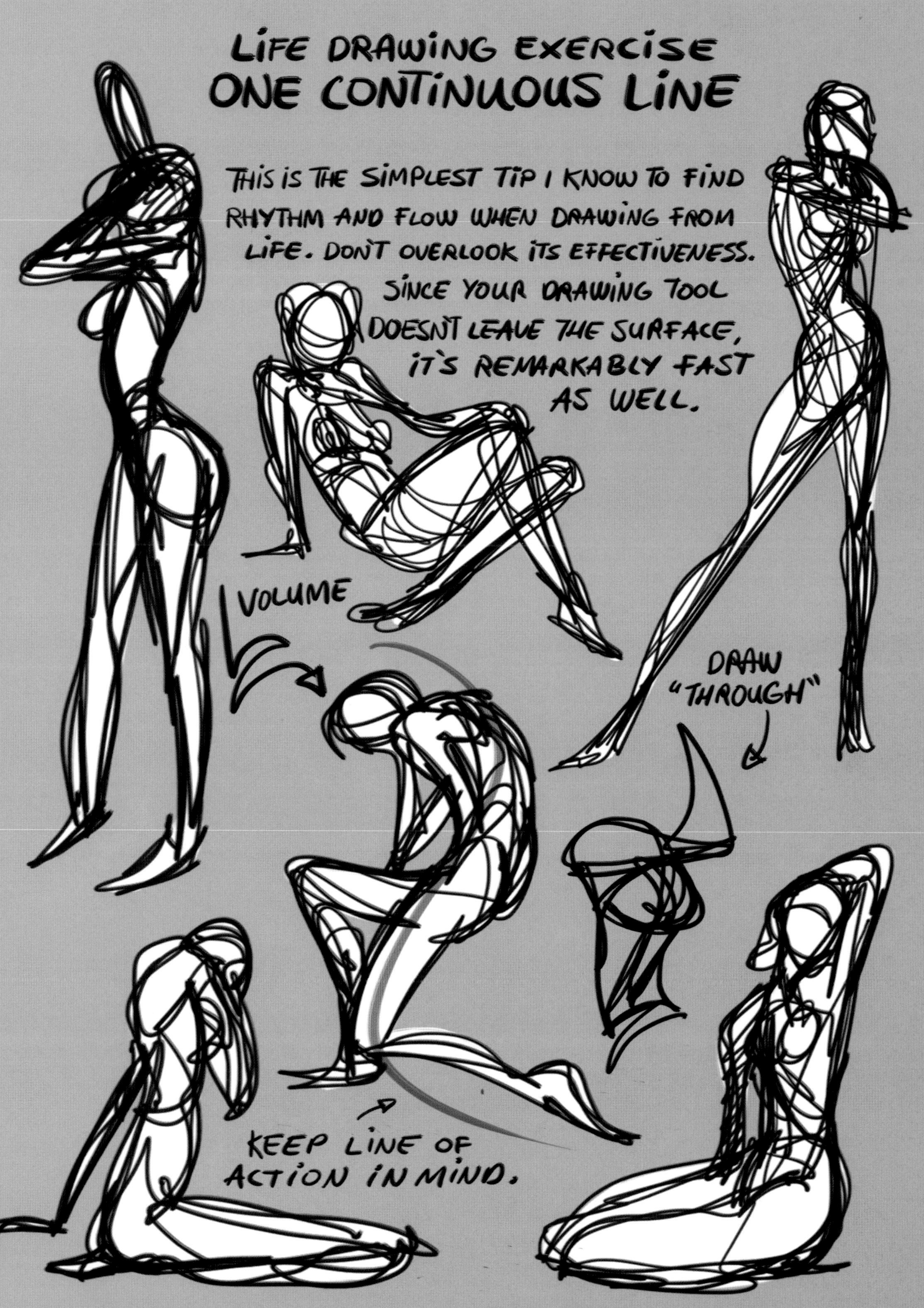
LIFE DRAWING EXERCISE
ONE CONTINUOUS LINE
THIS IS THE SIMPLEST TIP I KNOW TO FIND RHYTHM AND FLOW WHEN DRAWING FROM LIFE. DON'T OVERLOOK ITS EFFECTIVENESS. SINCE YOUR DRAWING TOOL DOESN'T LEAVE THE SURFACE, IT'S REMARKABLY FAST AS WELL.
VOLUME
DRAW "THROUGH"
KEEP LINE OF ACTION IN MIND.

Beware of TANGENTS

Most common tangents:

① Continuous long line (straight or curve)

continuous line w/ hair shape

continuous line w/ umbrella & hair

continuous line w/ the torso outline & umbrella handle

② Touch each other / tension points (within the drawing itself or the edge of your canvas

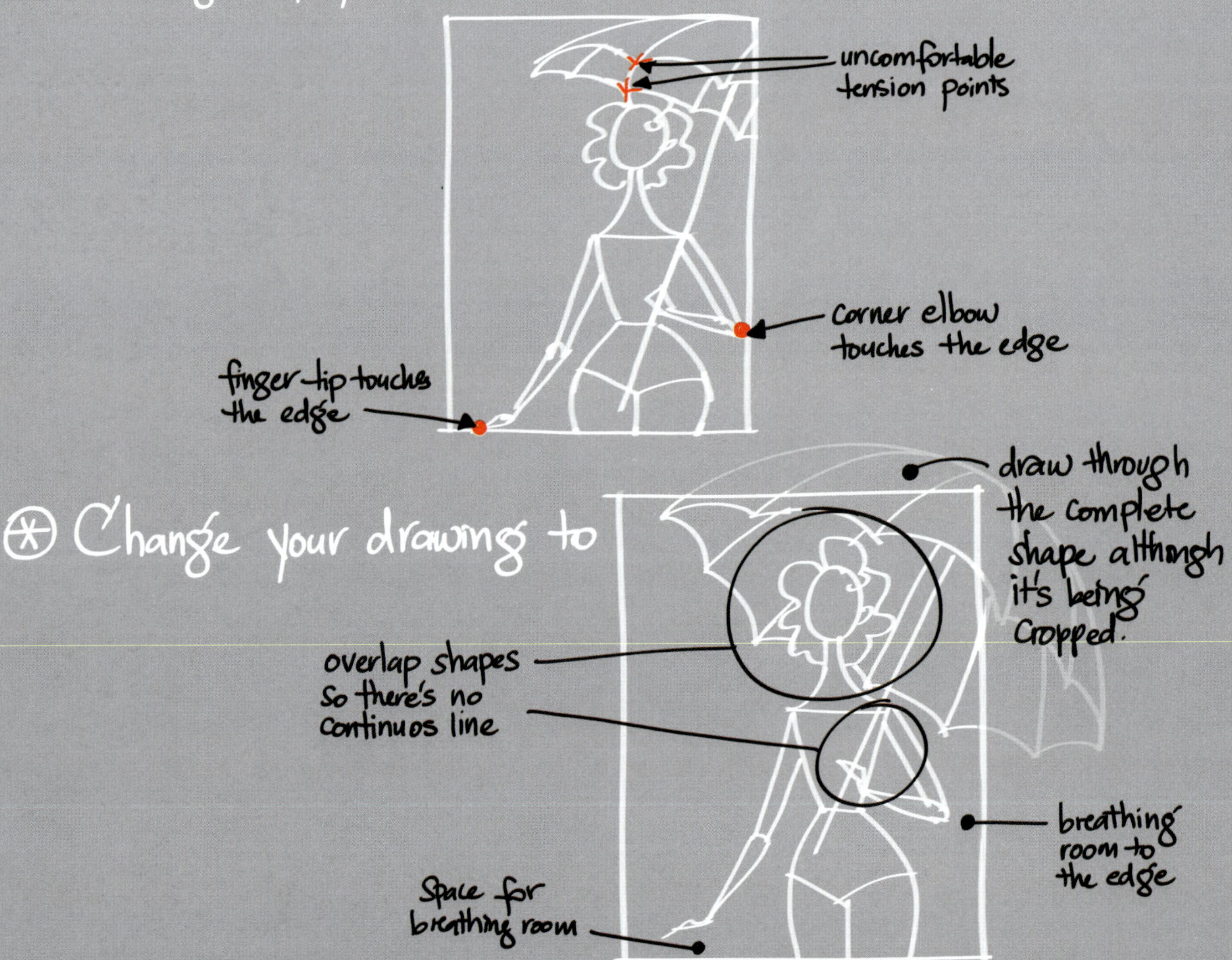

Rules of CROPPING

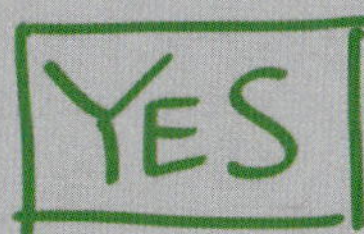

NO

⊛ Crop at 2/3 or 3/4

→ gives a nice & comfortable breathing room.

⊛ At any joint or edge

→ gives an unconformitable illusion as if something is missing

→ feels like a mistake

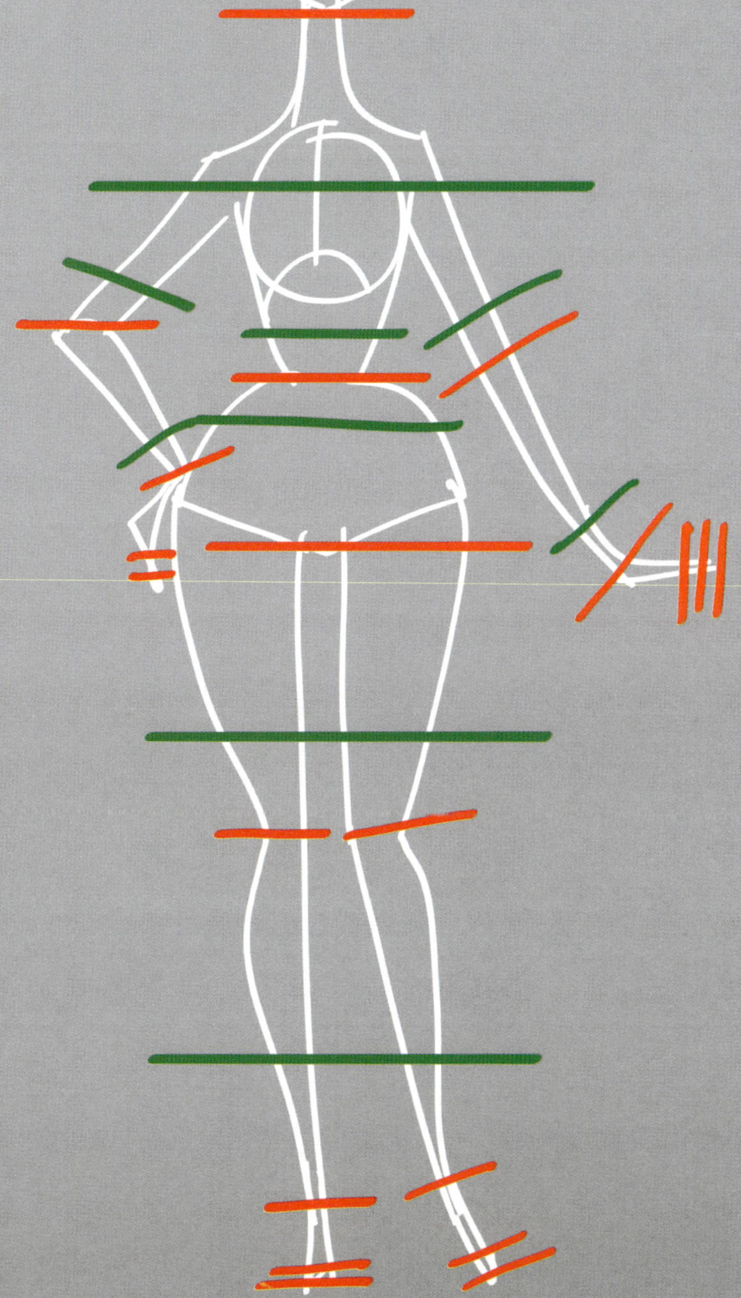

SILHOUETTES IN STORYTELLING

• CREATE CONTRAST AND DRAMA.

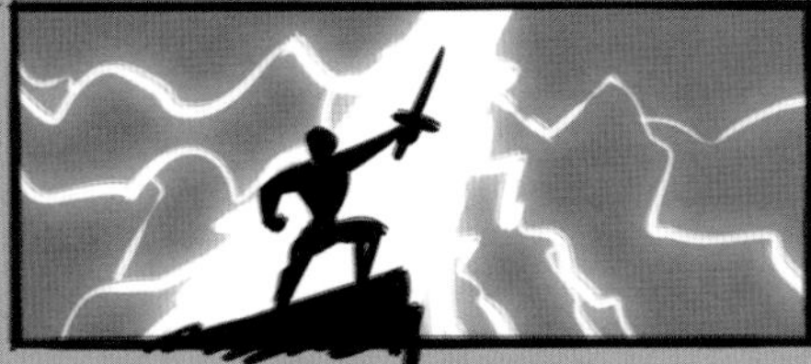
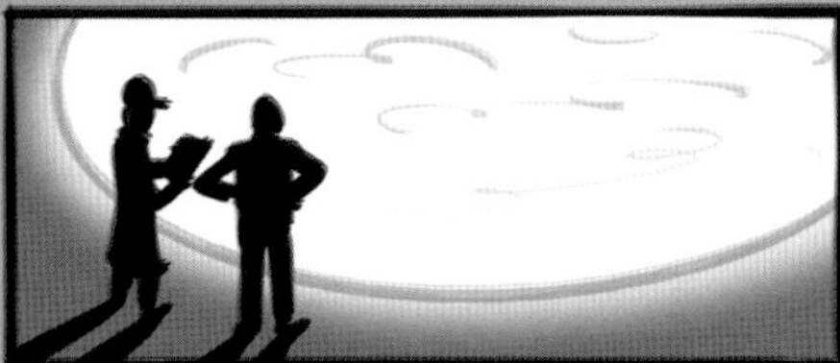
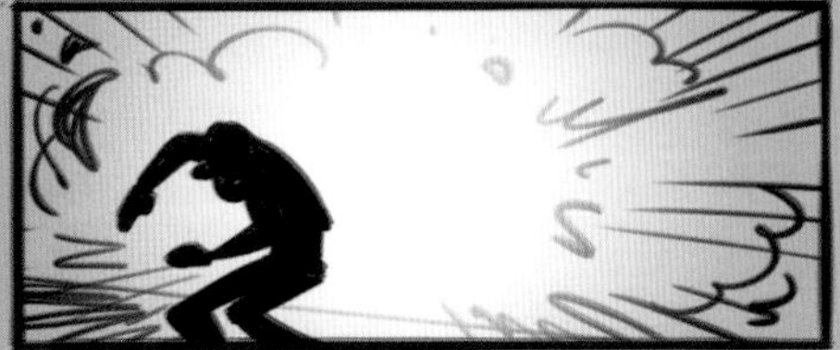

• CAN BE USED TO INTRODUCE A MYSTERIOUS CHARACTER.

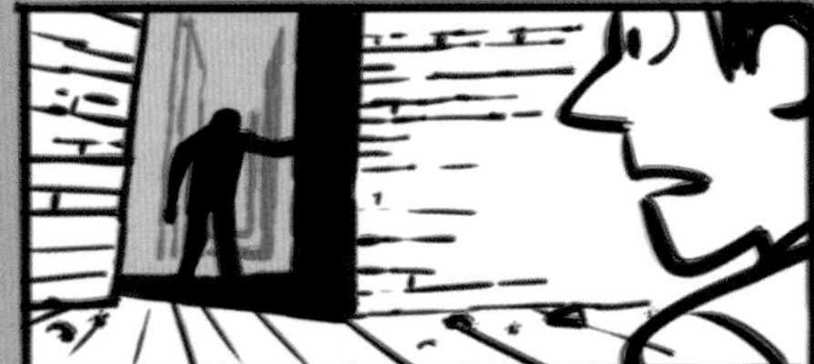
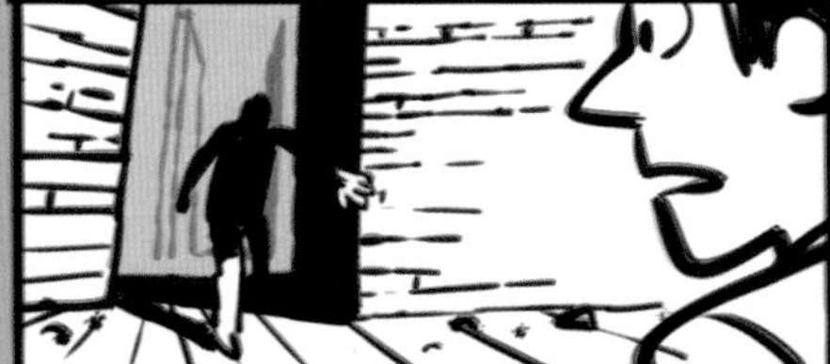
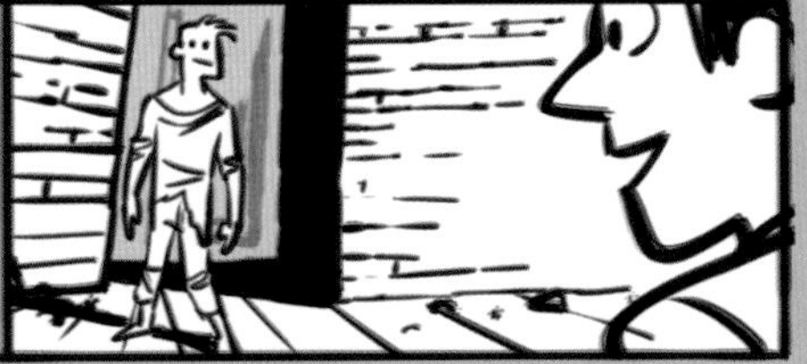

• PUT AN EMPHASIS ON WHAT A CHARACTER IS LOOKING AT.

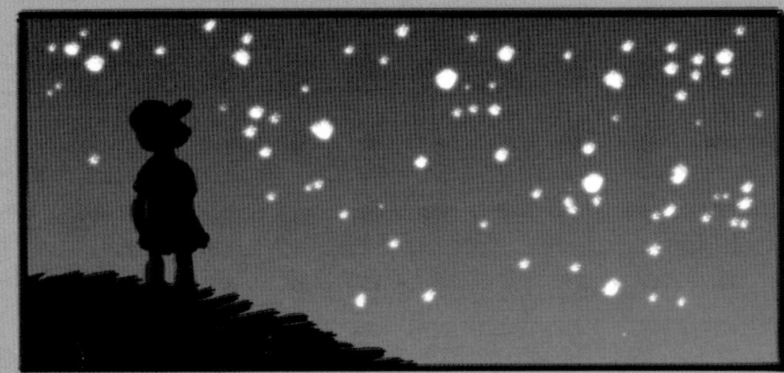
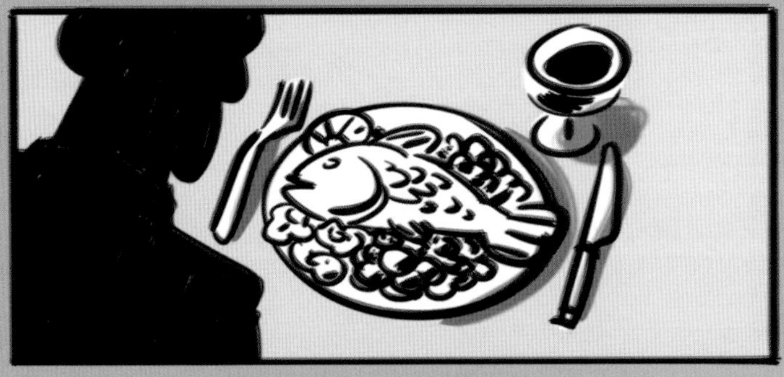

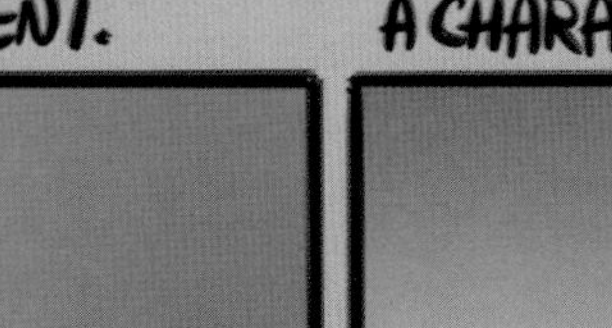

• SYMBOLIZE AN INTIMATE MOMENT.

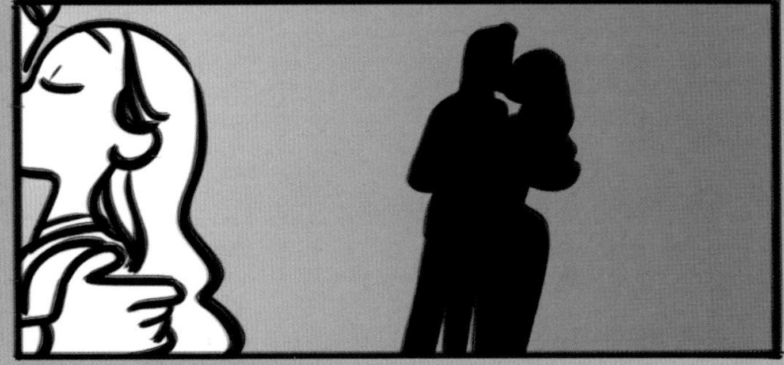

• GIVE A SENSE OF IMPORTANCE TO A CHARACTER OR GROUP OF CHARACTERS.

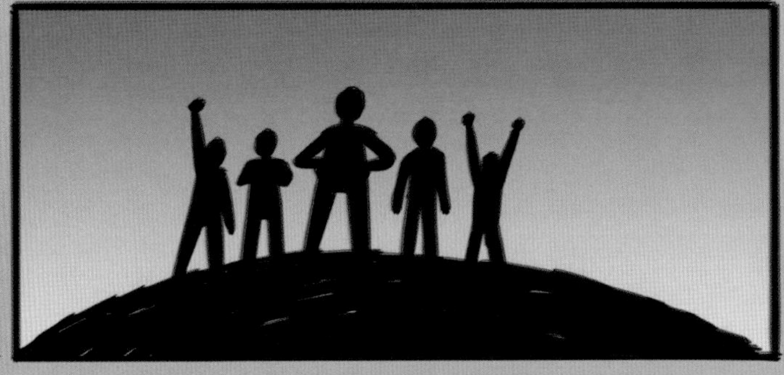

• MAKE SOMETHING MORE THREATENING.

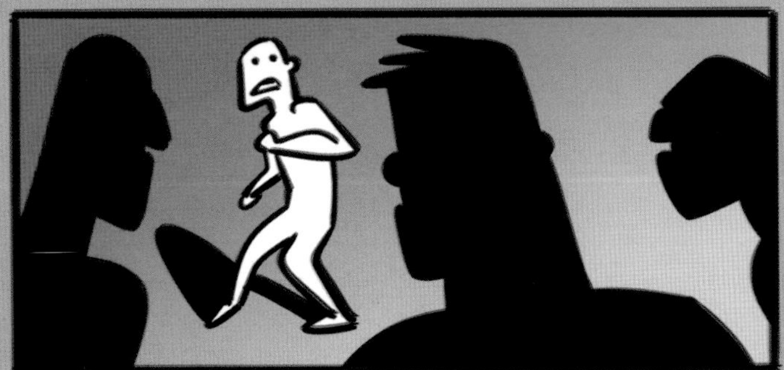

• SHOW LESS AND MAKE THE AUDIENCE FEEL MORE.

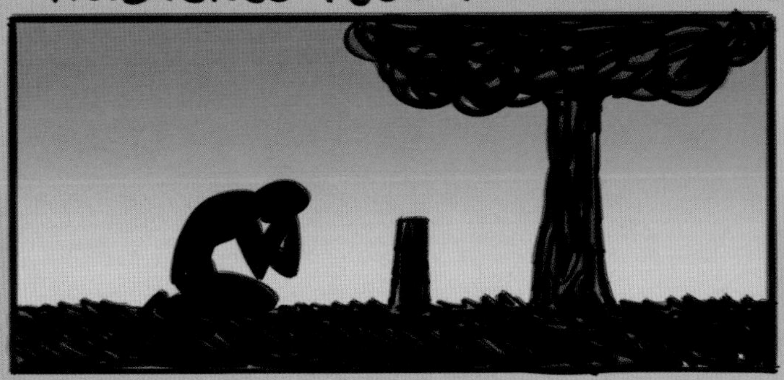

Film Study

Film study is another great exercise to do. When I do mine, I assign a specific area to focus on; ie: texture, light/dark, shape, color, etc...

TIPS Keep it simple & time yourself !!! Also, watch the movie first.

⊛ Example → "Babe" — study on texture

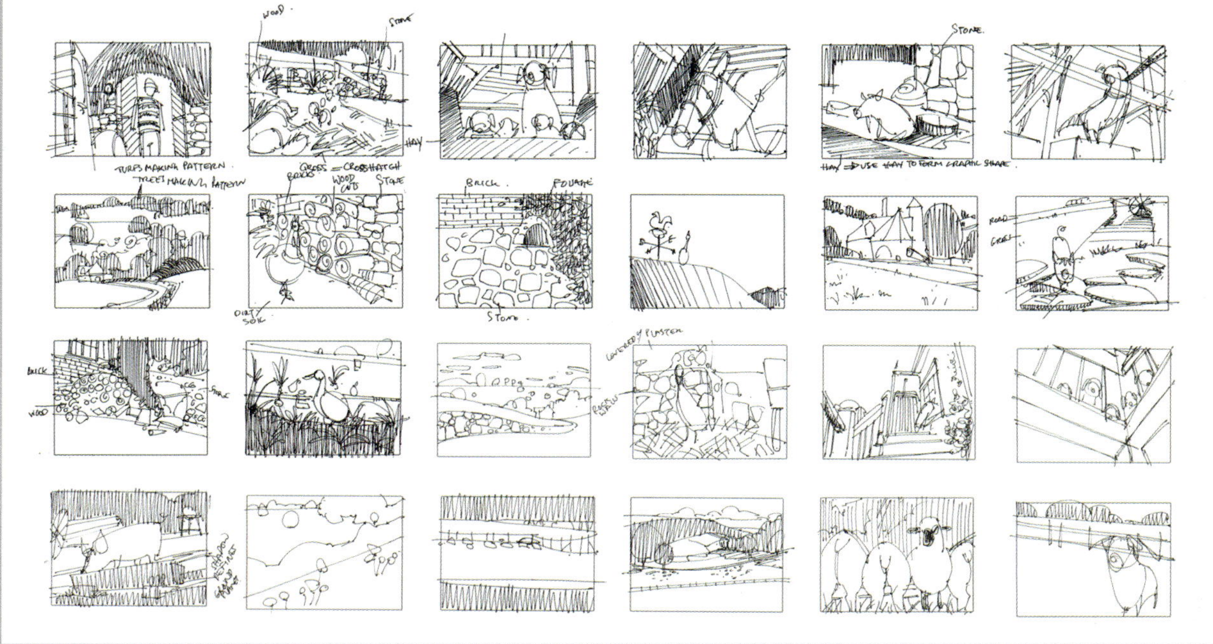

⊛ Example → "Rebecca" -- study on light shape

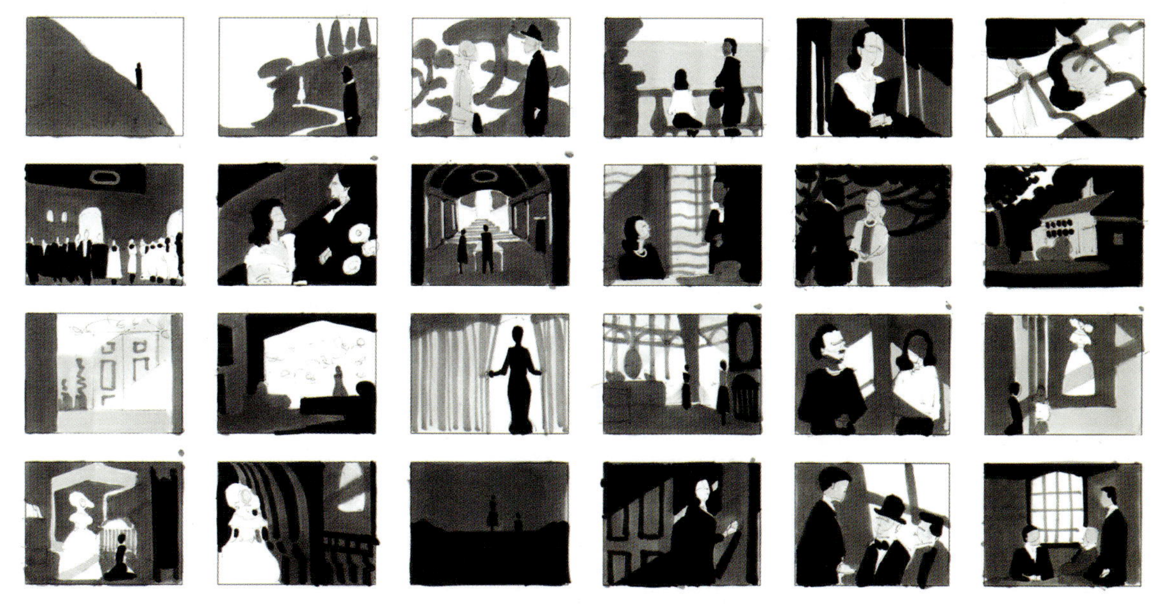

CONTOUR LINES IN LIFE DRAWING MAKES YOU AWARE OF THE BODY'S INNATE SHAPES AND ANGLES.

IT BECOMES EASIER TO DEVELOP "SHORT HANDS" FOR TYPICALLY HARD TO DRAW AREAS.

FINDING A CLEAR SILHOUETTE BECOMES ESSENTIAL WITH A CONTOUR LINE.

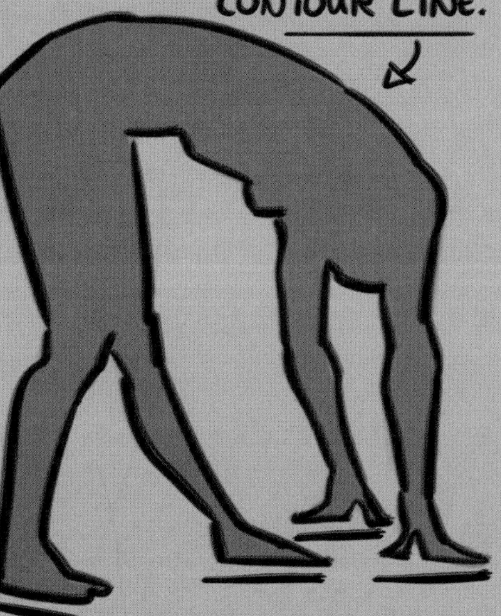

SIMPLIFY NEGATIVE SPACE IN CLOSED FIGURES.

THE PRINCIPLE OF SQUASH AND STRETCH REVEALS ITSELF ON A CONTOURED FIGURE.

SQUASH

STRETCH

FACE IN PROFILE.

WEIGHT DISTRIBUTION BECOMES CLEAR.

NOTICE ANGLES ON THE BODY, LIKE THE RIB CAGE AND PELVIC CREST.

YOU CAN SIMPLIFY WITH LONGER LINES OR NOTICE SUBTLE SHAPE/VOLUME DETAILS.

YOU CAN APPLY THE TECHNIQUE WITHIN ALREADY "CONTOURED" SHAPES.

PAY ATTENTION TO ALL ANGLES AND SHAPES OF THE FOOT.

LOOK FOR PRESSED FLESH TO INDICATE AND EXPRESS WEIGHT.

WHEN PRESSED ON THE GROUND, THE OVERALL SHAPES OF HANDS AND FEET REVEAL THEMSELVES.

THE GROUPING OF FINGERS AND TOES CREATE DISTINCT SHAPES.

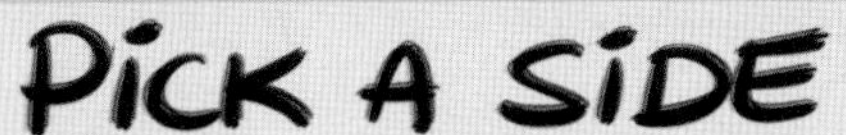

PICK A SIDE

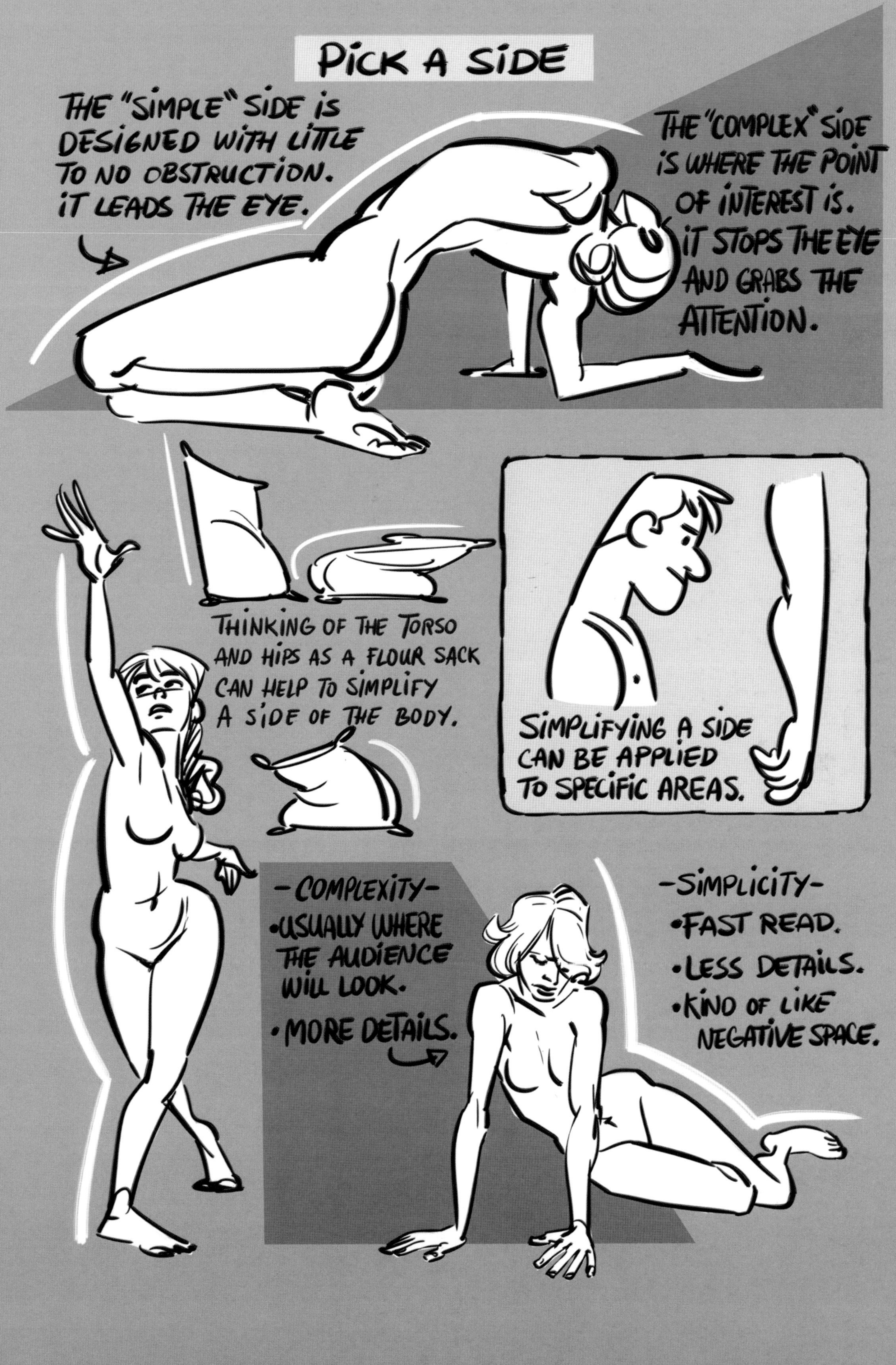

THE "SIMPLE" SIDE IS DESIGNED WITH LITTLE TO NO OBSTRUCTION. IT LEADS THE EYE.

THE "COMPLEX" SIDE IS WHERE THE POINT OF INTEREST IS. IT STOPS THE EYE AND GRABS THE ATTENTION.

THINKING OF THE TORSO AND HIPS AS A FLOUR SACK CAN HELP TO SIMPLIFY A SIDE OF THE BODY.

SIMPLIFYING A SIDE CAN BE APPLIED TO SPECIFIC AREAS.

-COMPLEXITY-
- USUALLY WHERE THE AUDIENCE WILL LOOK.
- MORE DETAILS.

-SIMPLICITY-
- FAST READ.
- LESS DETAILS.
- KIND OF LIKE NEGATIVE SPACE.

Stylized Female Body Proportion

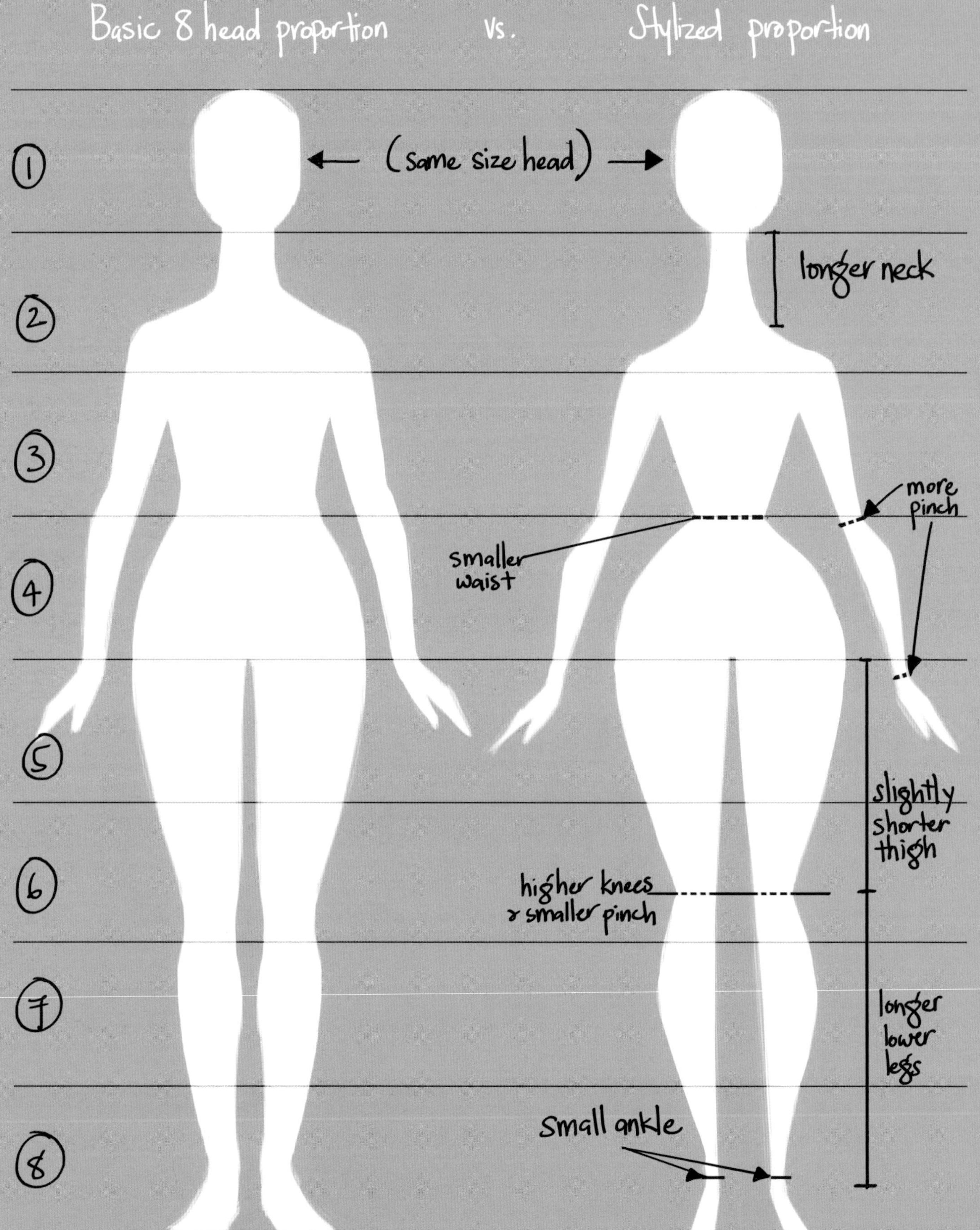

HAND DESIGN : MASCULINE VS. FEMININE

⊛ MASS -- WIDE VS. LEAN

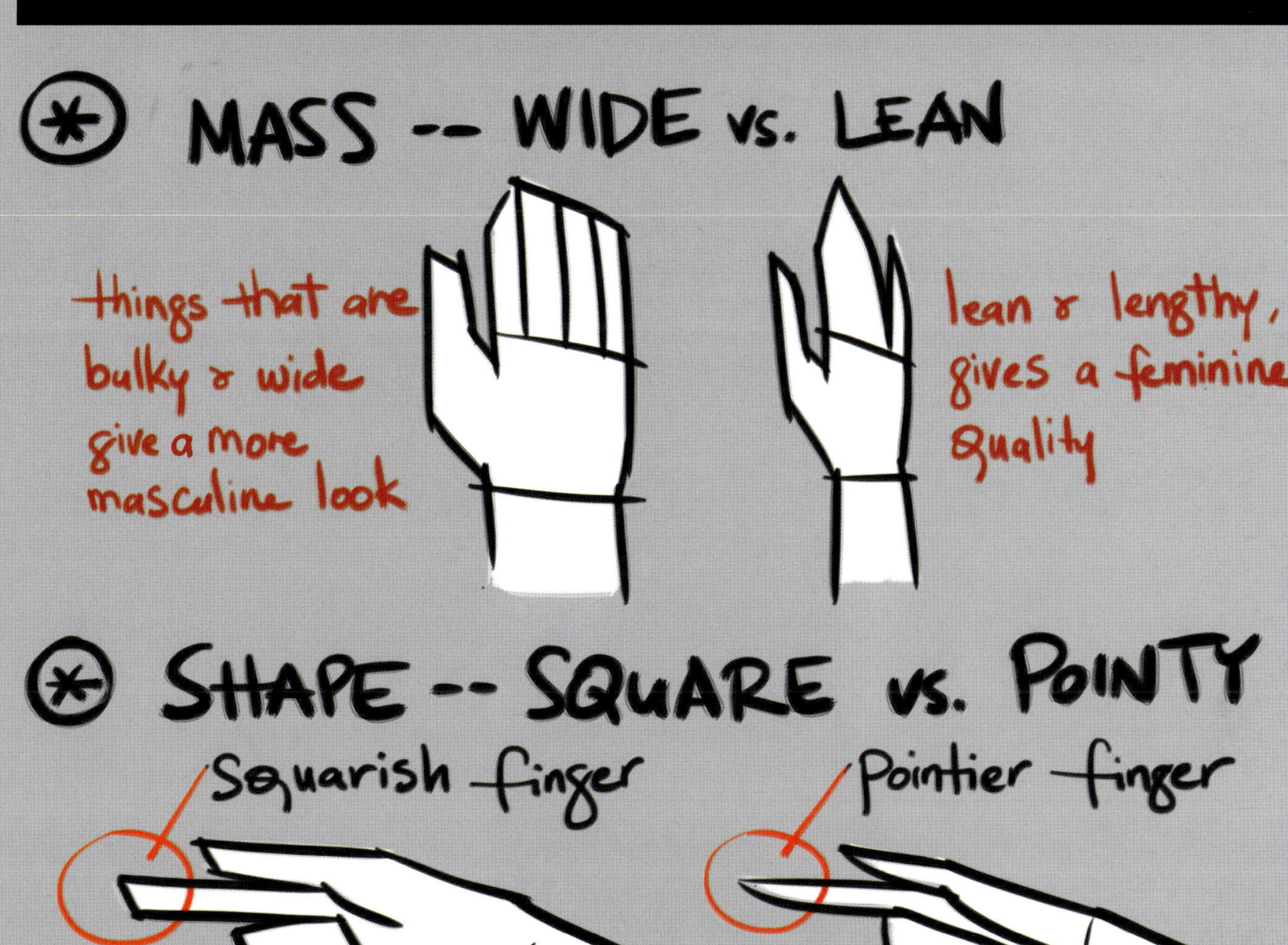

⊛ NEUTRAL POSE -- IN VS. OUT

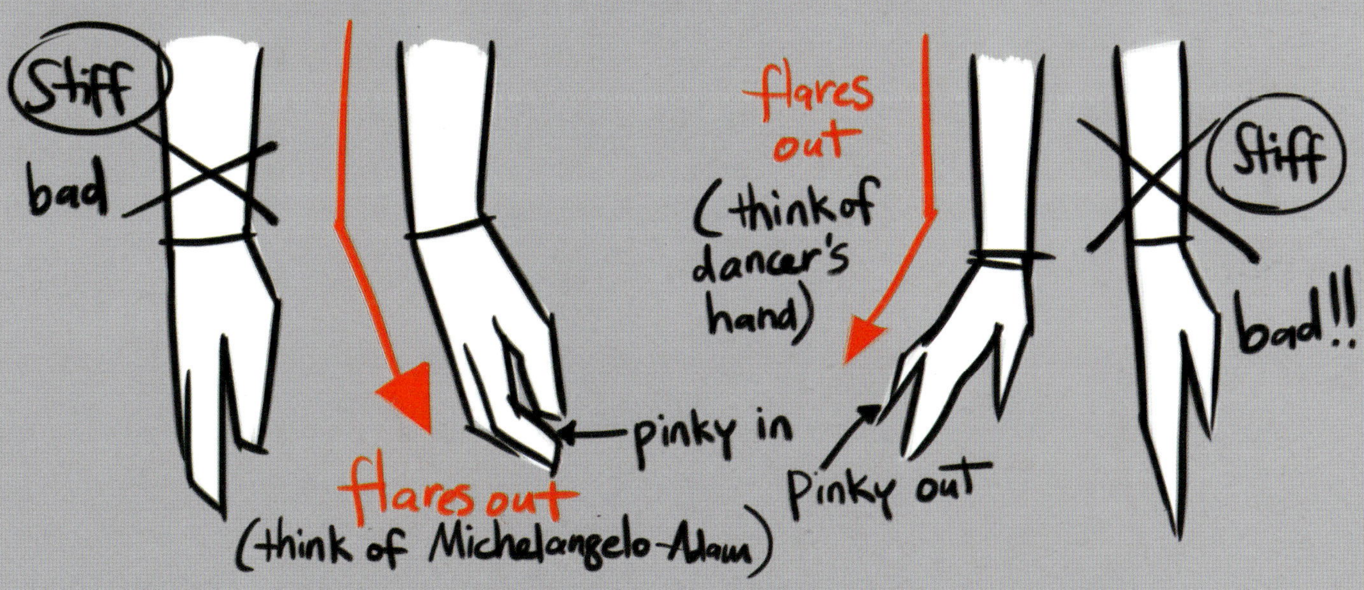

HEAD BASICS

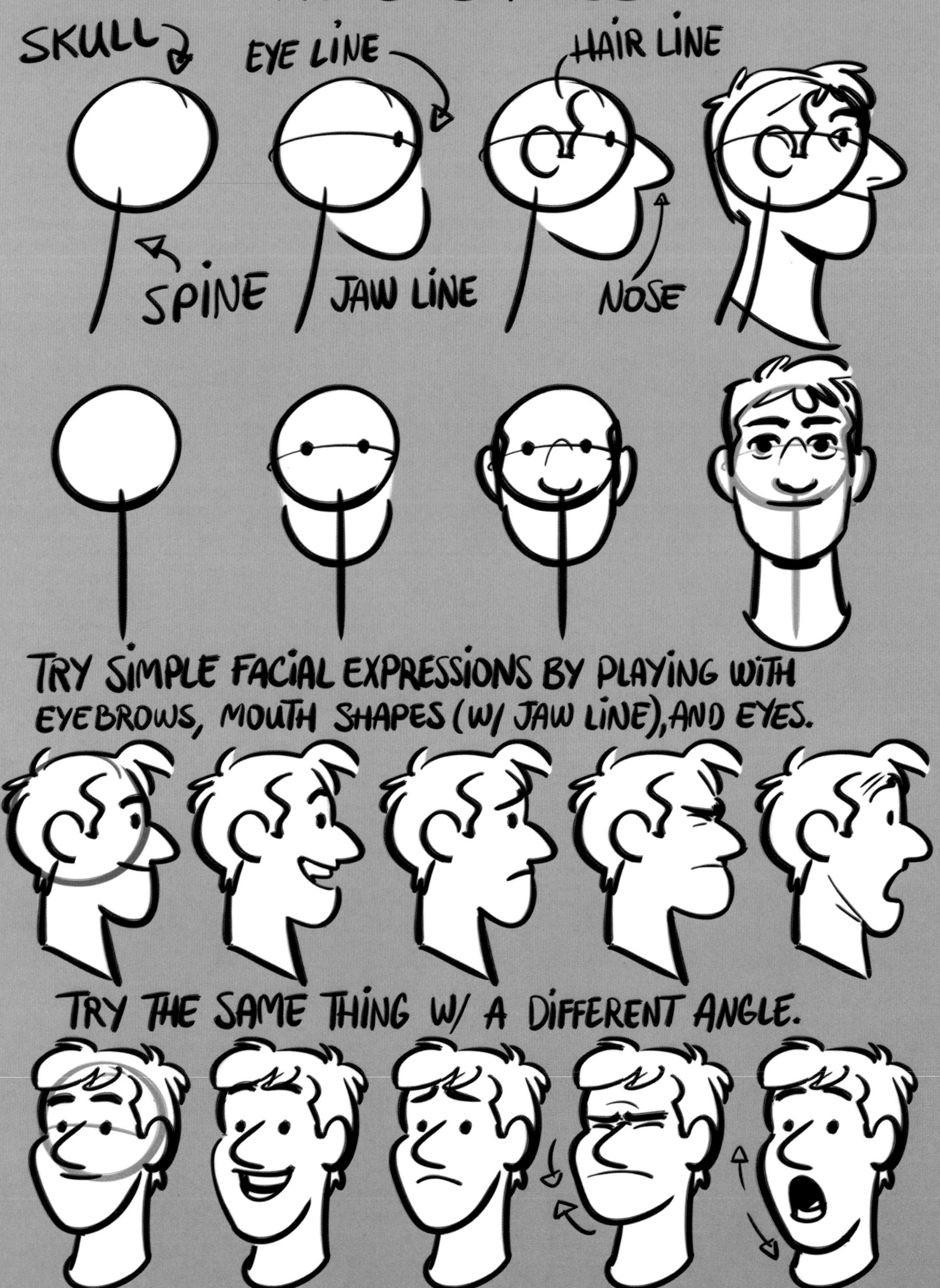
SKULL
EYE LINE
HAIR LINE
SPINE
JAW LINE
NOSE
TRY SIMPLE FACIAL EXPRESSIONS BY PLAYING WITH EYEBROWS, MOUTH SHAPES (W/ JAW LINE), AND EYES.
TRY THE SAME THING W/ A DIFFERENT ANGLE.

HEAD FOUNDATION

THE 2 ESSENTIALS:

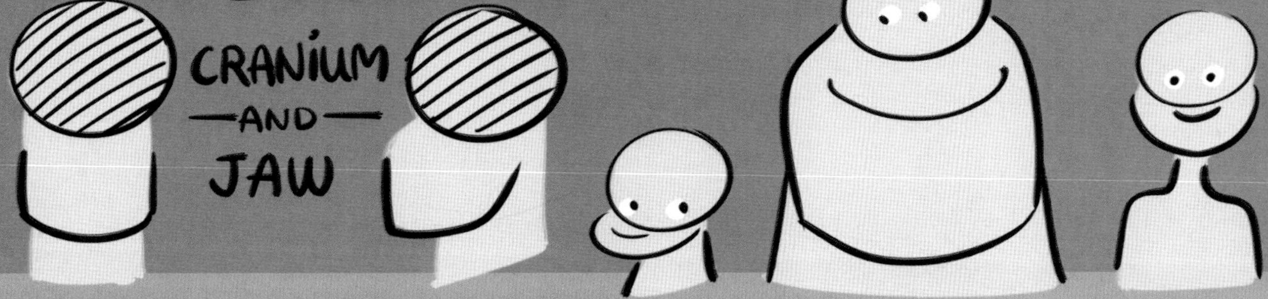

CRANIUM
—AND—
JAW

TRANSLATING INTO VOLUMES:

KEEP CUTTING FOR MORE DETAILS...

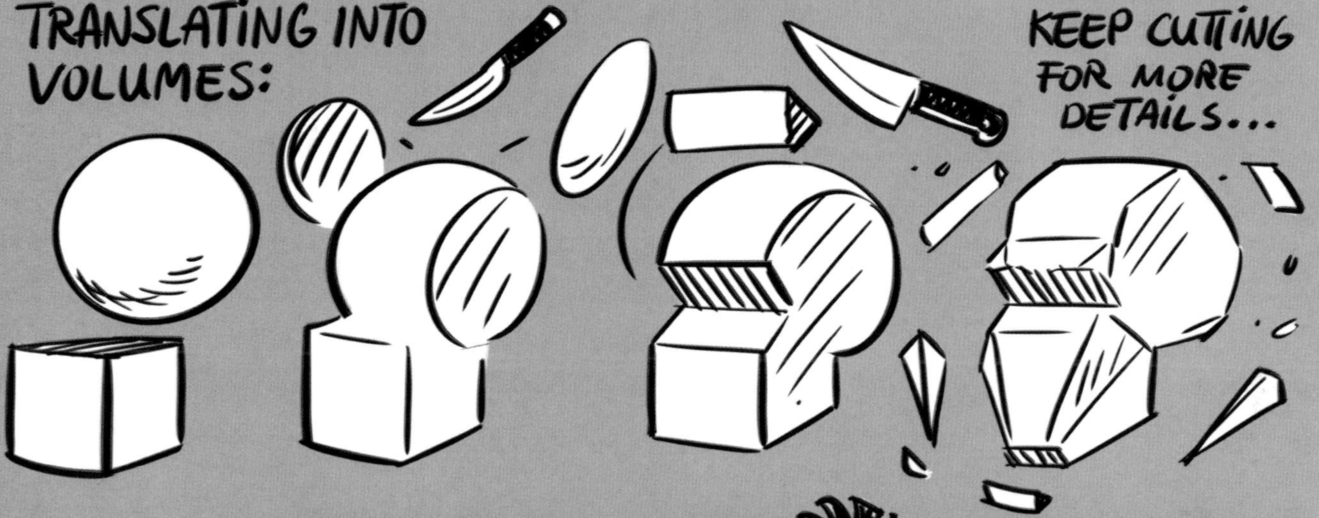

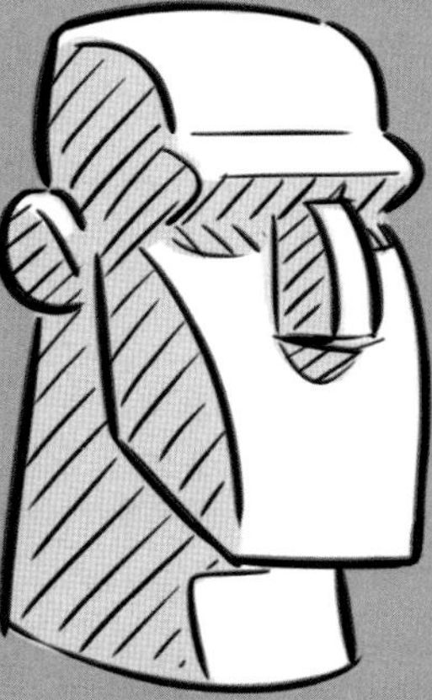

ONCE YOU HAVE A BASIC FOUNDATION, YOU CAN ADD ADDITIONAL FEATURES.

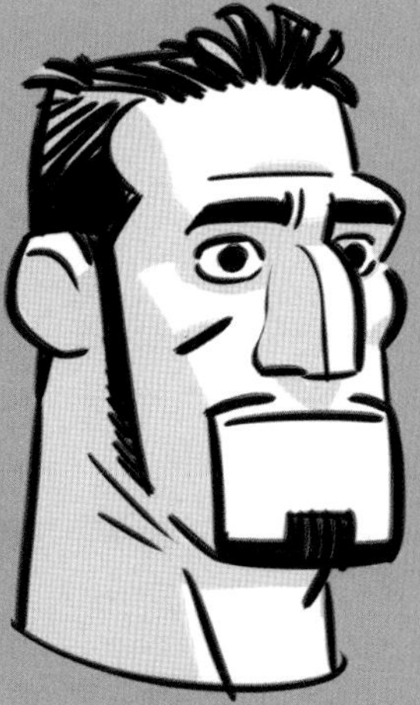

TRY TO ADD FEATURES THAT WILL ACCENTUATE THE BASIC FOUNDATION.

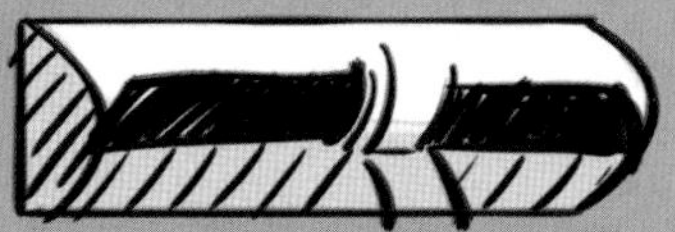

THE BEST WAY TO "TEST" YOUR DESIGN IS TO DRAW IT FROM DIFFERENT ANGLES. USE GUIDES TO KEEP PROPORTIONS.

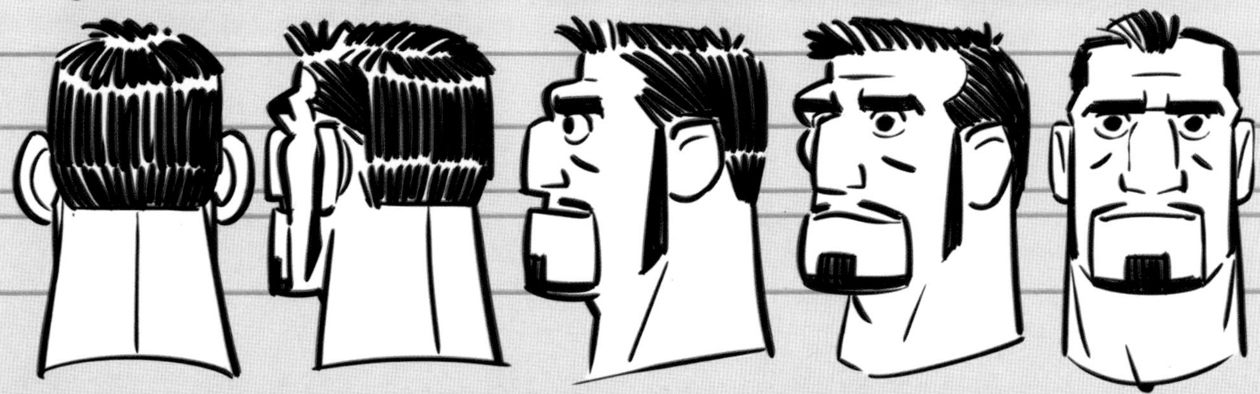

How do you paint?

Advice from Bob Kato -- BACK to FRONT
DARK to LIGHT
DULL to BRIGHT
GENERAL to DETAIL

example:

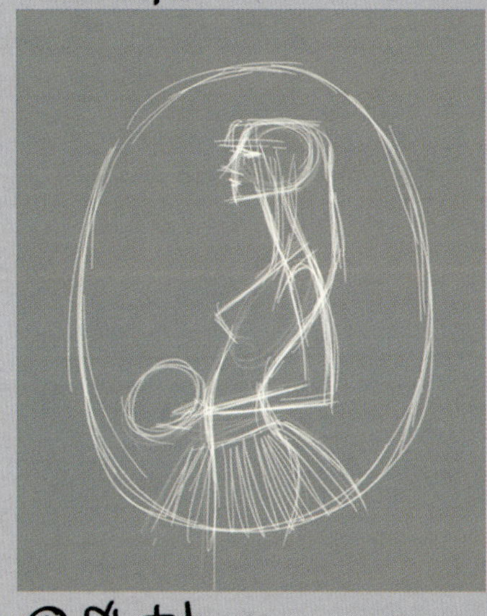

① Sketch

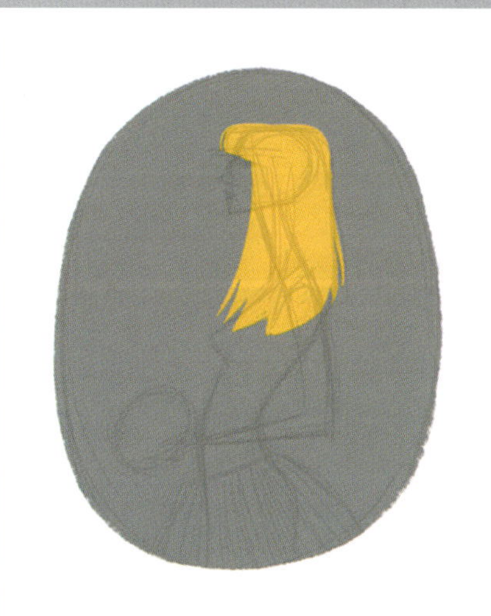

② Paint the furthest shape. In this ptg, it's the hair

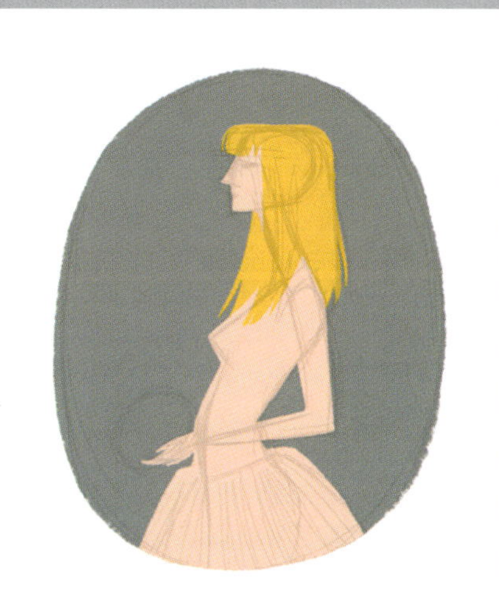

③ The 2nd furthest shape.
✱ I like painting the body & clothing as <u>one</u> shape.

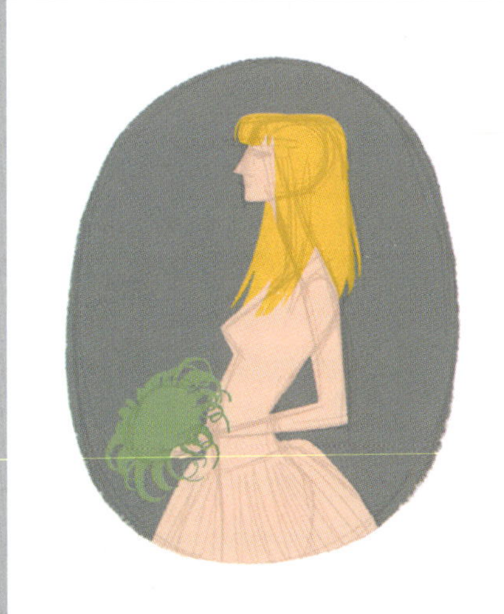

④ another layer on top

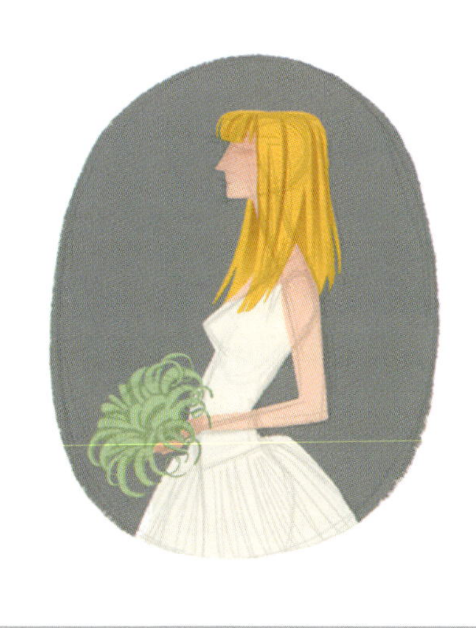

⑤ add graphic detail

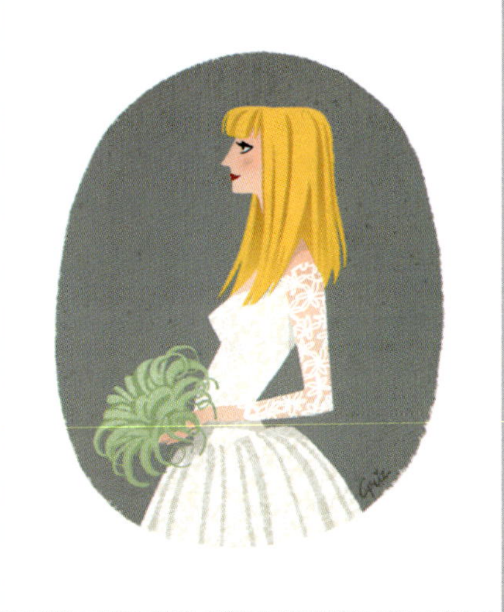

⑥ finishing touches

Bob Kato created "The Drawing Club", please go to www.thedrawingclub.com

Painting EYES 101

① Know your light source -- type, color, angle

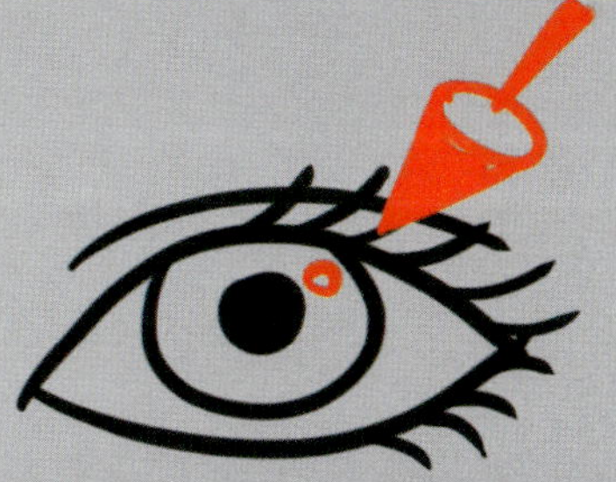

ie. the sun gives a round & warm highlight; rectangular flourescent light gives a cool & rectangular highlight, ... etc

② Think BASIC MATERIAL

✱ The sclera (white part) is a SEMI-GLOSSY SPHERE

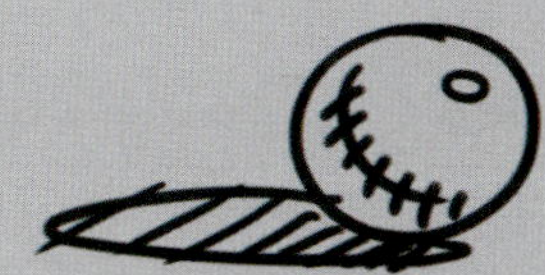

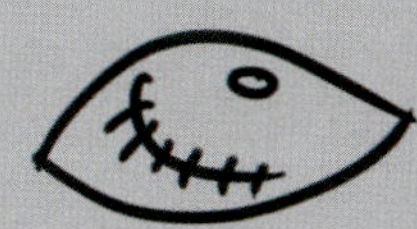

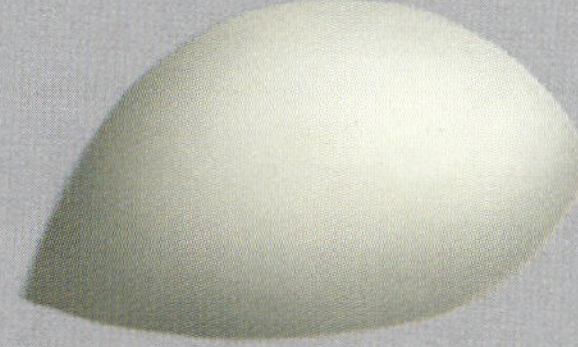

✱ The IRIS (color part) is GLASS; cornea is basically a glass dome.

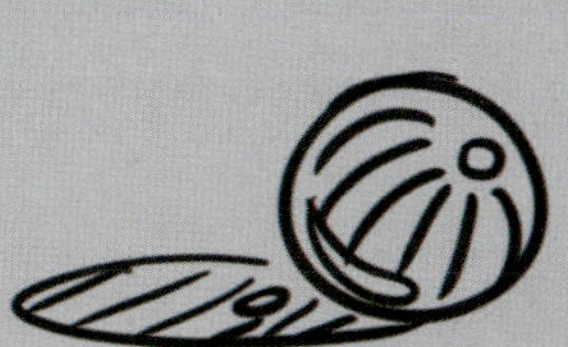

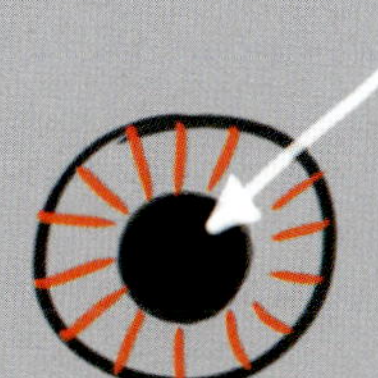

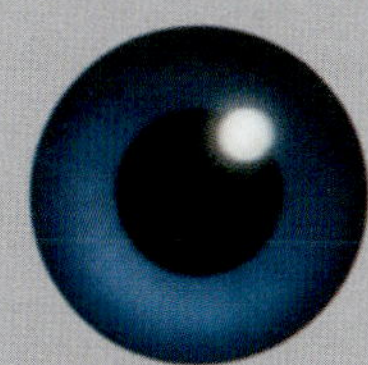

There is a starburst pattern that usually goes darker as it goes outside

③ Combine them & add detail ⇒ eyelash & shadow

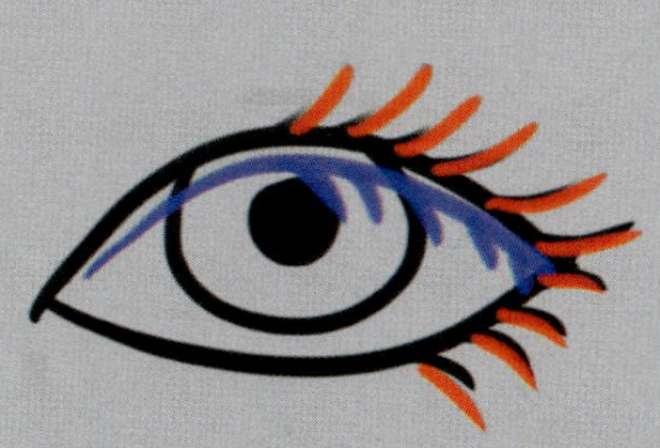

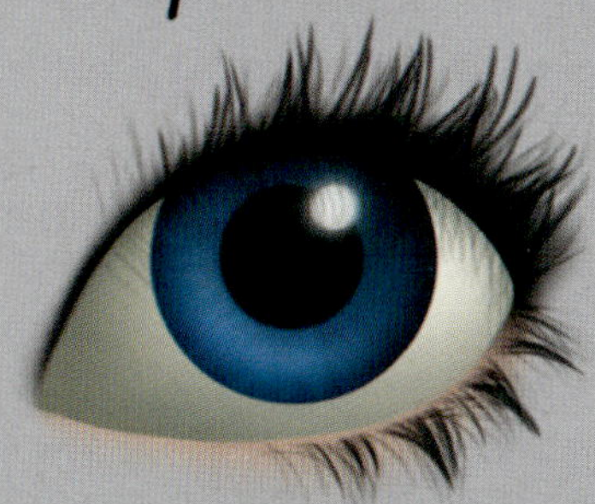

NO STRAIGHT LINES!

NOTHING KILLS A POSE QUICKER THAN A PURE, STRAIGHT LINE.

"KIND OF STRAIGHT" IS MUCH BETTER. THERE IS ENERGY, DIRECTION, AND POTENTIAL TO IT.

A COMBINATION OF CURVED LINES GIVES A LOT MORE INFORMATION THAN STRAIGHT LINES.

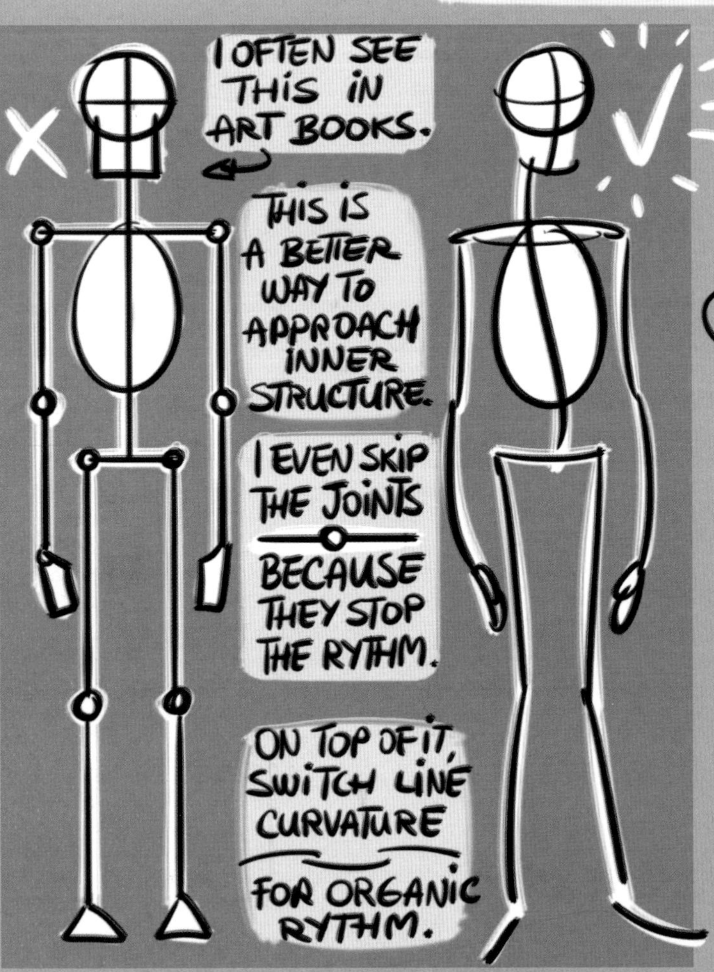

THESE 4 CURVED LINES GIVE A TON OF INFORMATION:

- CRANIUM POSITION/VOLUME.
- EYELINE PERSPECTIVE.
- ANGLE OF HEAD/FACE.
- JAW LINE.

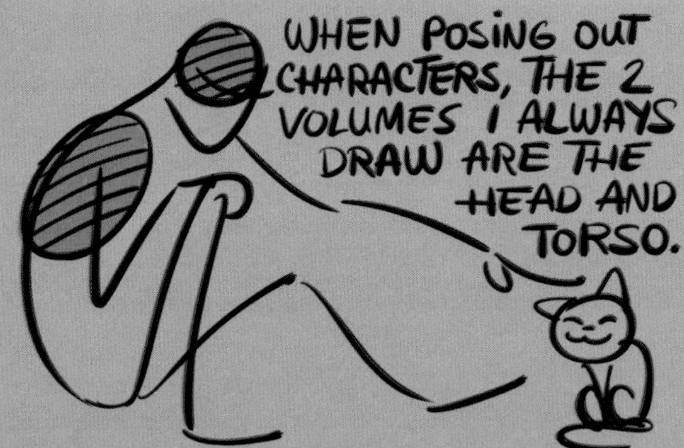

SWITCH LINE CURVATURE TO CREATE A NATURAL RHYTHM.

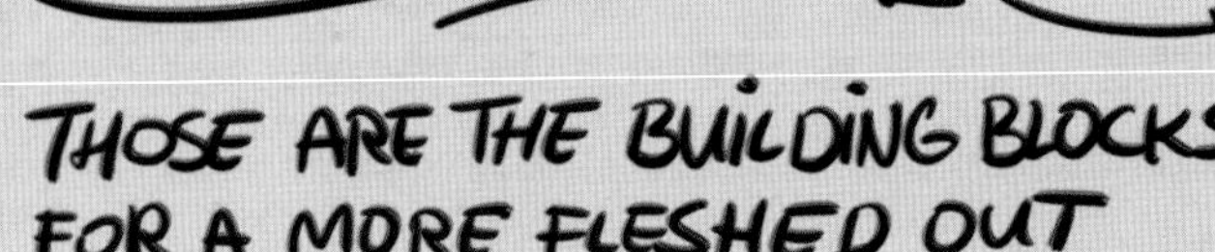

THOSE ARE THE BUILDING BLOCKS FOR A MORE FLESHED OUT DRAWING.

PERSPECTIVE W/ SIMPLE CURVED LINES:

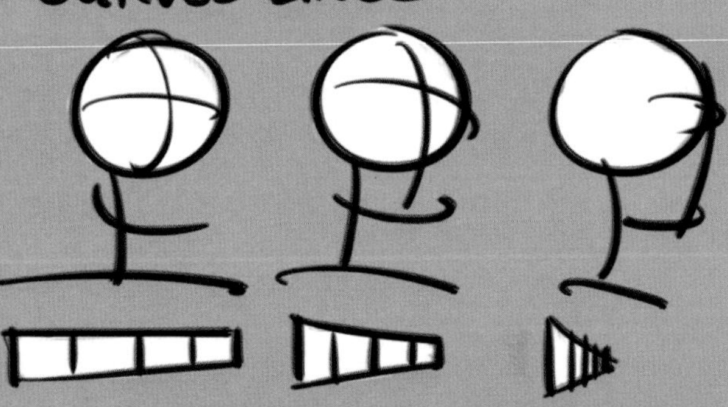

FLOATING HANDS

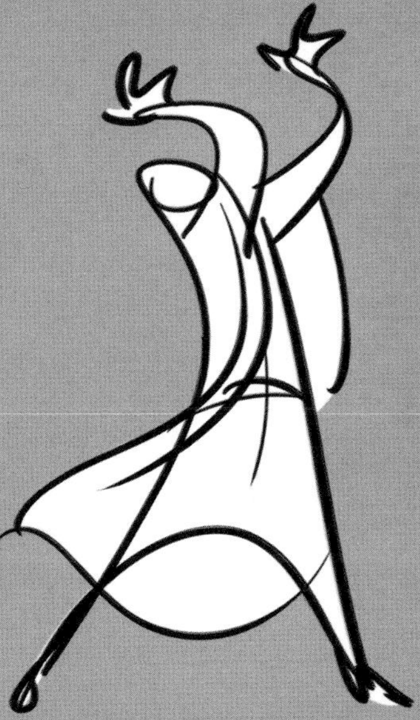

GESTURE AND STRUCTURE CAN SOMETIMES CLASH. IT CAN BE HARD TO FIND A GOOD BALANCE. DRAWING HANDS FIRST CAN HELP.

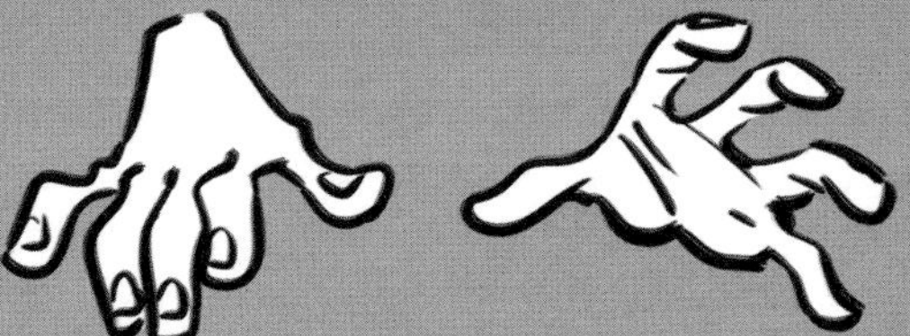

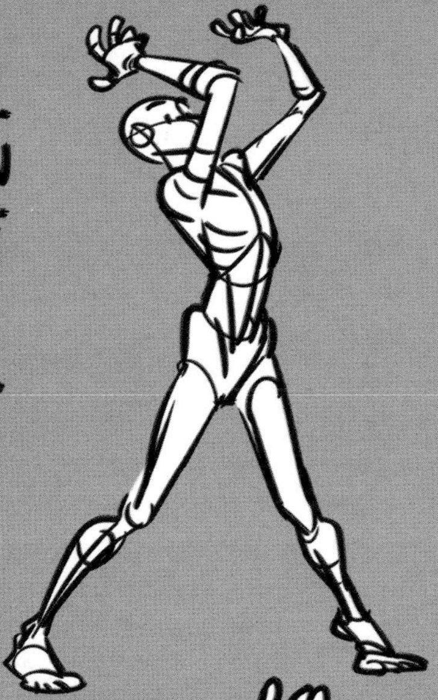

DRAW HANDS WITHIN RANGE OF MOTION, AND THEN CONNECT TO BODY.

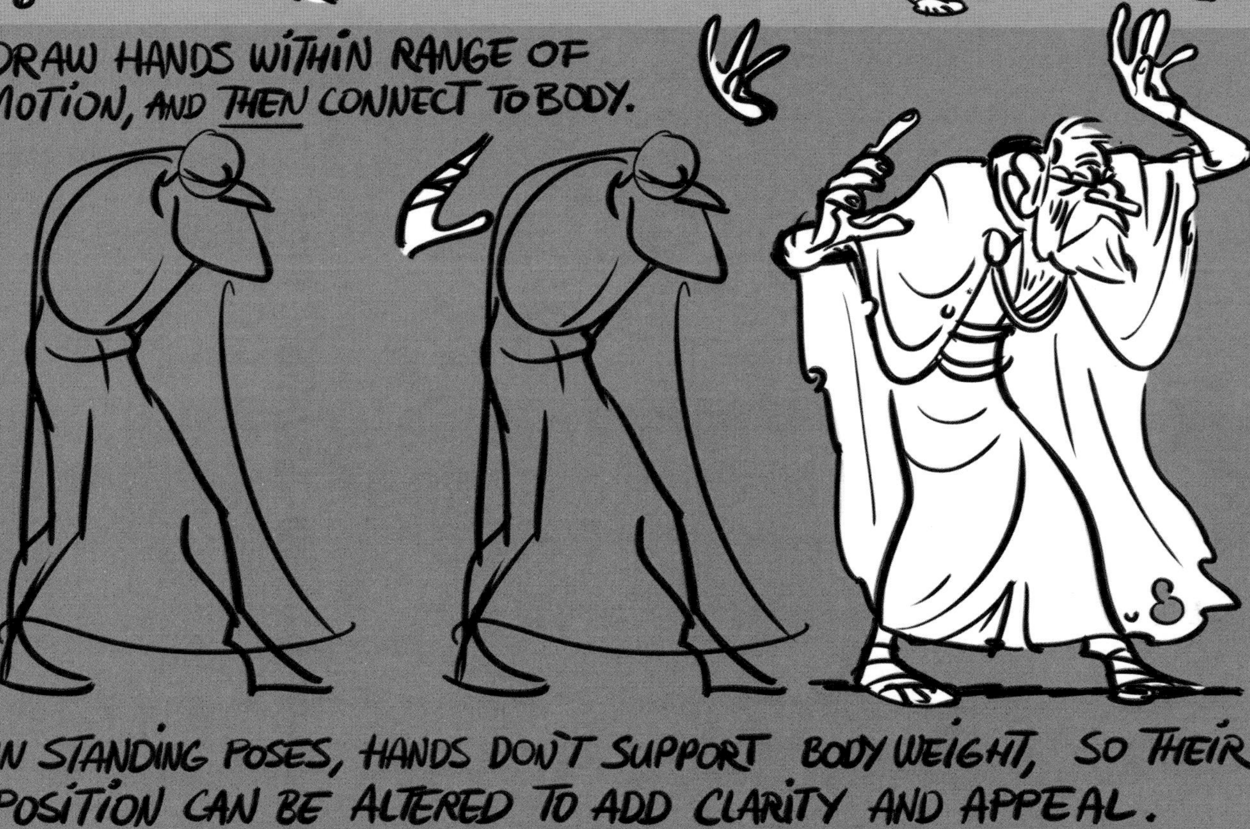

IN STANDING POSES, HANDS DON'T SUPPORT BODY WEIGHT, SO THEIR POSITION CAN BE ALTERED TO ADD CLARITY AND APPEAL.

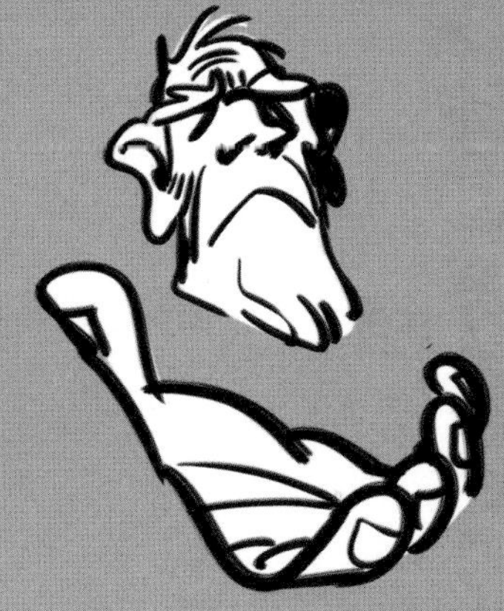

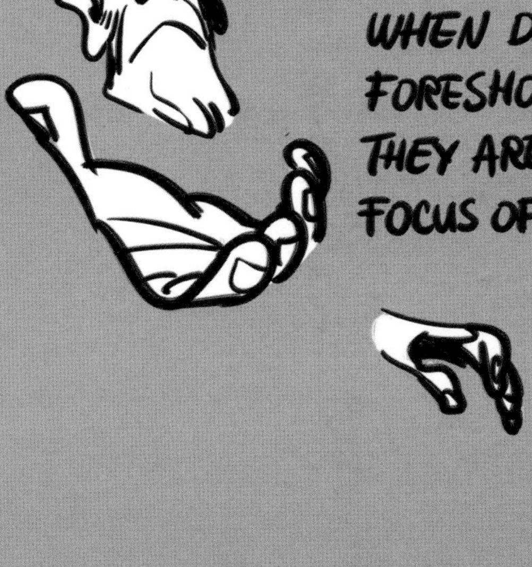

STAGE HANDS FIRST WHEN DEALING WITH FORESHORTENING, SINCE THEY ARE THE MAIN FOCUS OF THE POSE.

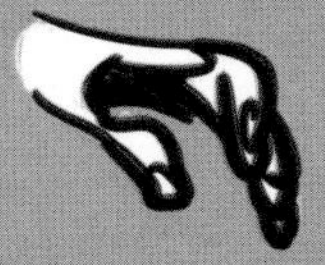

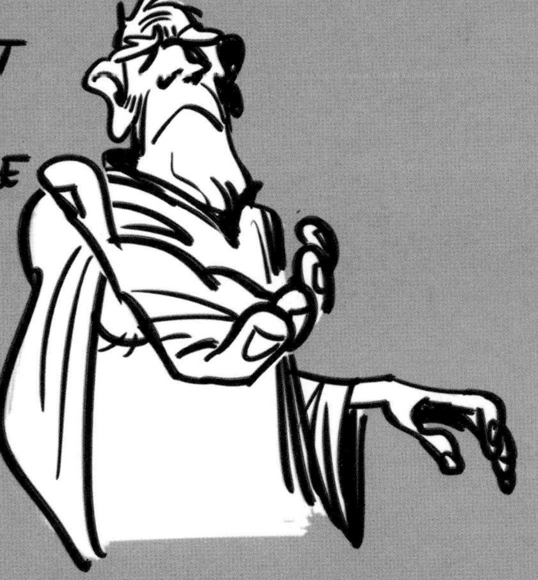

HUE, VALUE, SATURATION

HUE -- the color itself -- red, blue, green, indigo, orange, ochre, cobalt, ... etc.

VALUE -- how dark or light the hue is in greyscale 0% - 100%

ie. yellow has a high value of 10% - 15%
true RED & true GREEN has a value of 50%
forest green has a rough value of 85%
lime green has a rough value of 35%

SATURATION -- how intense the brightness of the hue.

ie. Neon lime green has HIGH saturation; dusty green has LOW saturation.

⊛ Exercises -- (3 different HUE)

1. contrast of VALUE
2. contrast of SATURATION
3. SAME VALUE & SATURATION

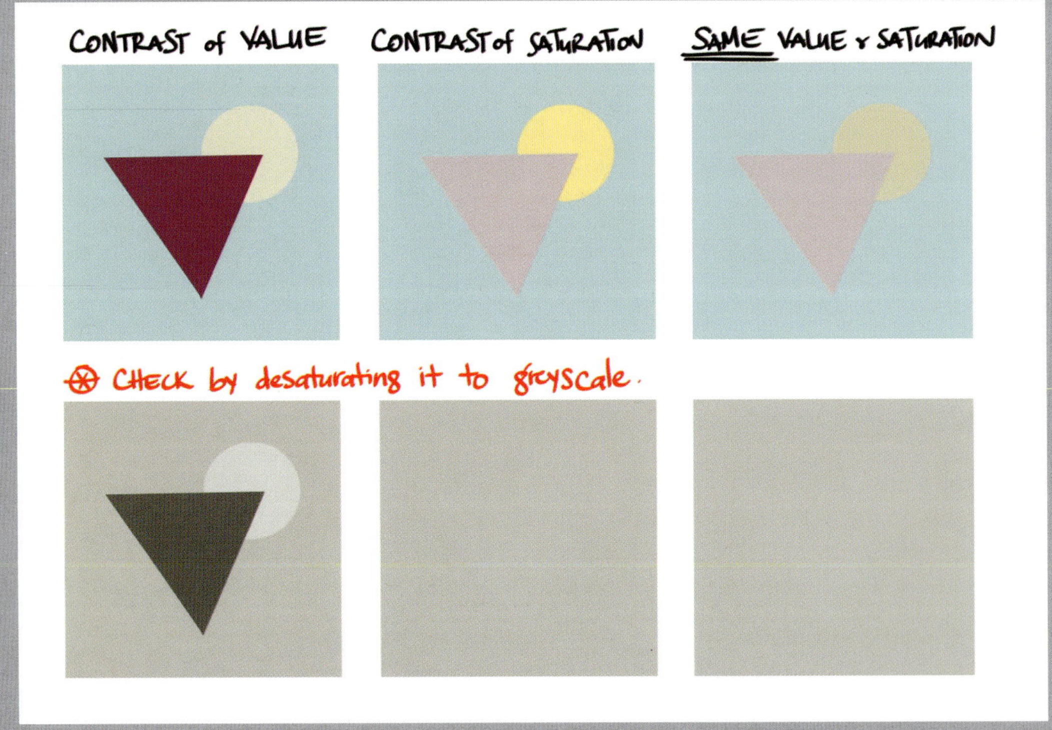

LIMITED PALETTE

Learning how to paint can be daunting & kind of scary. Use a limited palette to ease your way into color.

⇒ Use 3 colors -- (2 complementary + white) to recreate a master copy from a photograph.
⇒ For this exercise, you MUST use real paint !!!

I used Liquitex heavy body (acrylic); I used ultramarine blue, cadmium orange, & titanium white. The original photo was from a travel book of Bali.

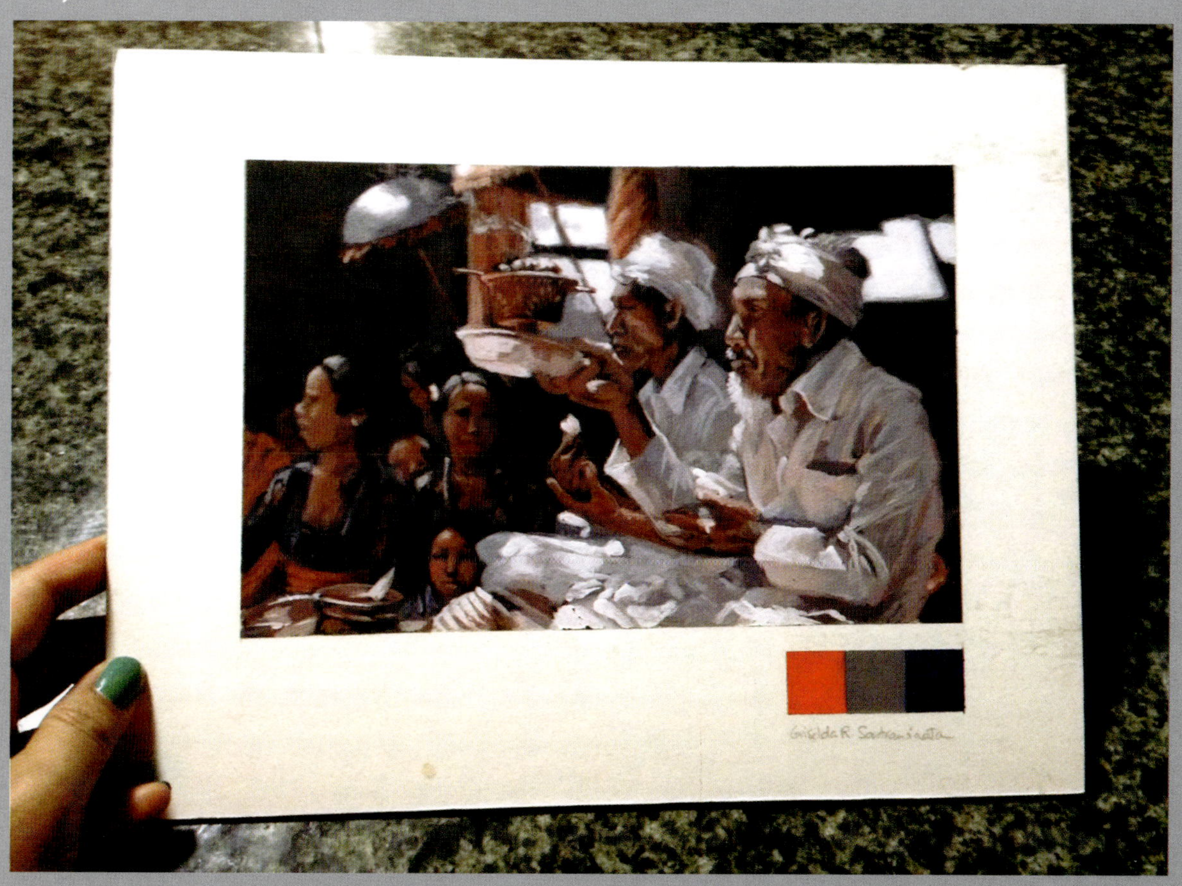

TIPS depending on your photograph, see what complementary color will suit your painting. Green vs. Red; Blue vs. Orange; Violet vs. Yellow.

EYES

TO CLARIFY OR ACCENTUATE A LOOK TO THE SIDE, TRY THIS:

- DON'T COMPLETE THE EYE SHAPE.
- ADD THE DOTS AT THE VERY EDGE.

VOILA!

OKAY. BETTER!

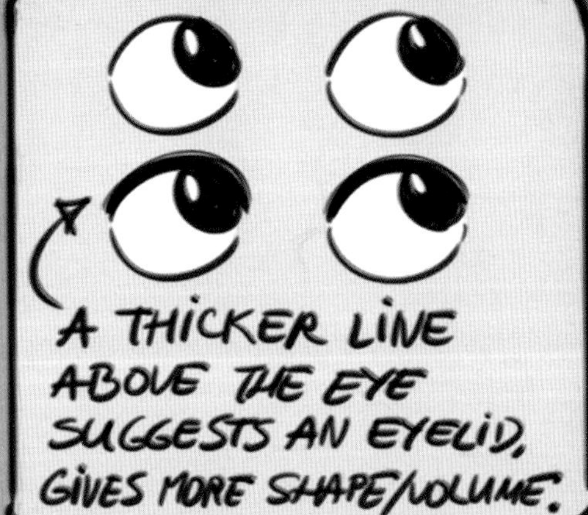

A THICKER LINE ABOVE THE EYE SUGGESTS AN EYELID, GIVES MORE SHAPE/VOLUME.

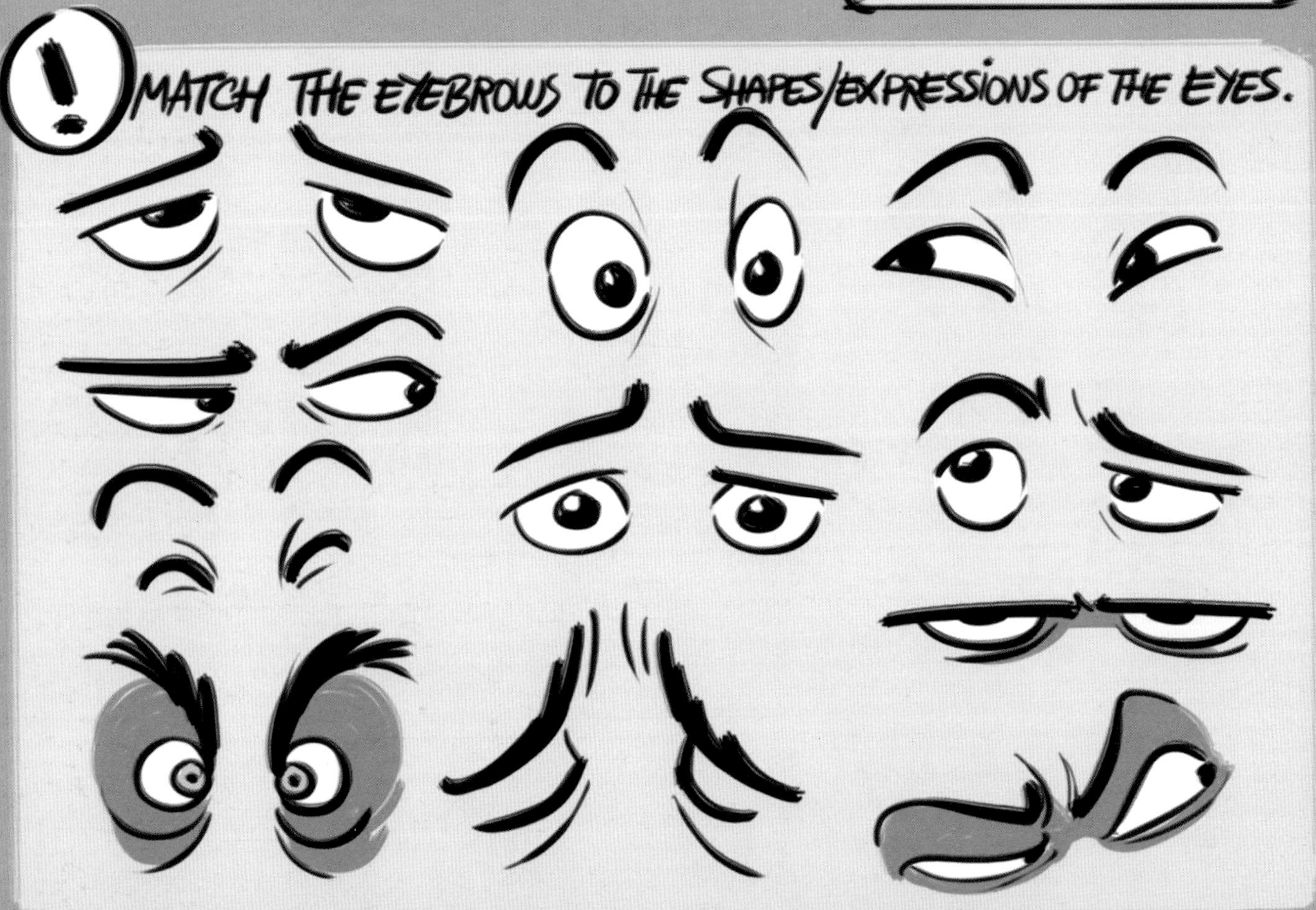

! MATCH THE EYEBROWS TO THE SHAPES/EXPRESSIONS OF THE EYES.

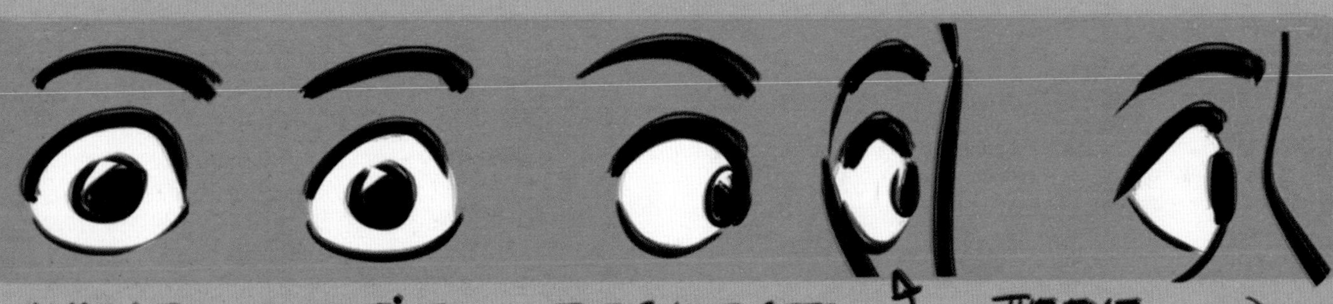

WHEN THE PERSPECTIVE CHANGES, TRACK THE WIDTH AND SHAPE OF EYE+EYEBROW.

EYE SHAPE GETS NARROWER AS THE ANGLE CHANGES.

THE EYE STAYS ROUND IN PROFILE.

EAR(S)

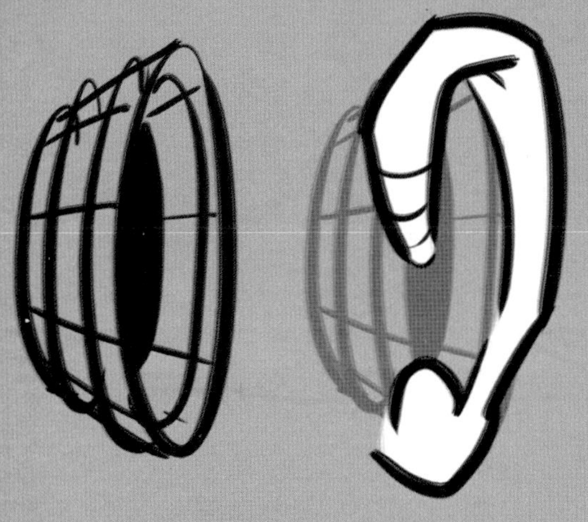
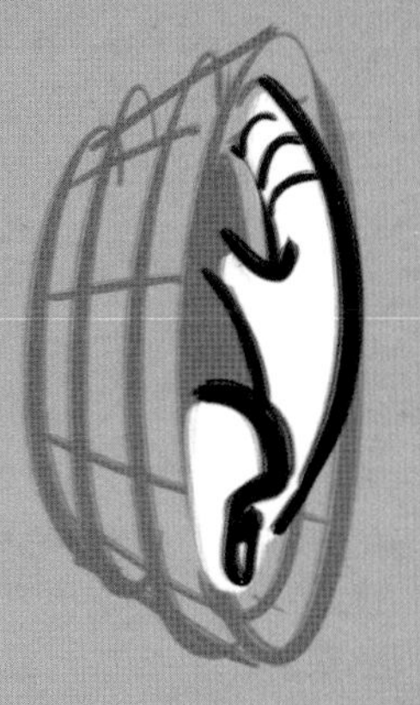
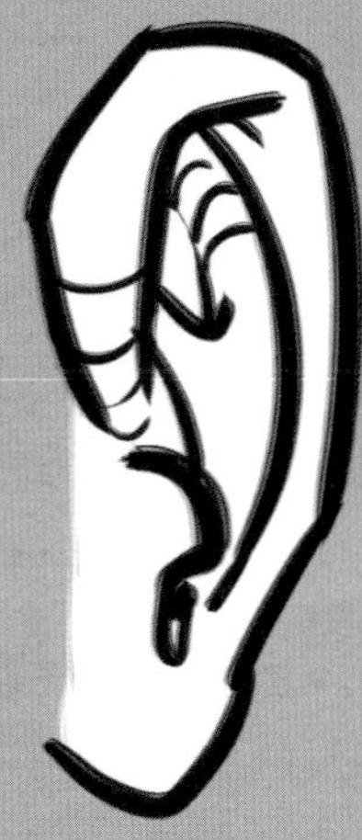
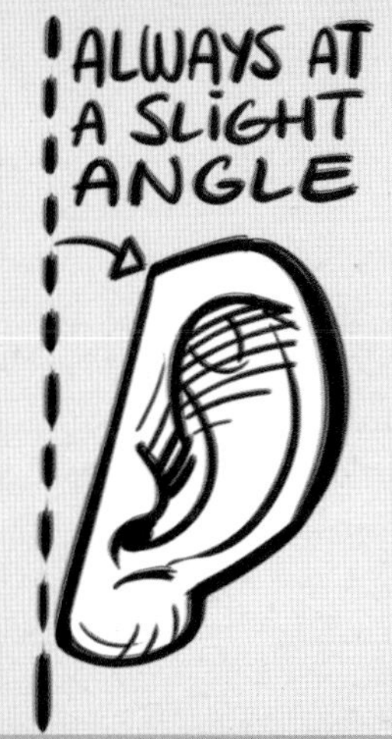

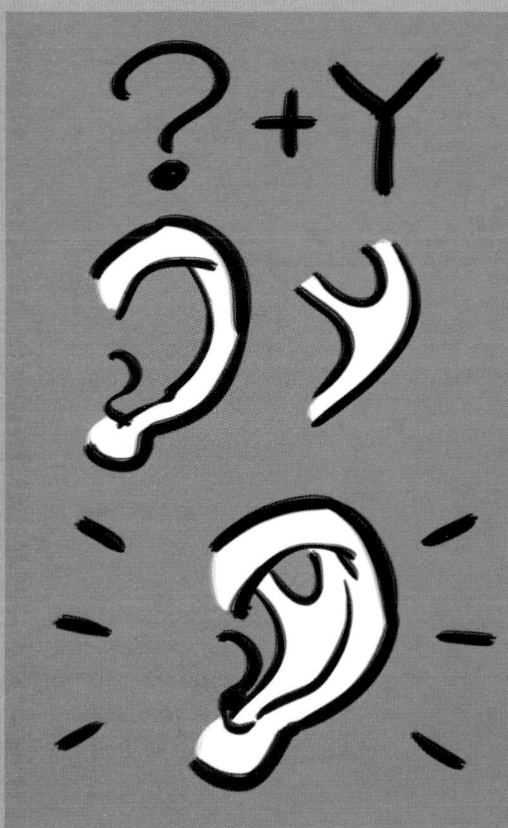

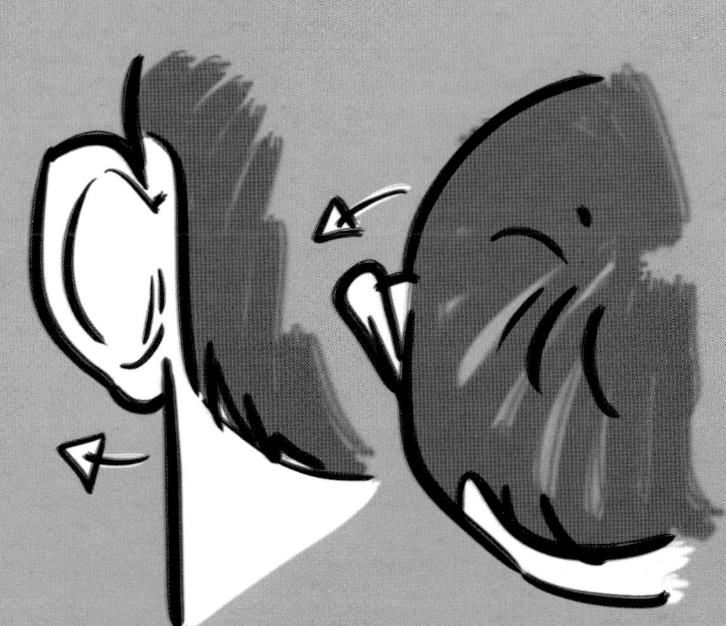

ALWAYS THINK OF THE EARS AS VOLUMES. VERY USEFUL FOR "OVER-THE-SHOULDER" SHOTS.

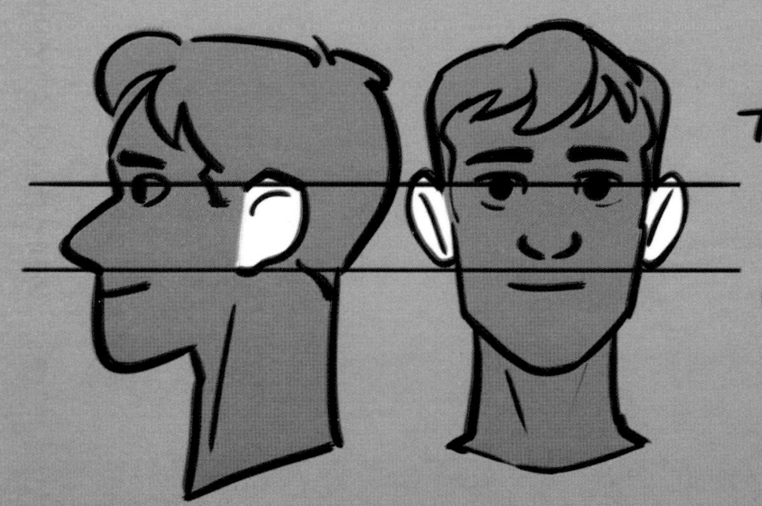

EYELINE/EARS POSITION TO SHOW HEAD PERSPECTIVE.

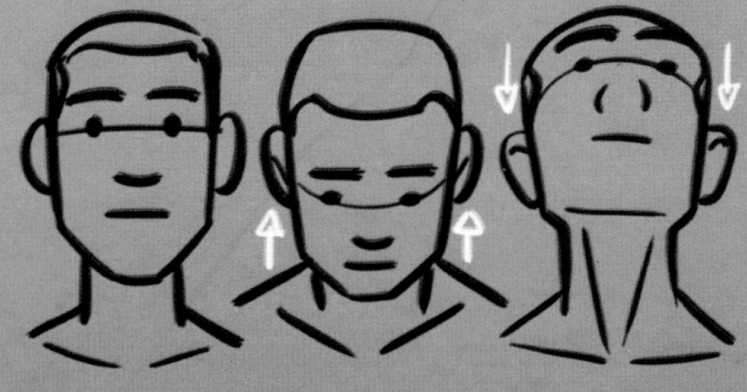

Drawing w/ PEN

Learned this from Dynamic Sketching. Having drawing skills is a MUST. It's about being a problem solver & having good ideas. One way to convey your ideas quickly is through sketches, & you can do this quickly if you train yourself to sketch with pen.

PROS of using PEN:
1. Faster (no noodling or erasing)
2. More confident sketches
3. Looks cool.

CONS: Can't erase !!! (which force you to be more confident)

exercise: Create value from 100 to 0 (black to white). Do as many different textures as you like

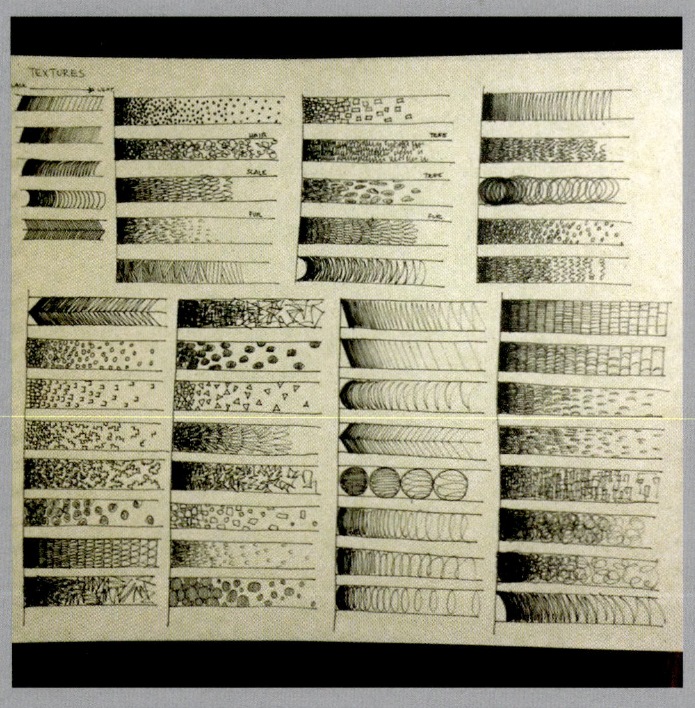

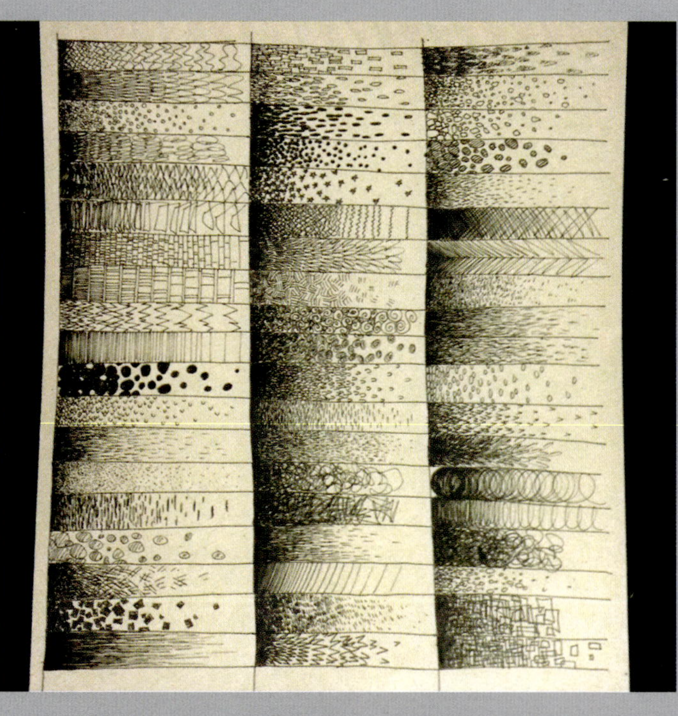

Indicating VOLUME

We show volume through contour lines & adding texture in a strategic way, because it's all about expressing your ideas quickly.

This exercise is very neat. You'll get the hang of it quickly & understand how much is enough, not enough, or too much. As long as it feels right, you're doing it right. And you can only get better through practice.

Steps : ① Abstract shape

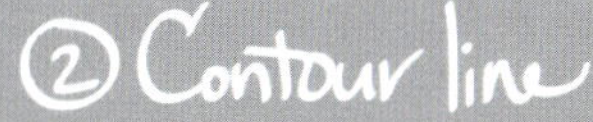

③ Texture

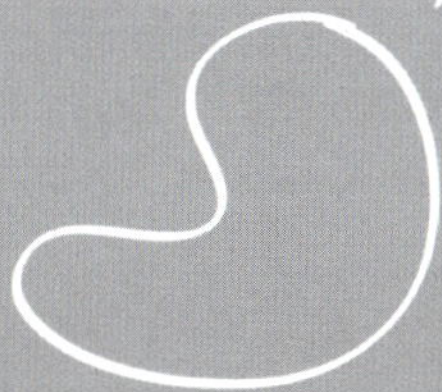

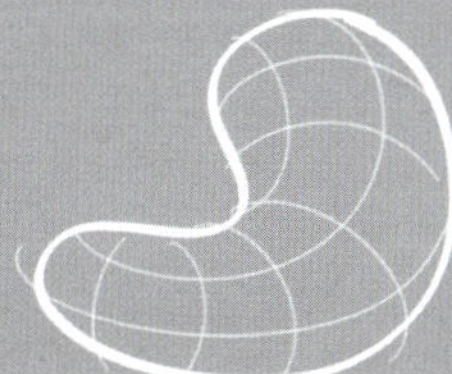

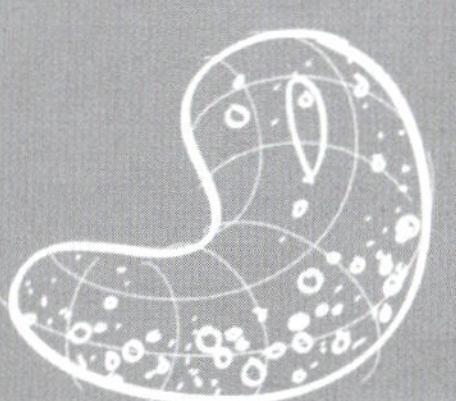

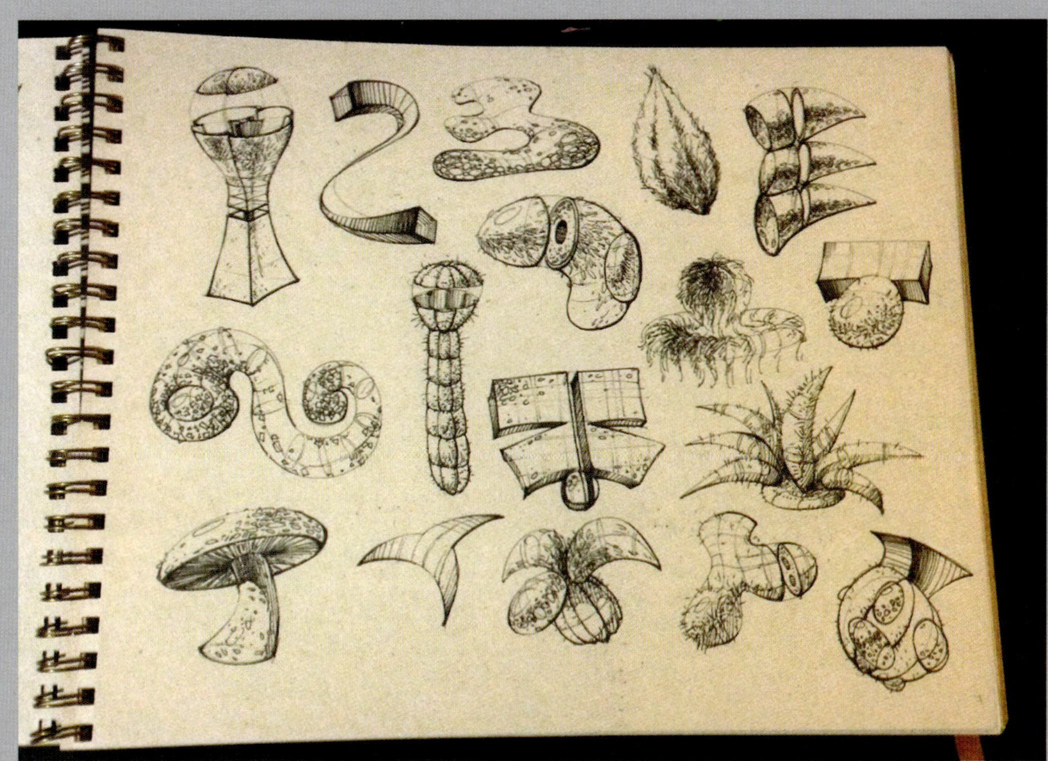

TIPS This is about showing idea, so there's no need to texture the whole object. Most of the texture will be around the CORE shadow

NOSE

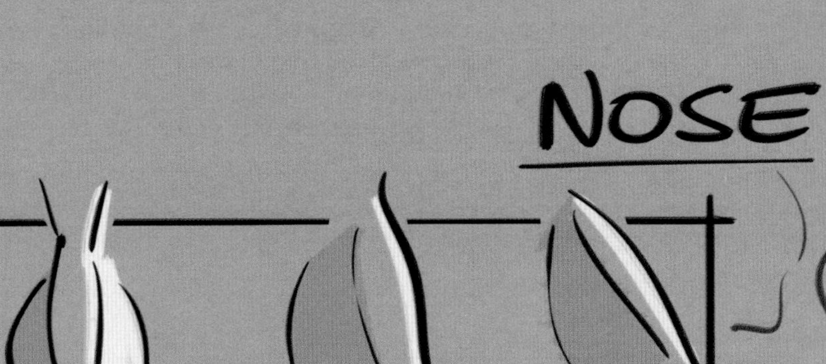

SIMPLIFICATION

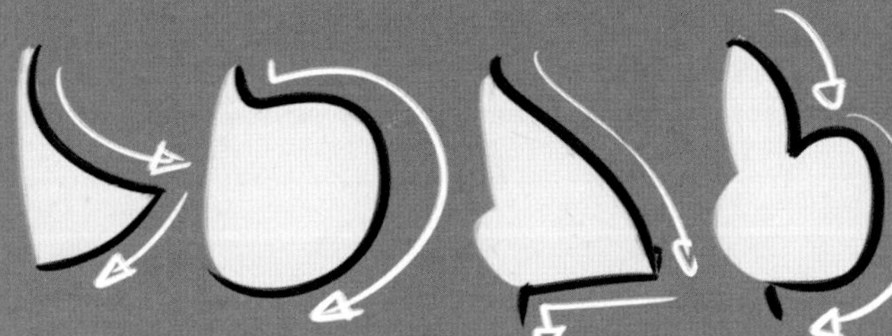

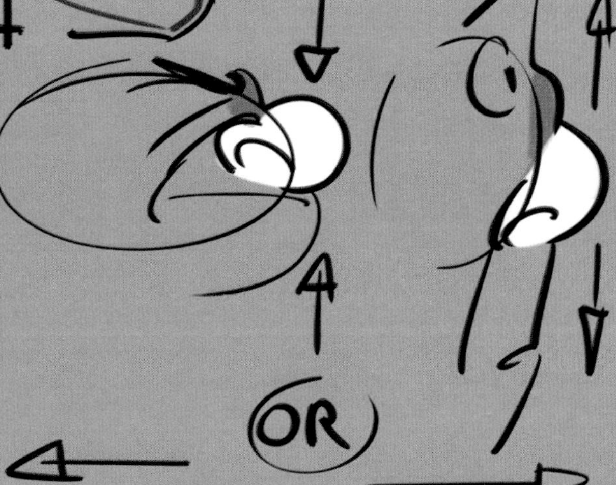

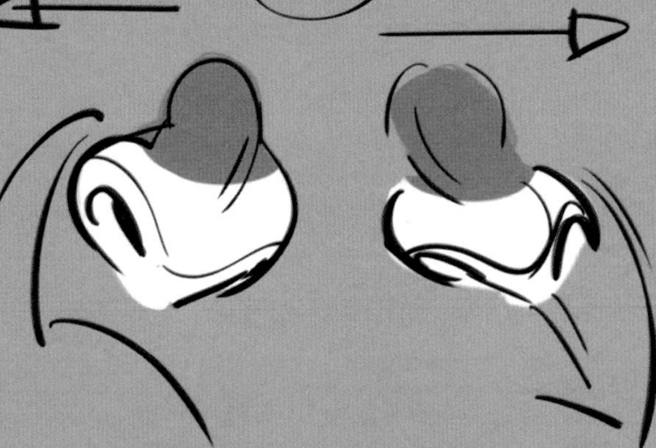

ANGLES / SHAPES / PROPORTIONS

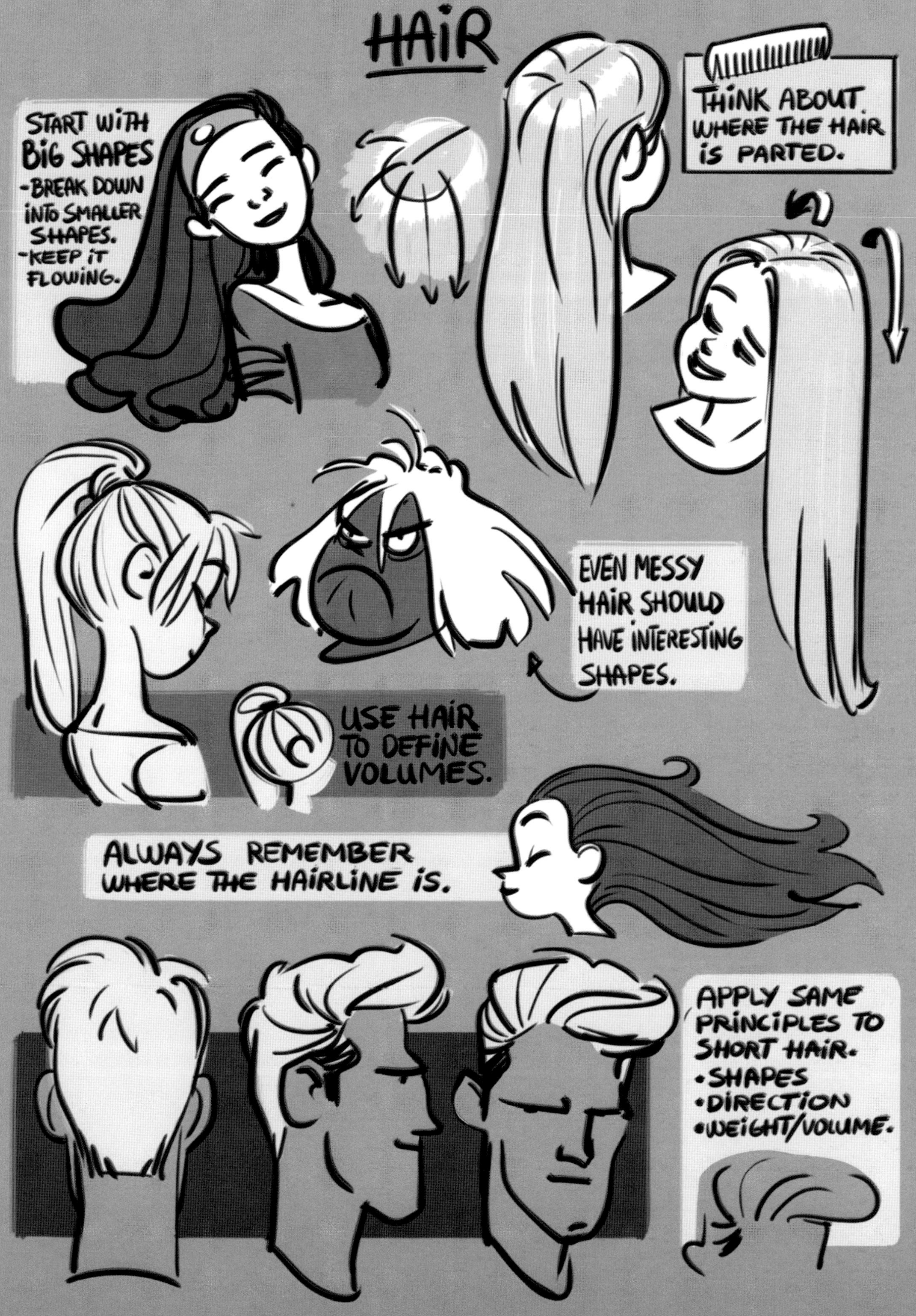
HAIR
START WITH BIG SHAPES
-BREAK DOWN INTO SMALLER SHAPES.
-KEEP IT FLOWING.
THINK ABOUT WHERE THE HAIR IS PARTED.
EVEN MESSY HAIR SHOULD HAVE INTERESTING SHAPES.
USE HAIR TO DEFINE VOLUMES.
ALWAYS REMEMBER WHERE THE HAIRLINE IS.
APPLY SAME PRINCIPLES TO SHORT HAIR.
•SHAPES
•DIRECTION
•WEIGHT/VOLUME.

Stylizing an Object

This is the J.C. Leyendecker way. He only does his final sketch from his study. He doesn't paint directly from the life model/object itself. He did his study from life, did tons of them; then composed his final sketch from his study.

Step 1: Set up a model / still life / etc.

Step 2: Do a study from it. Edit & Stylized shape right away.
Change angle / perspective / size, ... etc; but make sure it "feels" the same.

TIPS PUSH the shape. ie. make things round to be rounder; straight to be straighter; tall to be taller; short to be shorter; ... etc.

Step 3: Only do your final sketch from your study

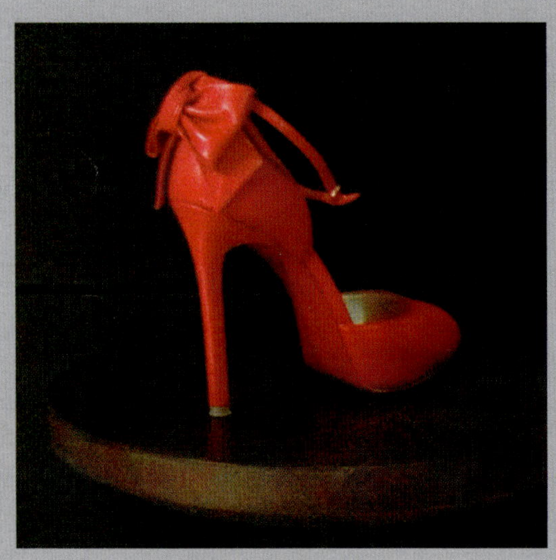

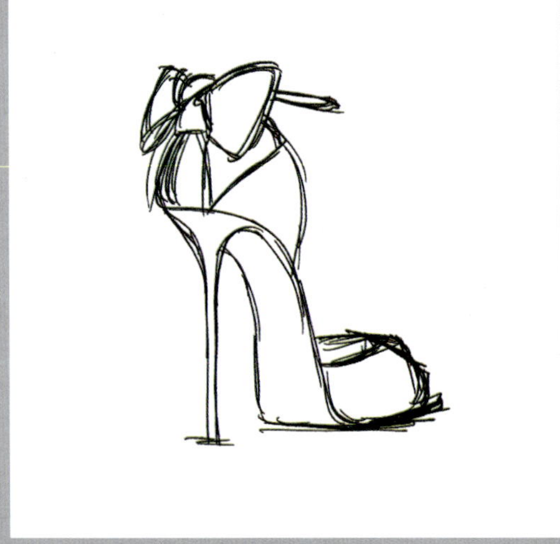

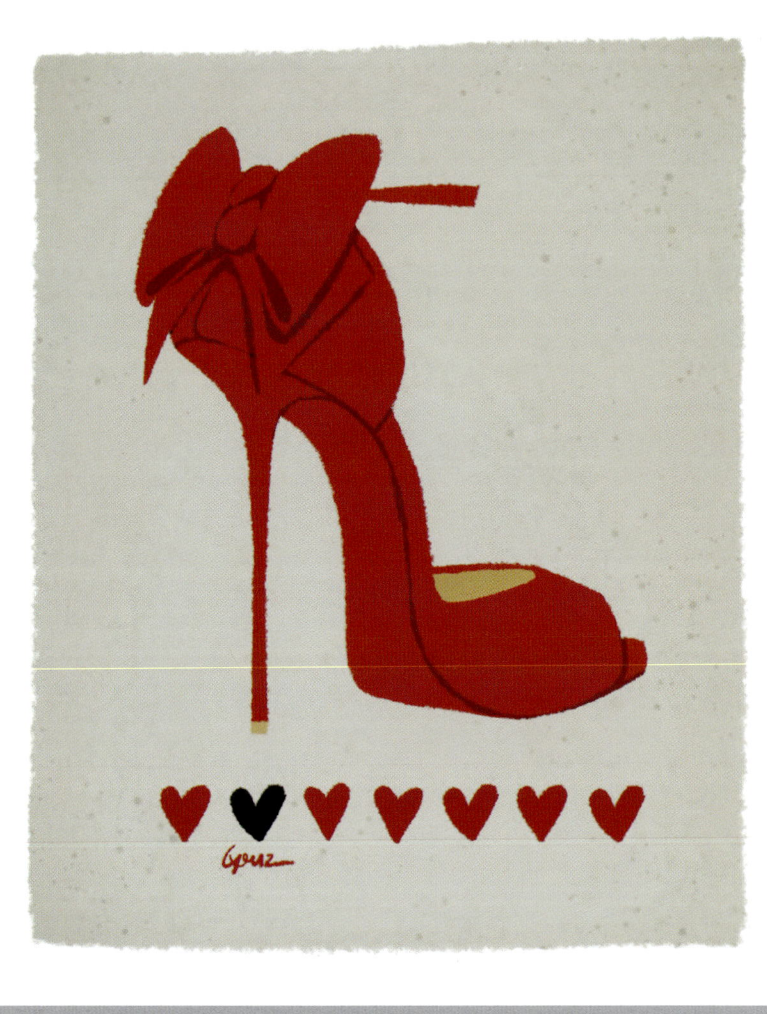

Shoes Vocabulary 101

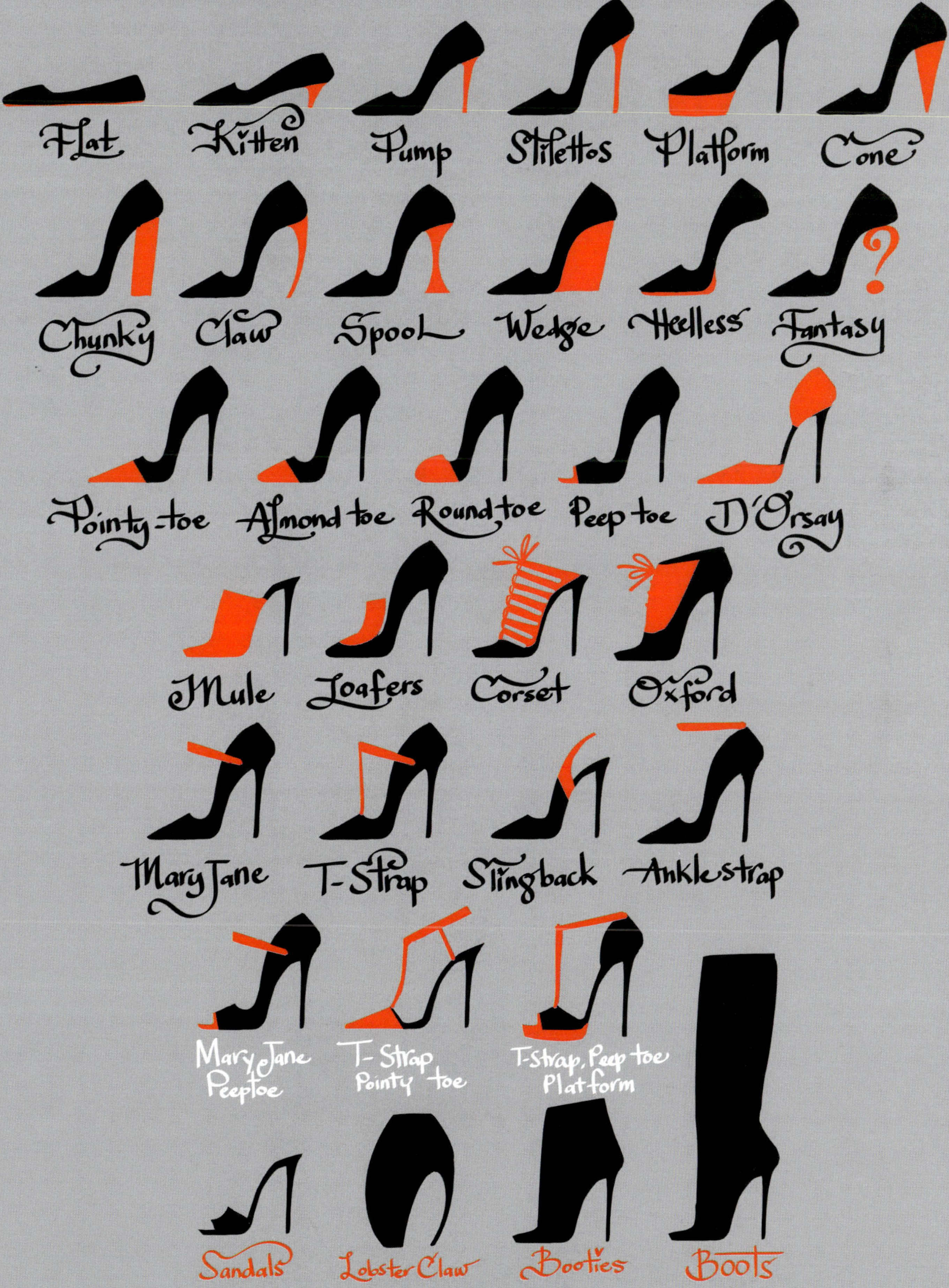

BEAT BOARDS • STORYBOARDS
(WHAT'S THE DIFFERENCE?)

BEATBOARDS ARE USED TO SHOW THE BIG STROKES OF A STORY. THEY ARE CLOSER IN CONCEPT TO AN ILLUSTRATED STORY BOOK.

FOR EXAMPLE:

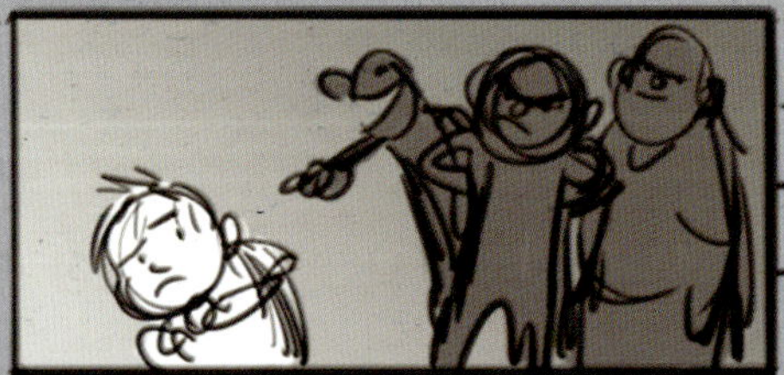

KID GETS BULLIED BY LARGER KIDS.

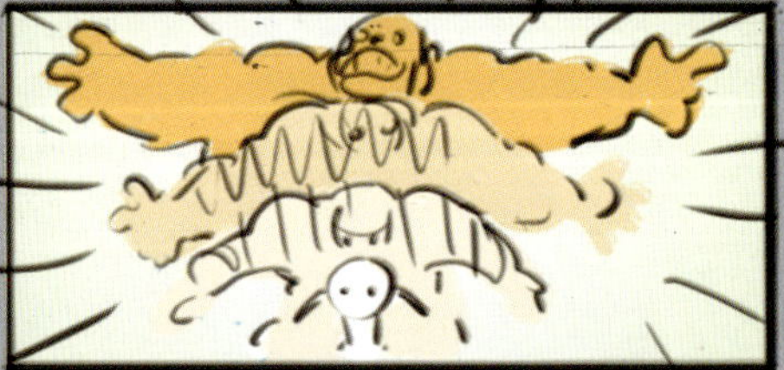

KID TRANSFORMS INTO A LARGE CREATURE.

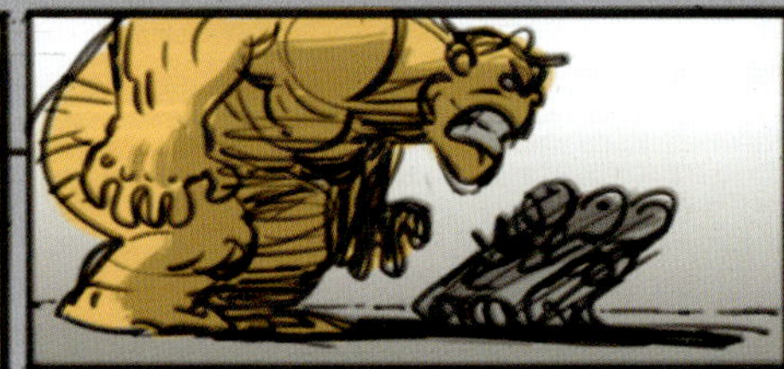

CREATURE SCARES BULLIES AWAY.

STORYBOARDS TELL THE STORY OF A MOVIE OR TV EPISODE THROUGH SEQUENCES CRAFTED WITH ATTENTION TO CAMERA ANGLES, CAMERA MOVES, ACTING, CUTS / TRANSITIONS, ETC

STORY-WISE, THEY GIVE A CLEAR PICTURE OF HOW THE MOVIE WILL PLAY OUT IN REAL-TIME, GIVING A BROAD SENSE OF LOCATION, ACTING, AND TIMING. WE CALL IT CONTINUITY.

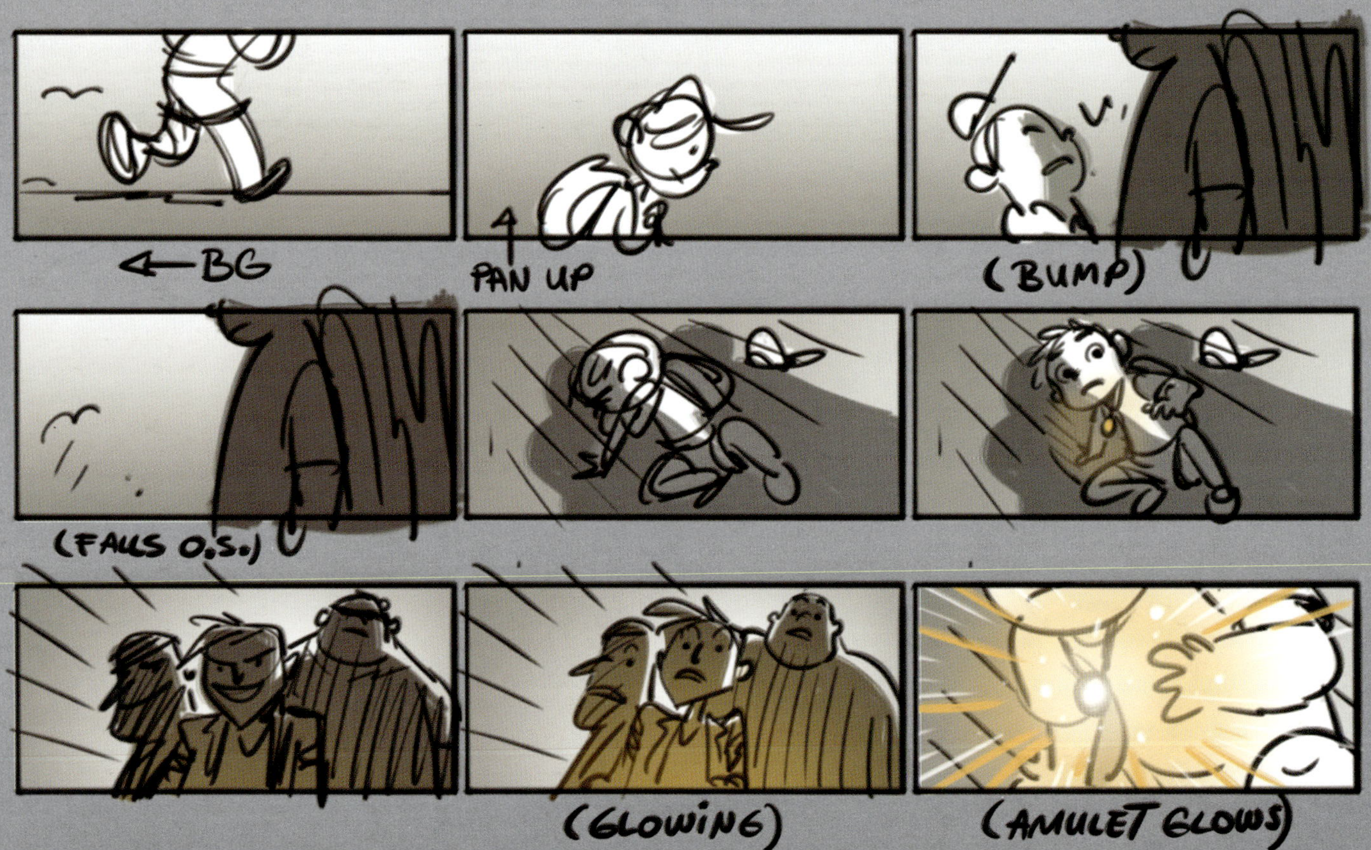

* STORYBOARDS CAN ALSO INCLUDE DIALOGUE AND SOUND FX.

2 BASIC STORYBOARD RULES

① MAINTAIN GENERAL SCREEN DIRECTION

WHEN A CHARACTER IS MOVING, KEEP HIM MOVING THE SAME WAY.

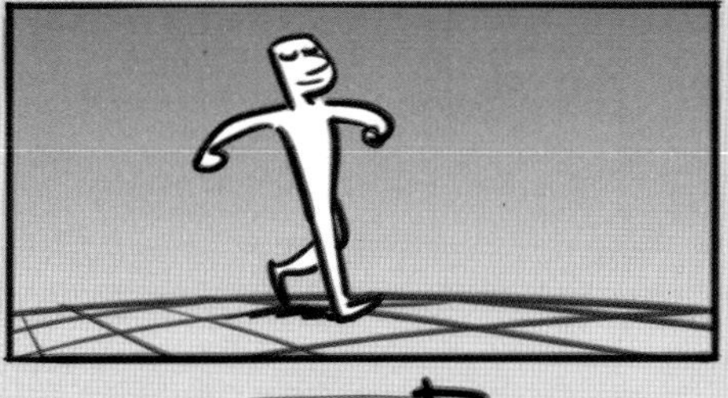
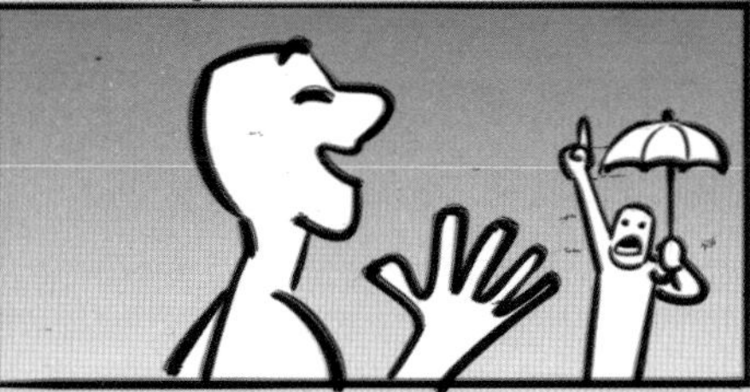
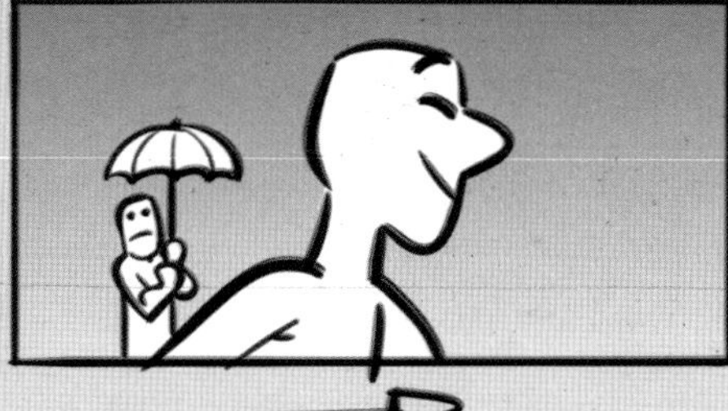

UNLESS... HE CHANGES DIRECTION ON-SCREEN.

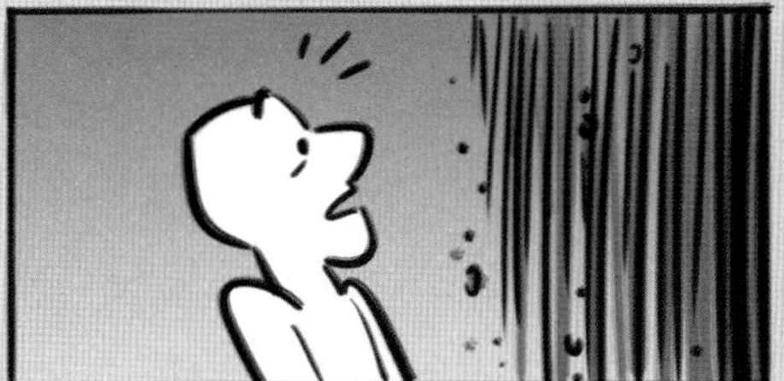
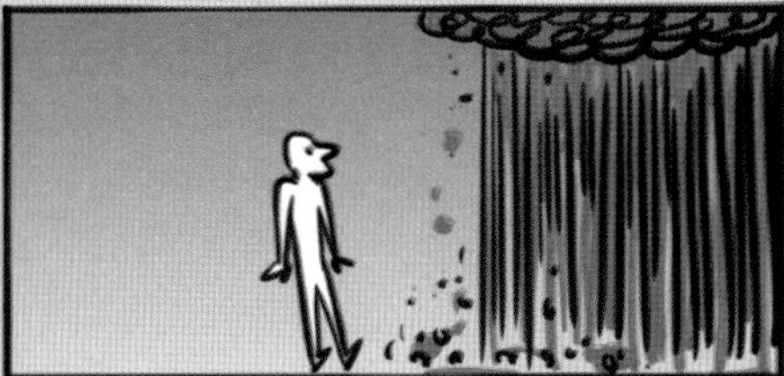
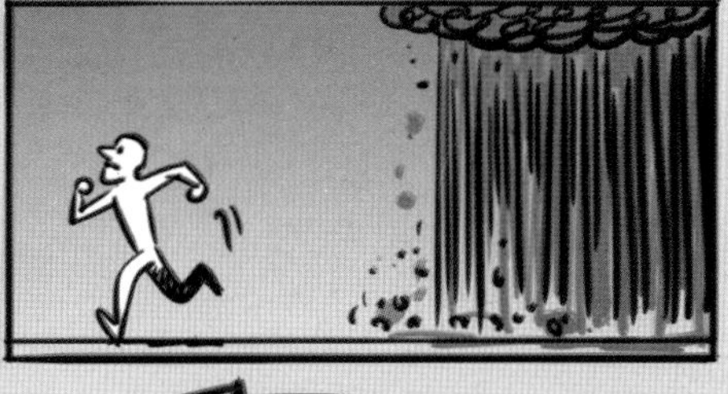

② MAINTAIN CHARACTER'S SCREEN POSITION

WHENEVER YOU "CUT", PLACE YOUR CHARACTER IN THE SAME GENERAL SCREEN POSITION.

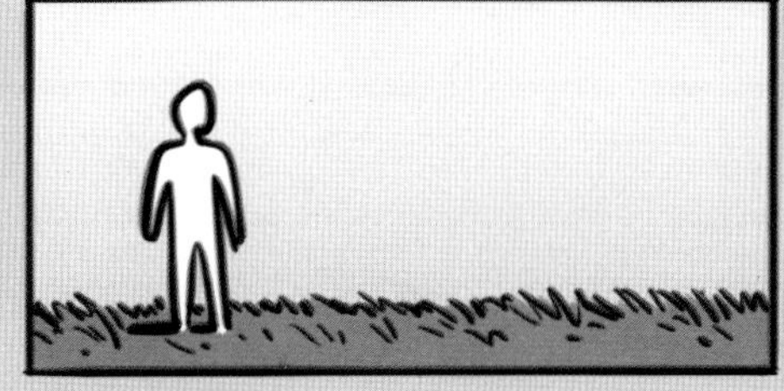
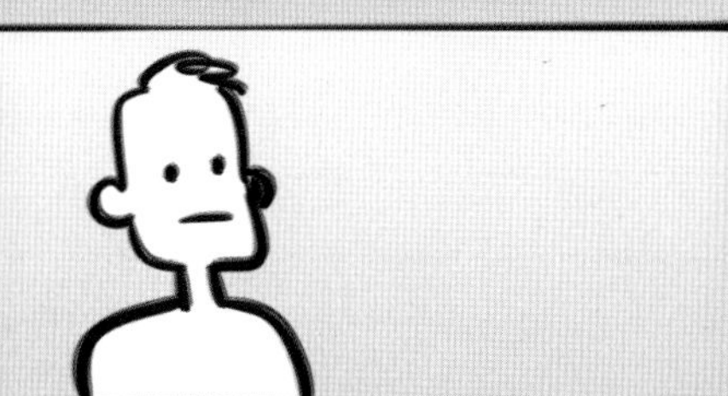
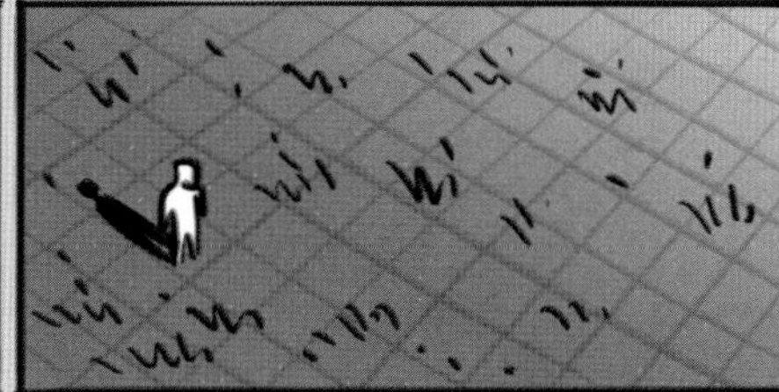

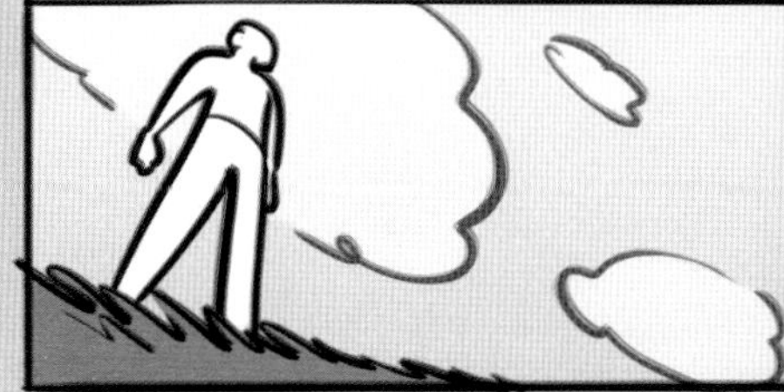
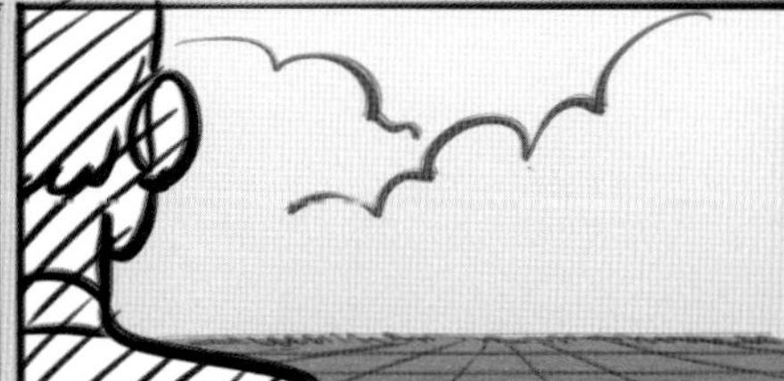
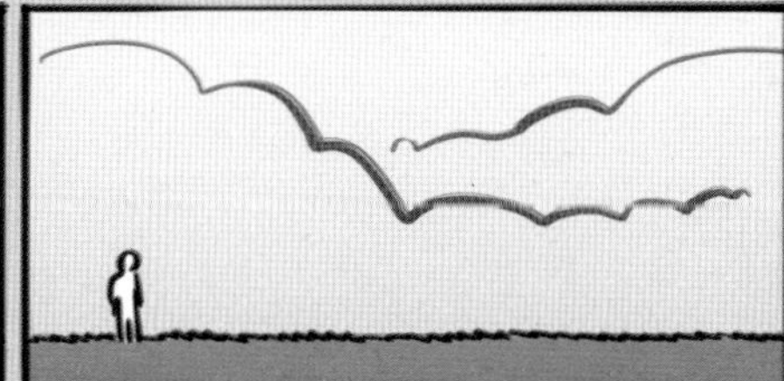

*ESPECIALLY USEFUL WHEN A CHARACTER IS MOVING.

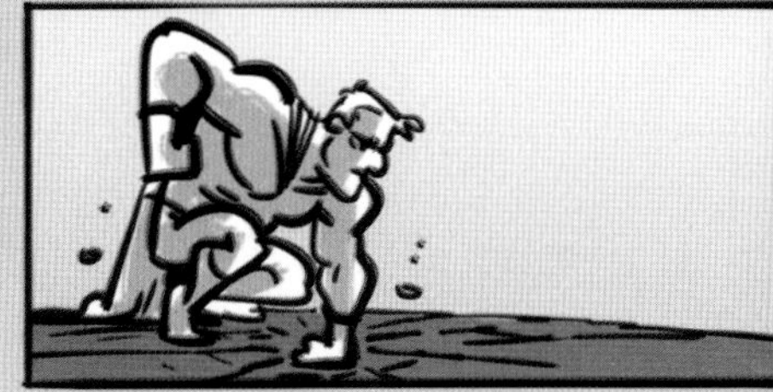
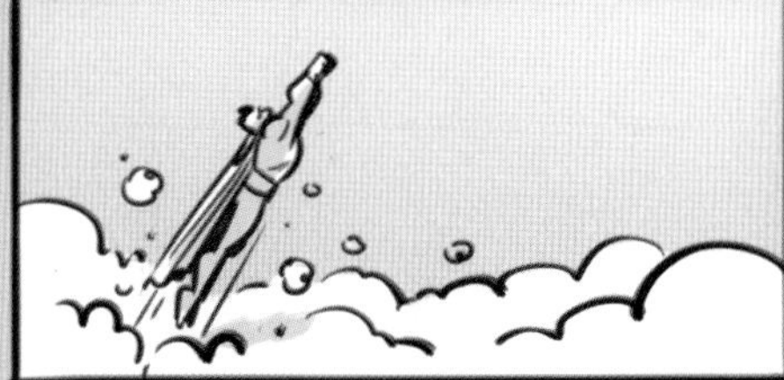
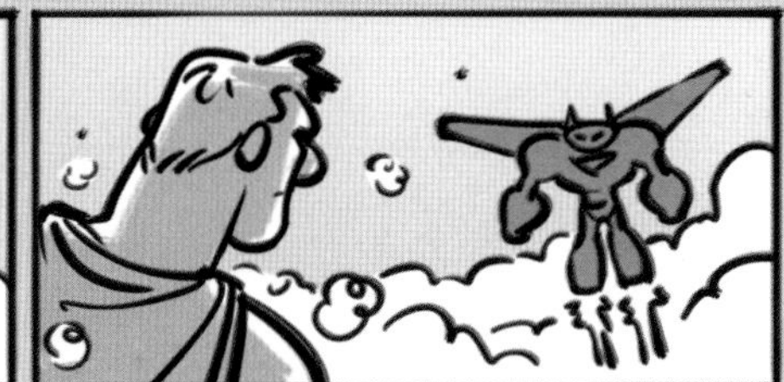

Sketchbook

Prismacolor
COL-ERASE
in Scarlet Red
PENTEL Arts
Pocket Brush Pen
MOLESKINE
Sketchbook

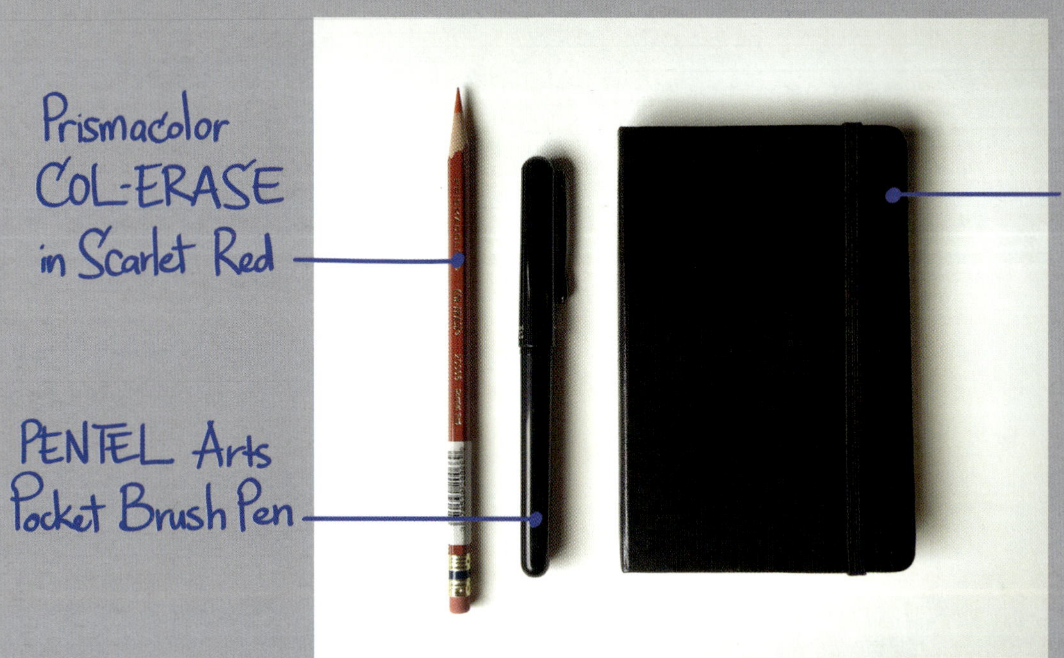

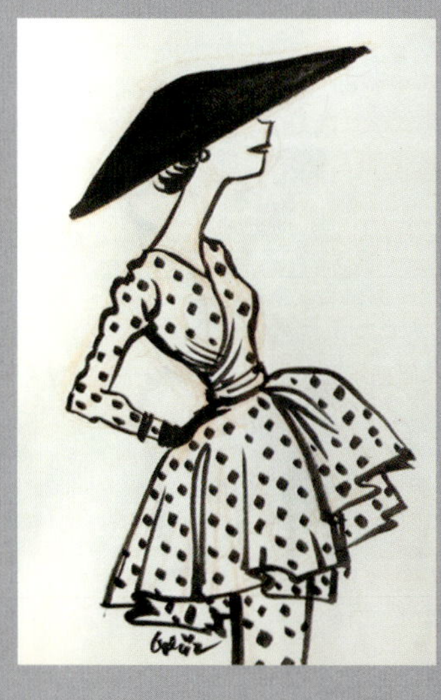

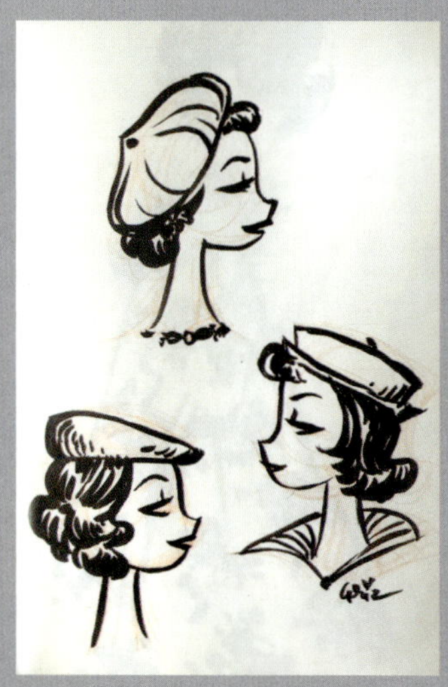

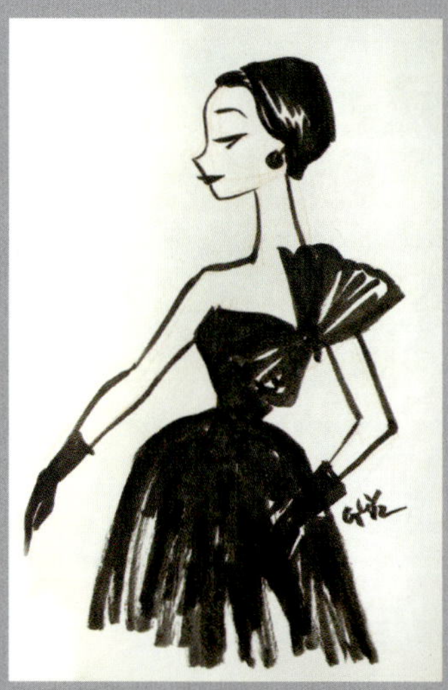

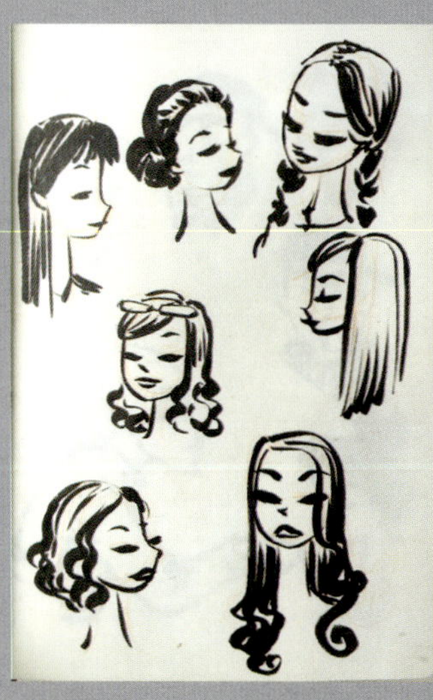

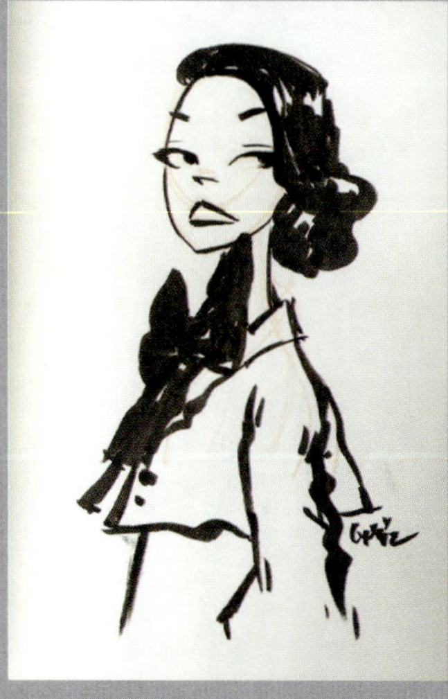

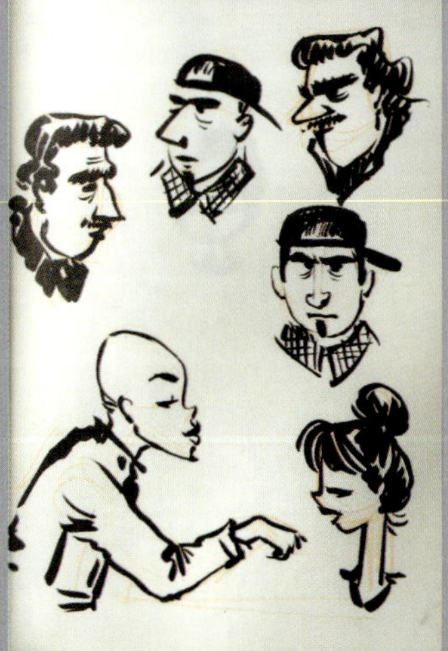

PEN & INK

My favorite pen & ink supplies that I learned from Dan Krall:

* litte plastic cups
* Black India Rapidograph
* Small ink nib pen (always have a few, they break easily)

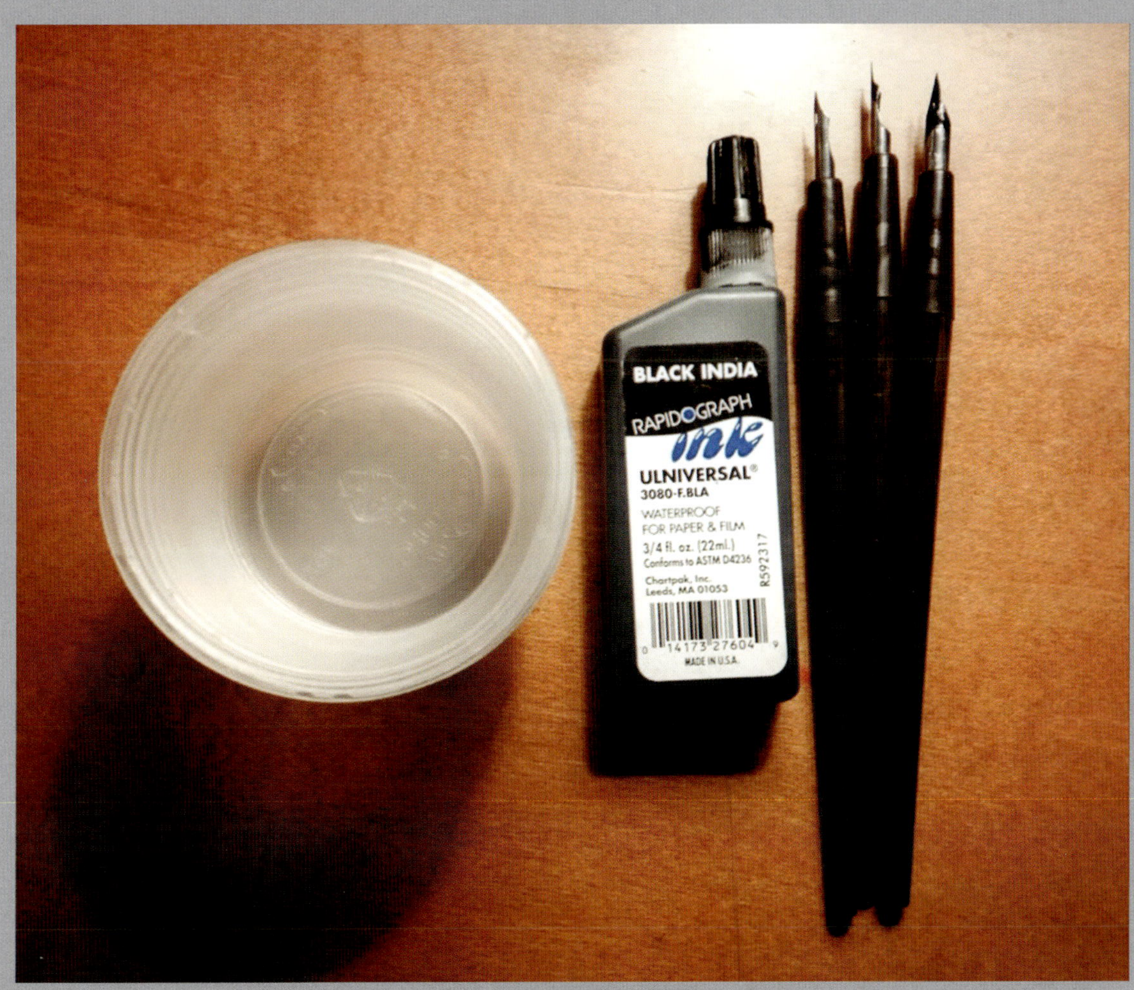

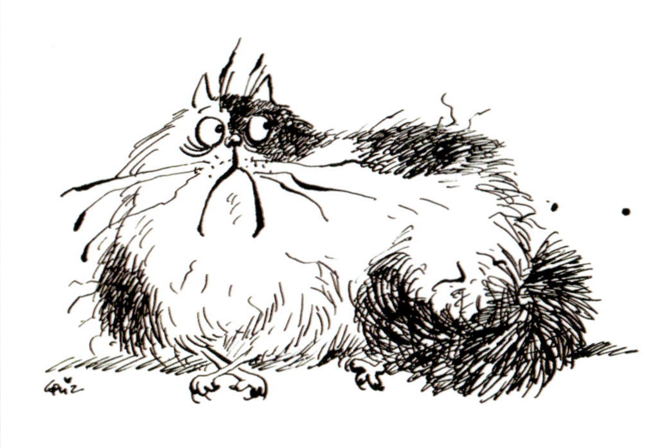

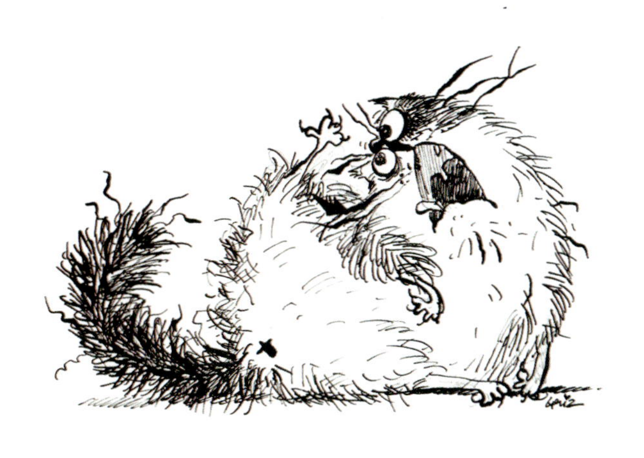

TYPES OF SHOTS (AND WHAT THEY SAY) PART ①

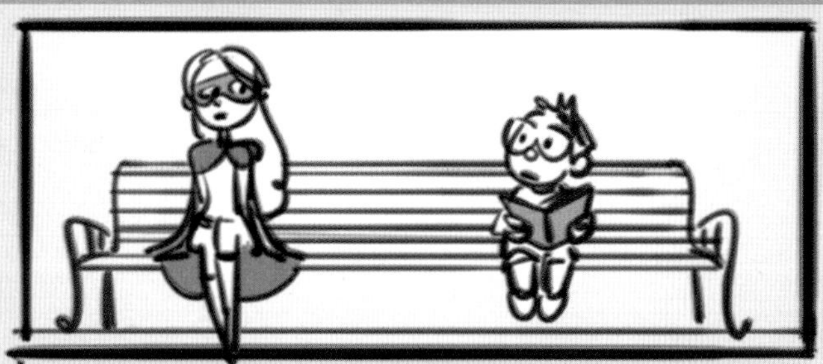

STRAIGHT-ON (FLAT)

- EYE-LEVEL CAMERA ANGLE

"FLAT" SHOTS ARE OFTEN USED IN COMEDIC SCENES OFTEN INCLUDING 2 CHARACTERS. THE FOCUS IS ON THE PERFORMANCE

- A PASSIVE TYPE OF SHOT (NEUTRAL)

EXTREME WIDE-SHOT

- OFTEN USED AS AN "ESTABLISHING SHOT"
- GIVES A LOT OF INFO ABOUT PHYSICAL SURROUNDINGS
- CAN CONVEY: ISOLATION (SOLITUDE), VASTNESS, SCOPE OF WHAT'S AT STAKE, RESULT OF ACCOMPLISHMENT OR FAILURE, ETC.

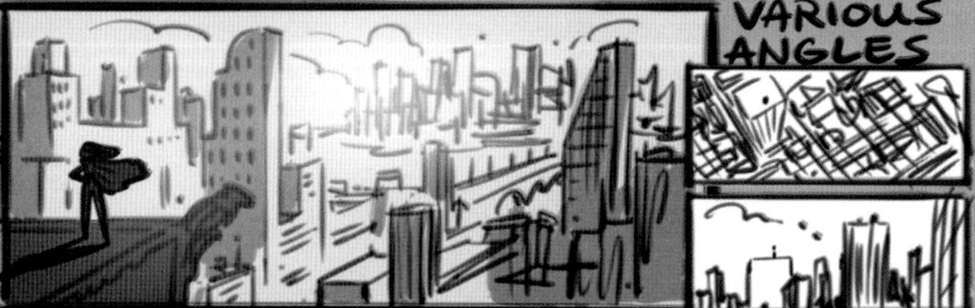

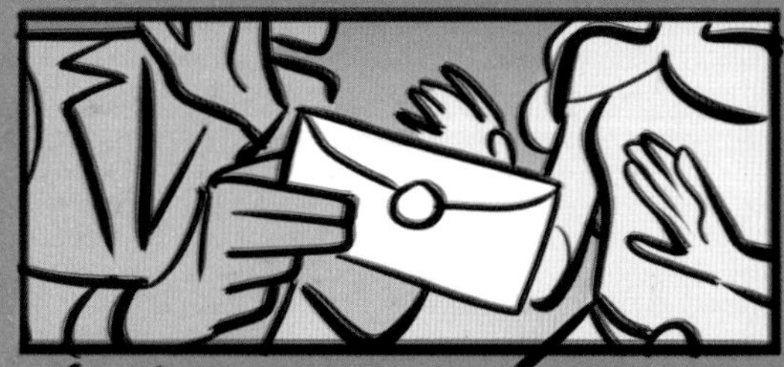

CLOSE-UP (C.U.)

- SHOWS SOMETHING/SOMEONE IN DETAIL
- CREATES INTIMACY
- DRAWS FOCUS ON A CHARACTER'S EXPRESSION

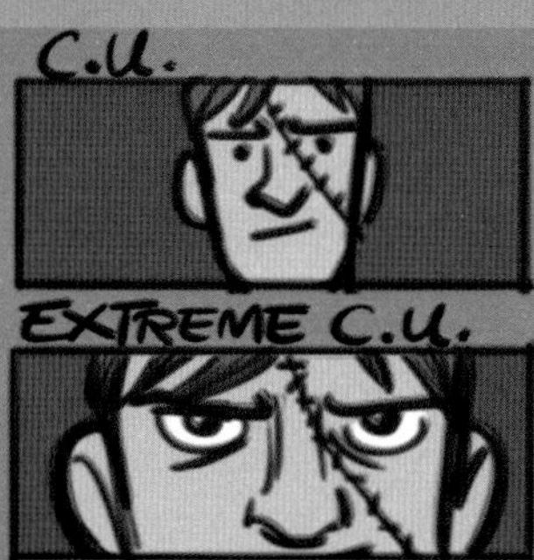

↰ IF IT'S AN OBJECT, IT'S USUALLY A STORY SET-UP.

DUTCH ANGLE (TILTED)

- DYNAMIC. CREATES TENSION. OUT OF BALANCE
- USED FOR ACTION, MYSTERY, DANGER

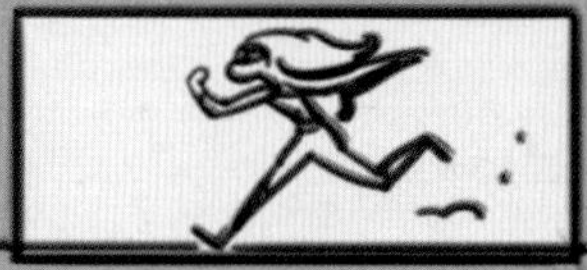

↰ SAME ACTION, FROM A FLAT ANGLE WOULD HAVE LESS TENSION. MIGHT BE COMEDIC.

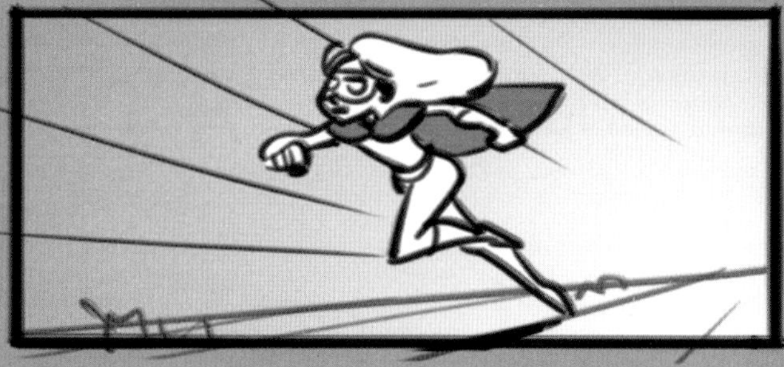

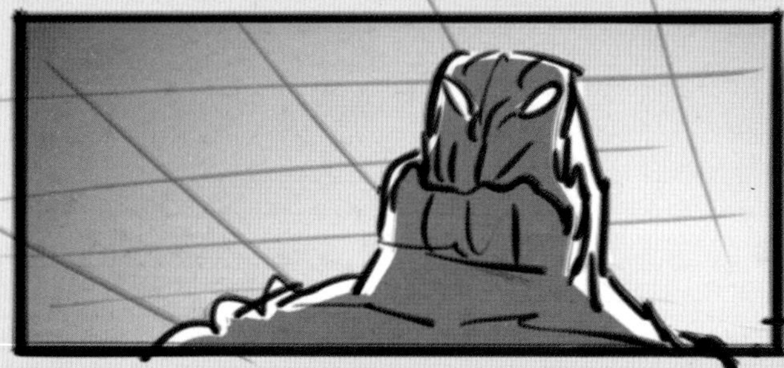

UPSHOT

ON CHARACTER: GIVES A SENSE OF IMPORTANCE, POWER, DOMINANCE.

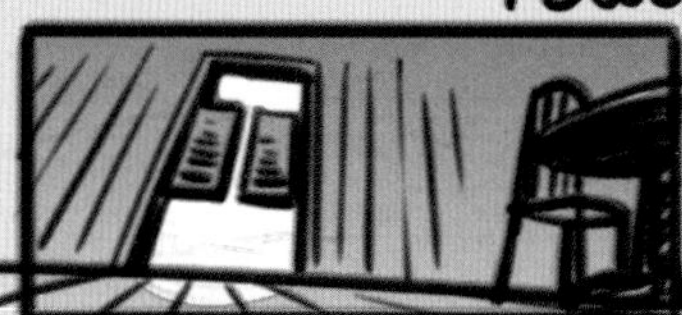

ON BACKGROUND:

- DRAMATIC
- CAN BE USED TO INTRODUCE A FEARED/MYSTERIOUS CHAR.

DOWNSHOT

- MAKES CHARACTER(S) FEEL:
  - SMALLER
  - DEFENSELESS (JUDGED?)
  - ACTED UPON

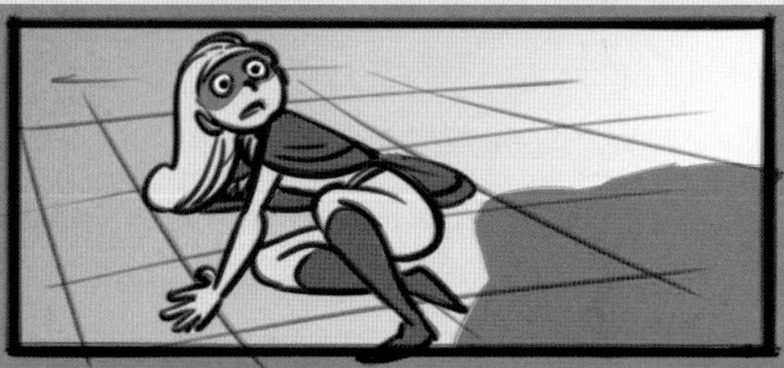

TYPES OF SHOTS (AND WHAT THEY SAY) PART ②

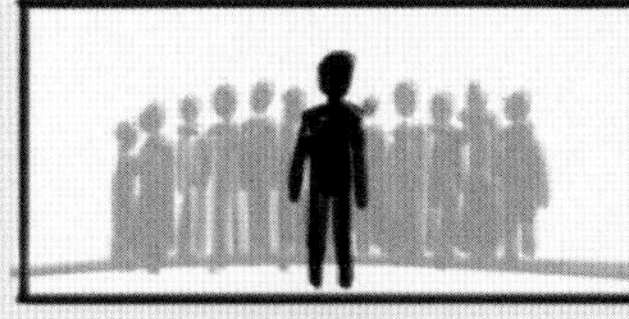
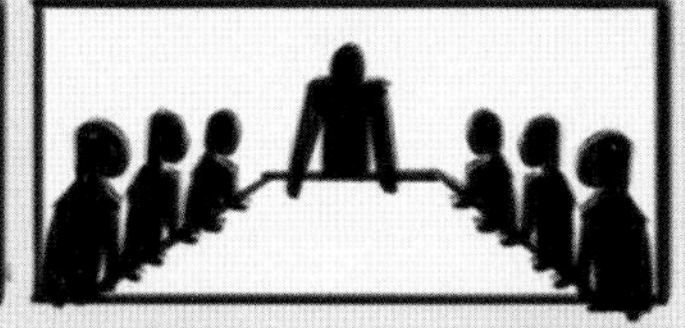
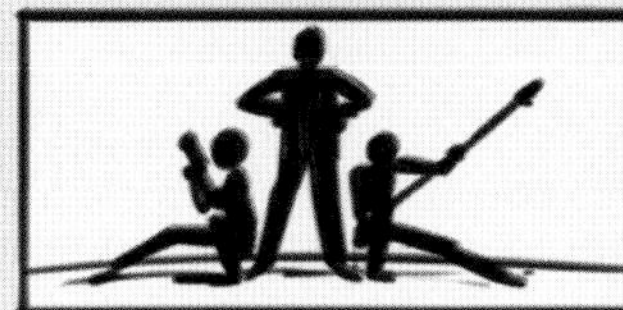
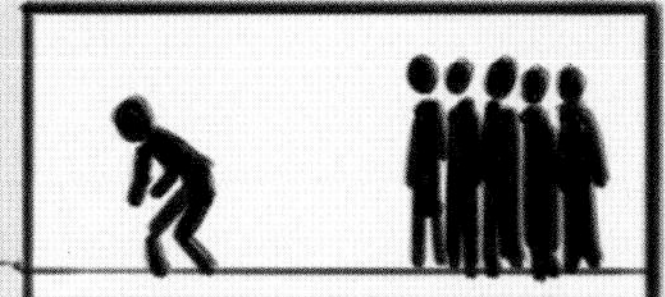

GROUP SHOT

- OFTEN STAGED TO SHOWCASE THE LEADER OF THE GROUP (OR THE OUTCAST)
- USED TO TAKE A BREATHER AND RE-ASSESS WHERE THE GROUP IS HEADED OR HOW THEY FEEL ABOUT THE SITUATION. KIND OF LIKE AN ESTABLISHING SHOT FOR CHARACTERS

OVER-THE-SHOULDER

- USED FOR DIALOGUE SEQUENCES

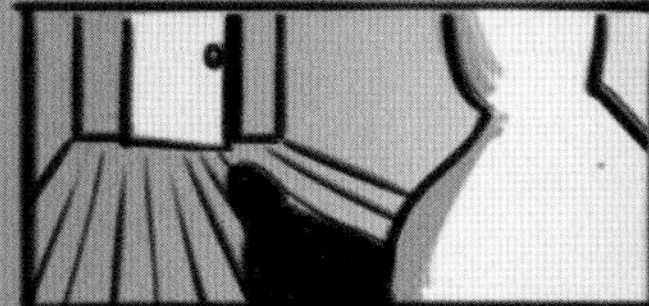

OR TO SHOW WHERE A CHARACTER IS LOOKING/NEEDS TO GO

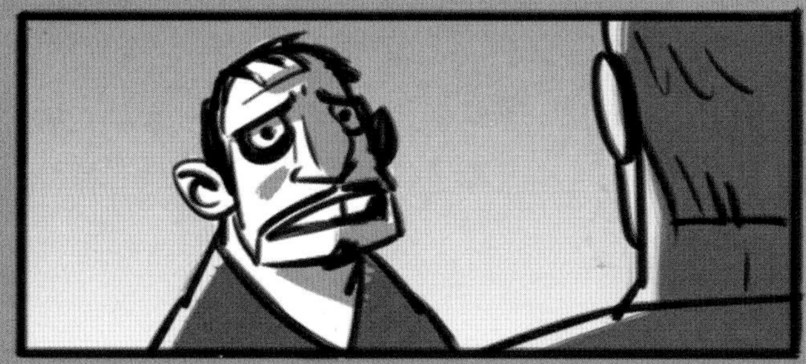

BACK TO THE CAMERA.

- OFTEN USED IN POSTER DESIGN
- AUDIENCE PROJECTS MEANING ON CHARACTER'S JOURNEY
- A WAY TO VICARIOUSLY GET INTO THE HERO/VILLAIN'S POV

LOOKING BACK OVER SHOULDER

- CREATES A SENSE OF INTIMACY
- A "ONE MORE THING" TYPE OF MOMENT
- CAN PROVIDE OPPORTUNITY TO REVEAL SECRET ABOUT A CHARACTER OR A CHANGE OF MIND

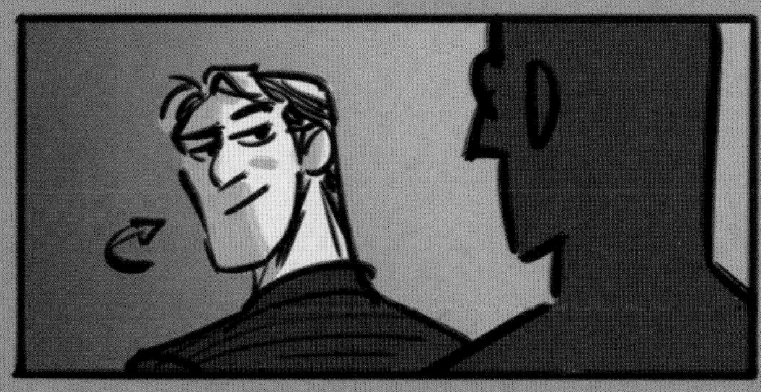

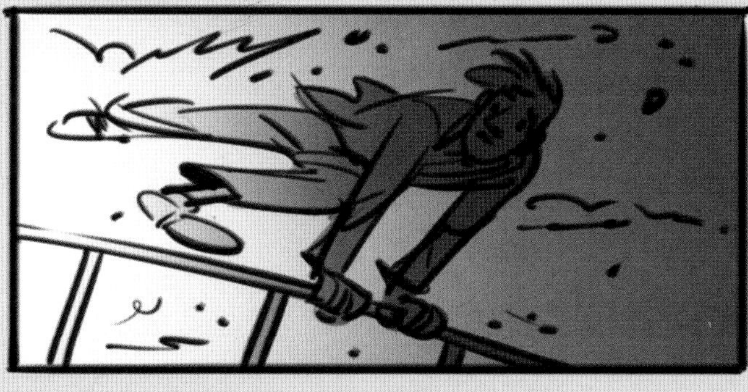

CUTTING ON ACTION.

- STARTING W/ AN ESTABLISHING SHOT ISN'T ALWAYS NECESSARY
- PUTS AUDIENCE IN THE MIDDLE OF THE ACTION, KEEPS THEM GUESSING, ON THE EDGE OF THEIR SEAT
- OFTEN USED IN THRILLERS AND ACTION FILMS

Stylized Fur (straight hair)

① Silhouette !!!

Put hair indication when there's a direction change

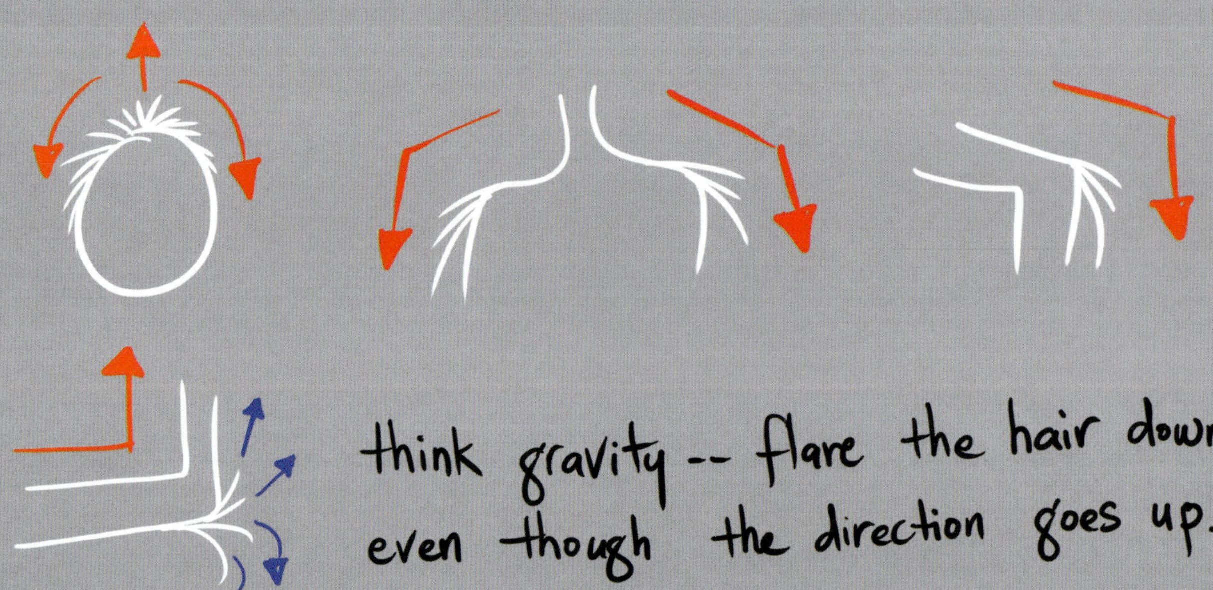

think gravity -- flare the hair down even though the direction goes up.

② Interior -- do indication

ex. 1:

Short hair

ex 2: s m b or s m b

Vary length; Think Big. Med. Sml

③ Combine both

Markers & Pencils

① Abstract shape with loose lines

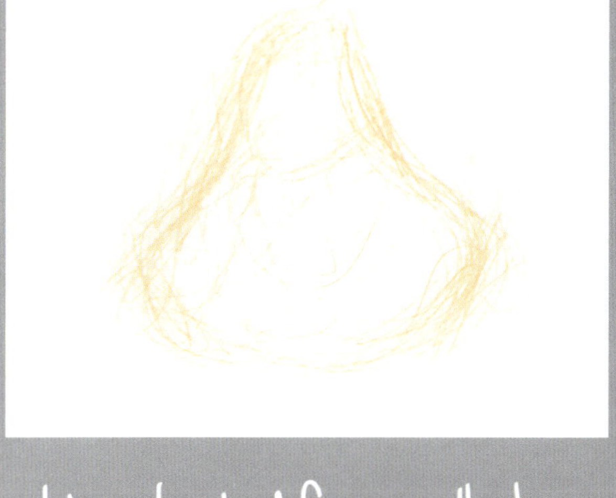

② Define shapes within

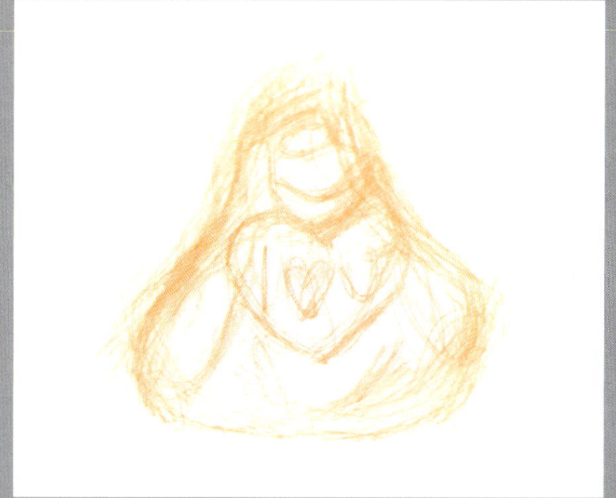

③ Light marker to define overall shape

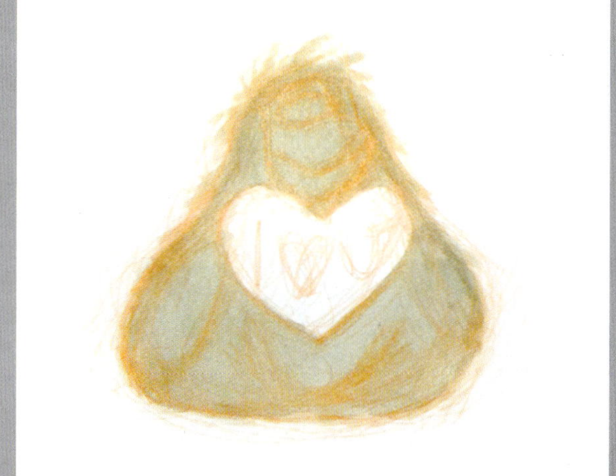

④ Medium value for more detail

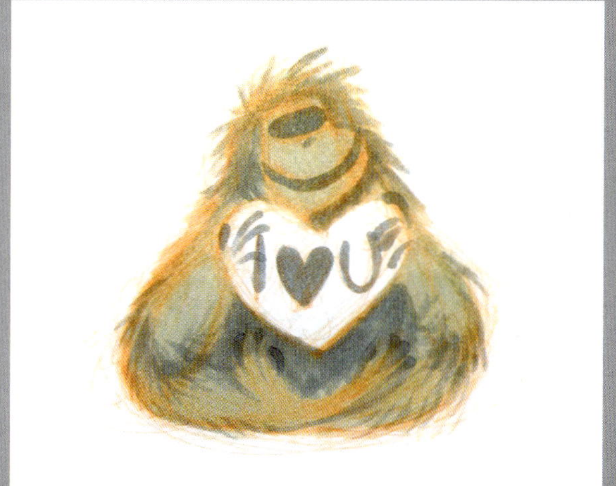

⑤ Dark value for more detail

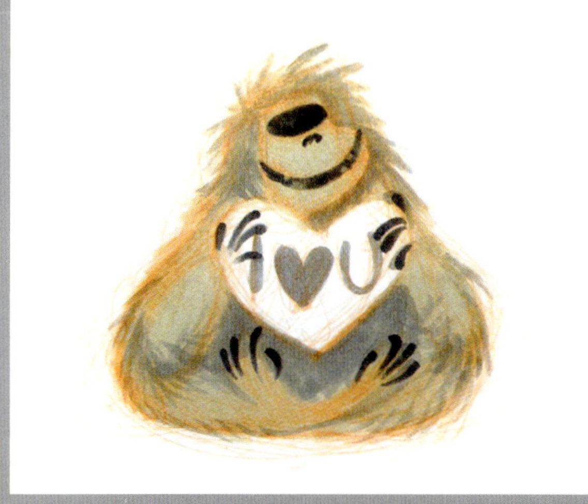

⑥ Black pencil & white pen for detail

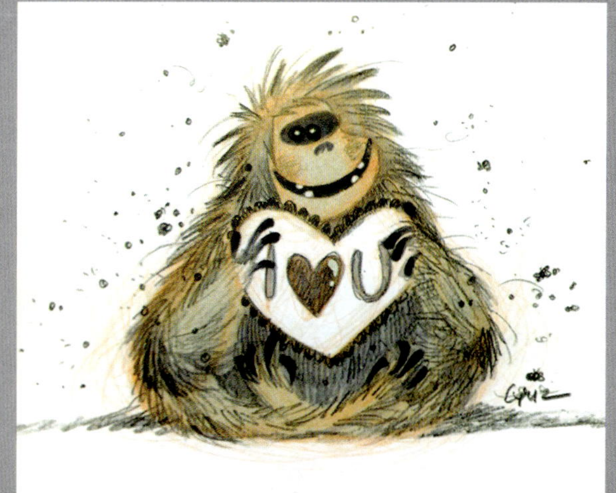

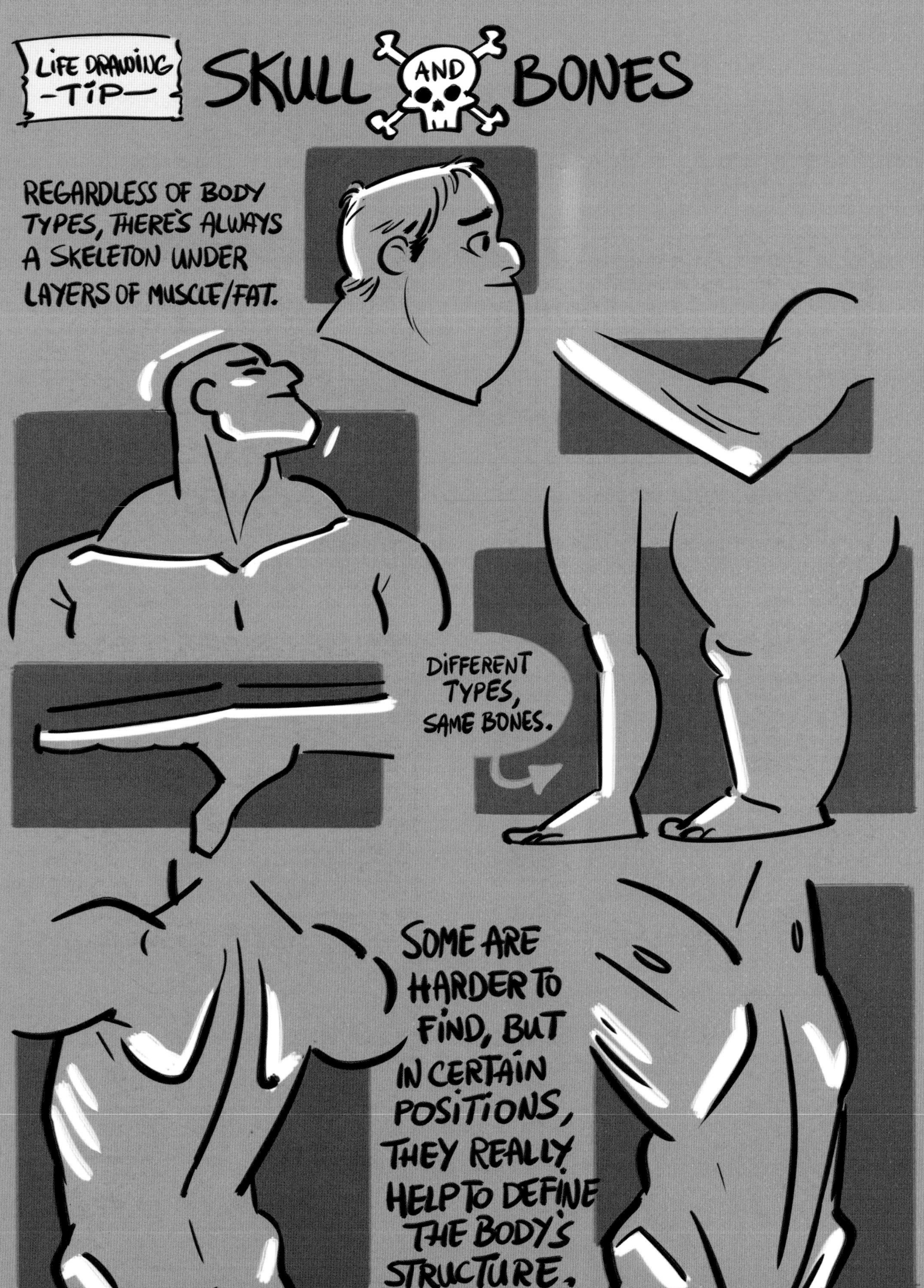

LIFE DRAWING -TIP-
SKULL AND BONES
REGARDLESS OF BODY TYPES, THERE'S ALWAYS A SKELETON UNDER LAYERS OF MUSCLE/FAT.
DIFFERENT TYPES, SAME BONES.
SOME ARE HARDER TO FIND, BUT IN CERTAIN POSITIONS, THEY REALLY HELP TO DEFINE THE BODY'S STRUCTURE.

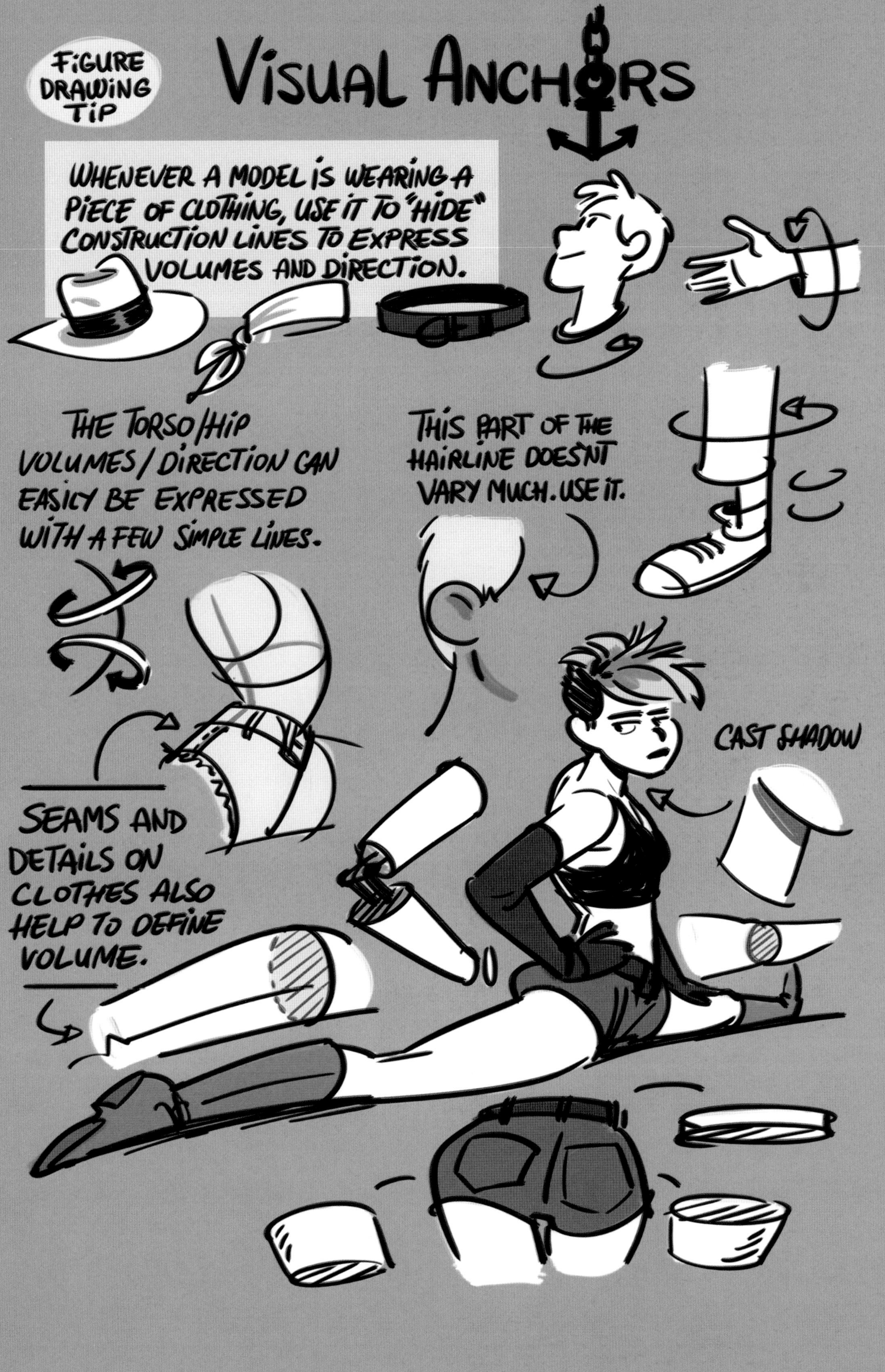

FIGURE DRAWING TIP

VISUAL ANCHORS

WHENEVER A MODEL IS WEARING A PIECE OF CLOTHING, USE IT TO "HIDE" CONSTRUCTION LINES TO EXPRESS VOLUMES AND DIRECTION.

THE TORSO/HIP VOLUMES/DIRECTION CAN EASILY BE EXPRESSED WITH A FEW SIMPLE LINES.

THIS PART OF THE HAIRLINE DOESN'T VARY MUCH. USE IT.

CAST SHADOW

SEAMS AND DETAILS ON CLOTHES ALSO HELP TO DEFINE VOLUME.

Painting Hair (stylized)

① Clean silhouette of the overall shape

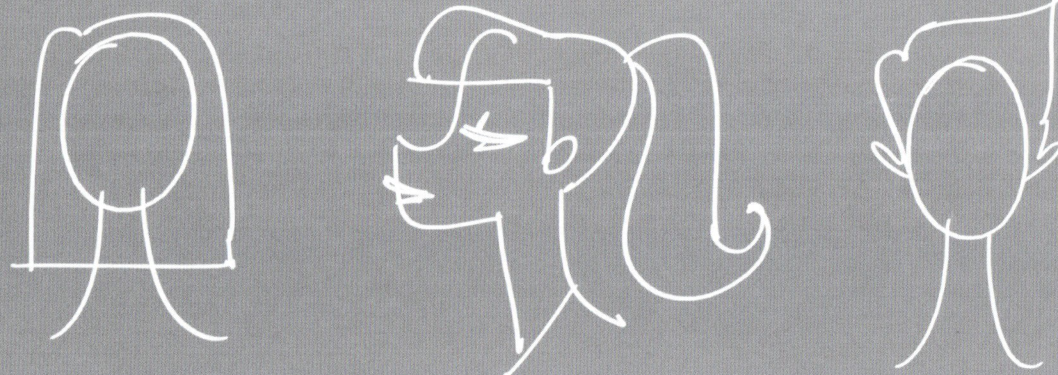

② Create shape w/in a shape. Do a combination of Big, Medium, Small.

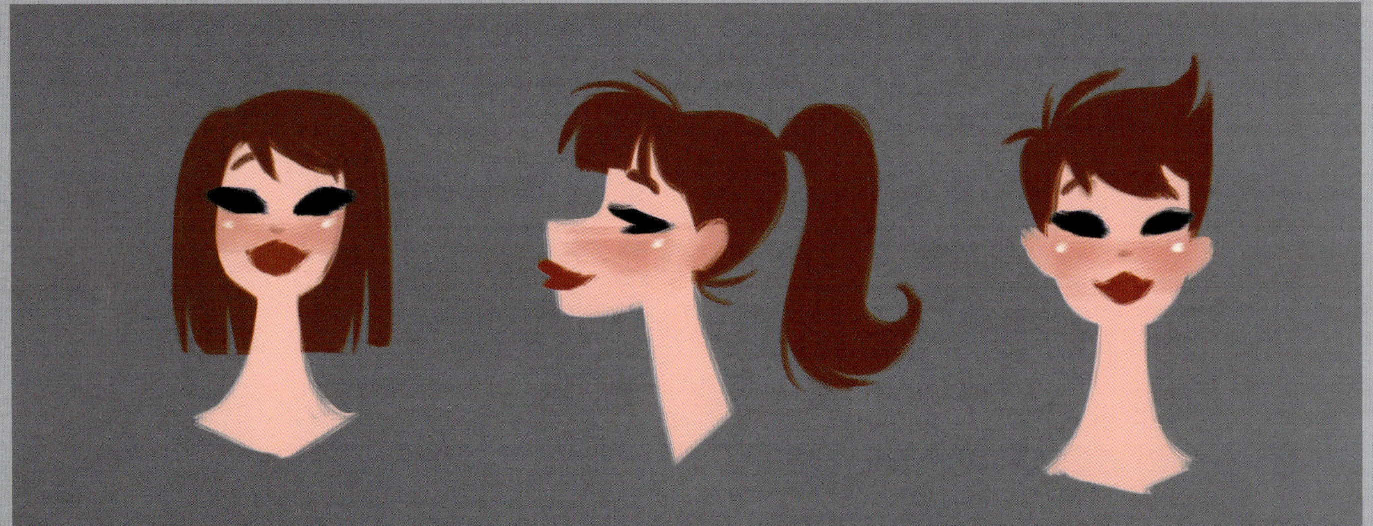

③ Add extra strands to make it look more organic

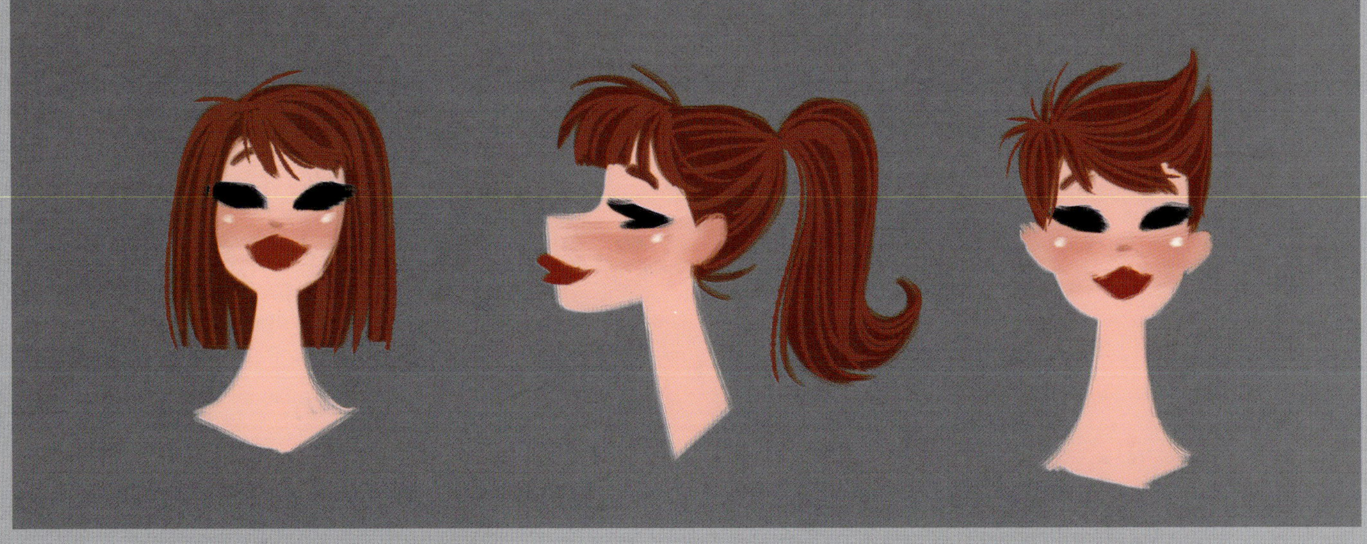

How to paint Hair

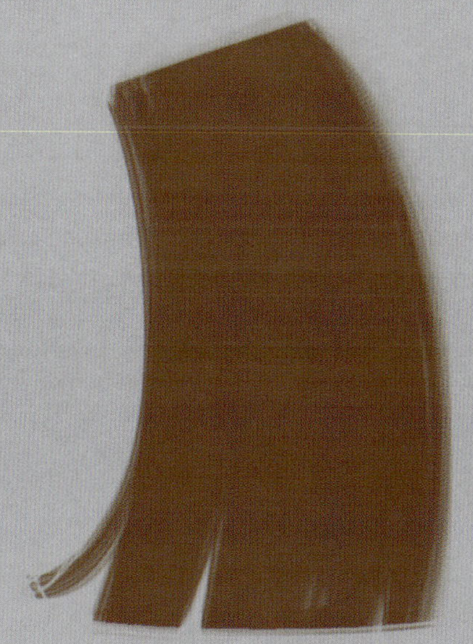

① Base color

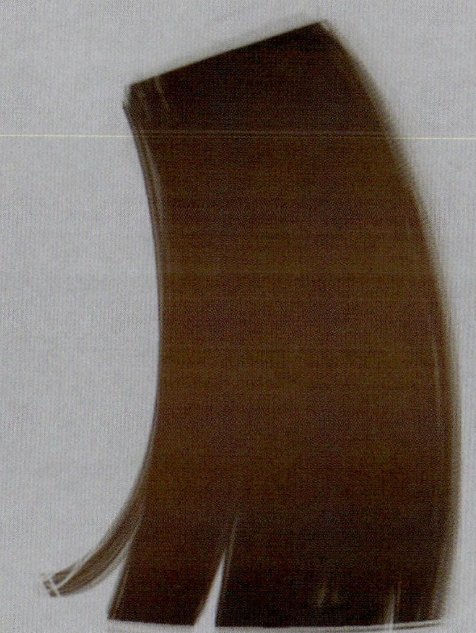

② Add dark w/ a soft brush (creating volume)

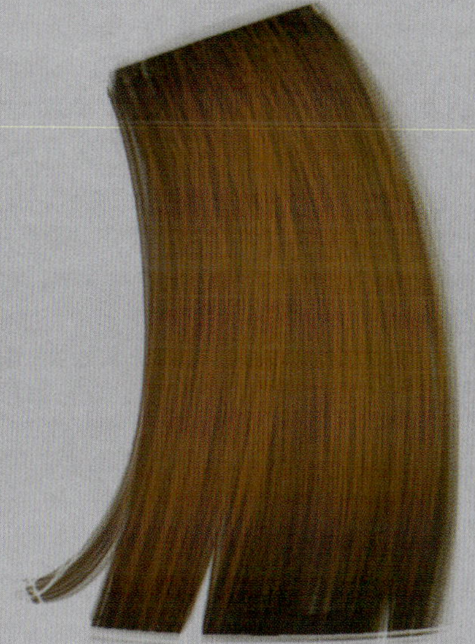

③ Paint hair on a separate layer, use a more saturated version of the base color

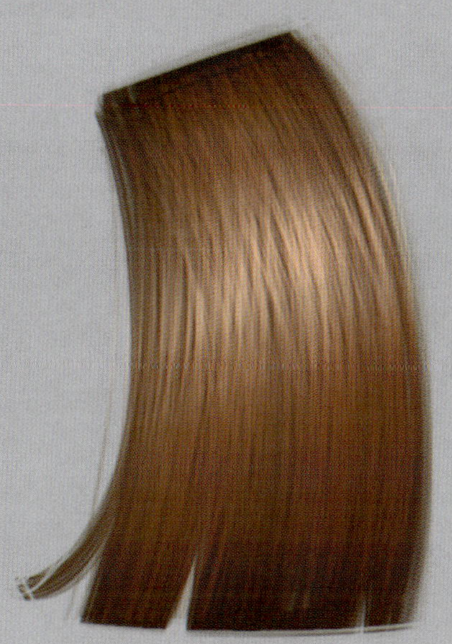

④ Add highlight

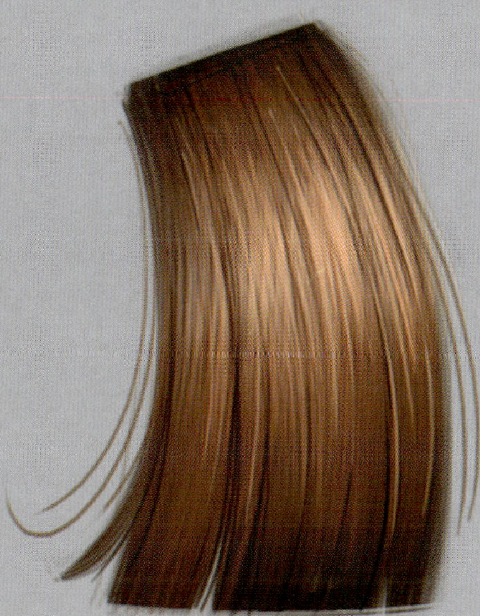

⑤ Add lines to create shape separation & hair strands

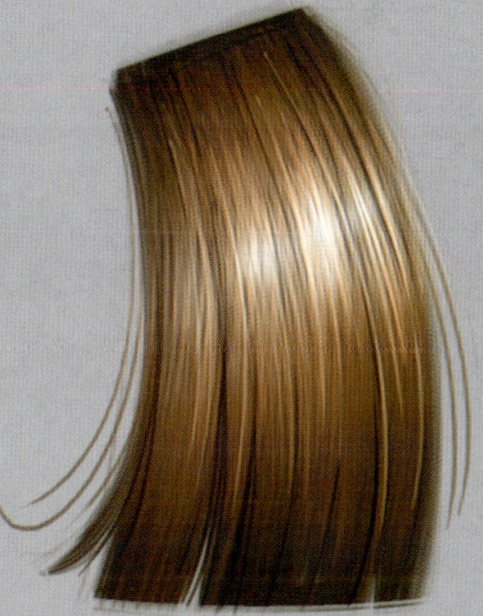

⑥ Final highlight

SHAPE CONTRAST IN CHARACTERS.

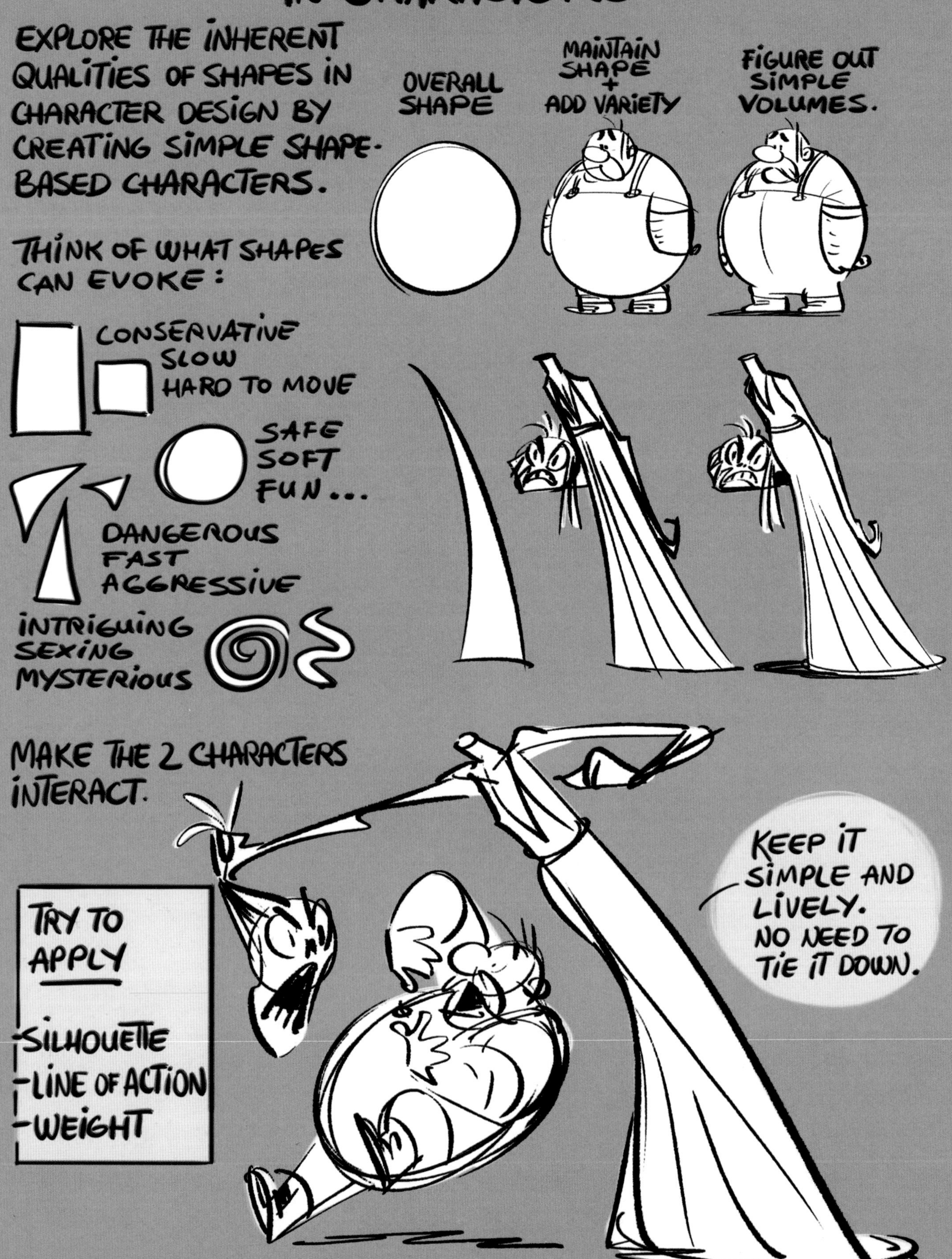

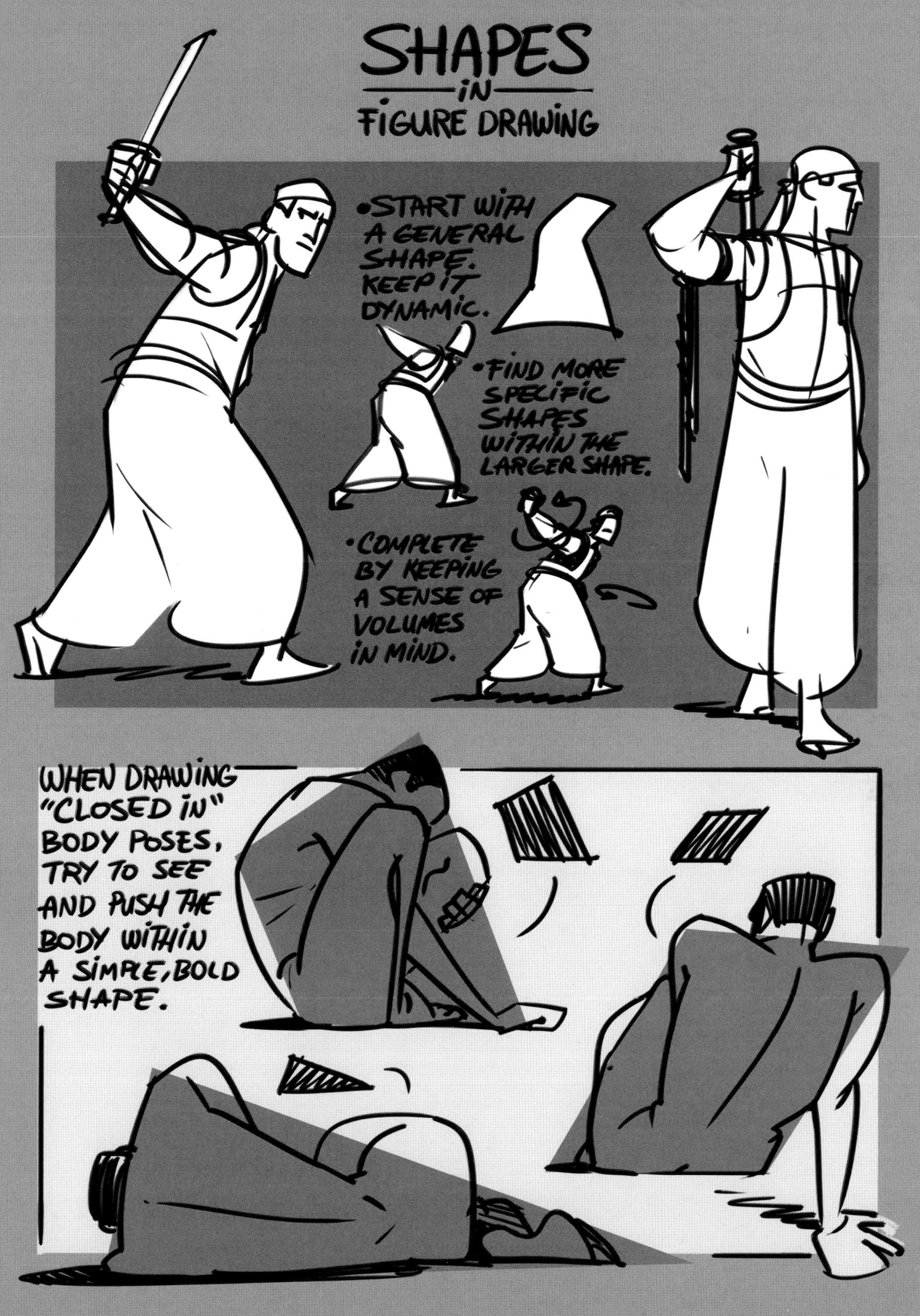
SHAPES in FIGURE DRAWING
•START WITH A GENERAL SHAPE. KEEP IT DYNAMIC.
•FIND MORE SPECIFIC SHAPES WITHIN THE LARGER SHAPE.
•COMPLETE BY KEEPING A SENSE OF VOLUMES IN MIND.
WHEN DRAWING "CLOSED IN" BODY POSES, TRY TO SEE AND PUSH THE BODY WITHIN A SIMPLE, BOLD SHAPE.

Basic Color Palette

Simple way to create color palette:
Black + White + warm & cool YELLOW
RED
BLUE
Orange (Earth Color)
Violet
Green

Example: Winsor & Newton Gouache

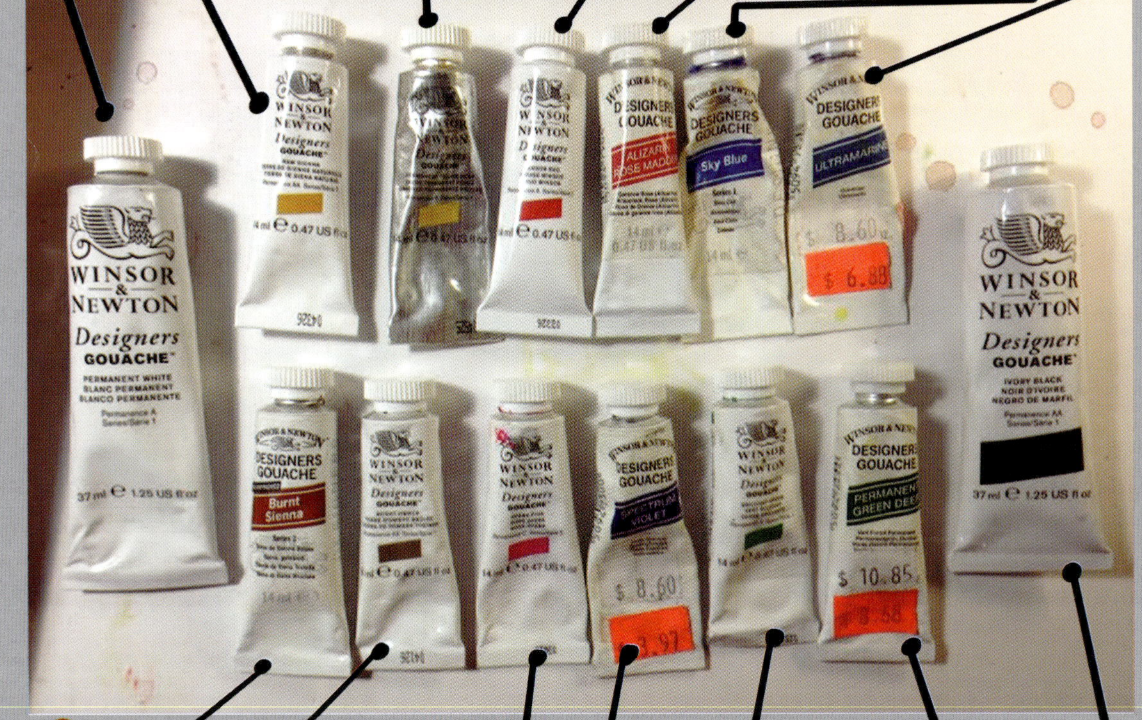

(*) this is my go to gouache palette, sometimes I change the color depending what I'm painting, but I always follow this simple warm & cool rule!

Gouache Set Up

Winsor & Newton gouache
organize them by color
Green Violet Orange/Brown Blk
Blue Red Yellow White

Large H_2O bucket
→ cut 2 holes & slip in envelope sorter to use as a brush holder

Brushes -- Winsor & Newton; Junior da Vinci

Rag

tooth pick
to mix paint

Small H_2O container
--for clean H_2O

Spray mister
→ to keep paint moist

Watercolor travel Palette

Crescent Illustration Board

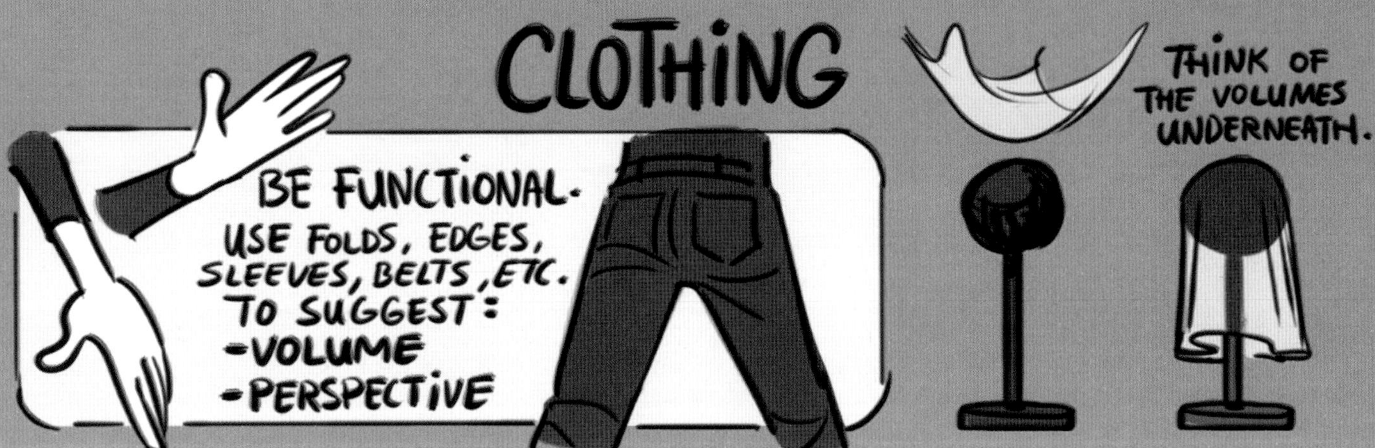

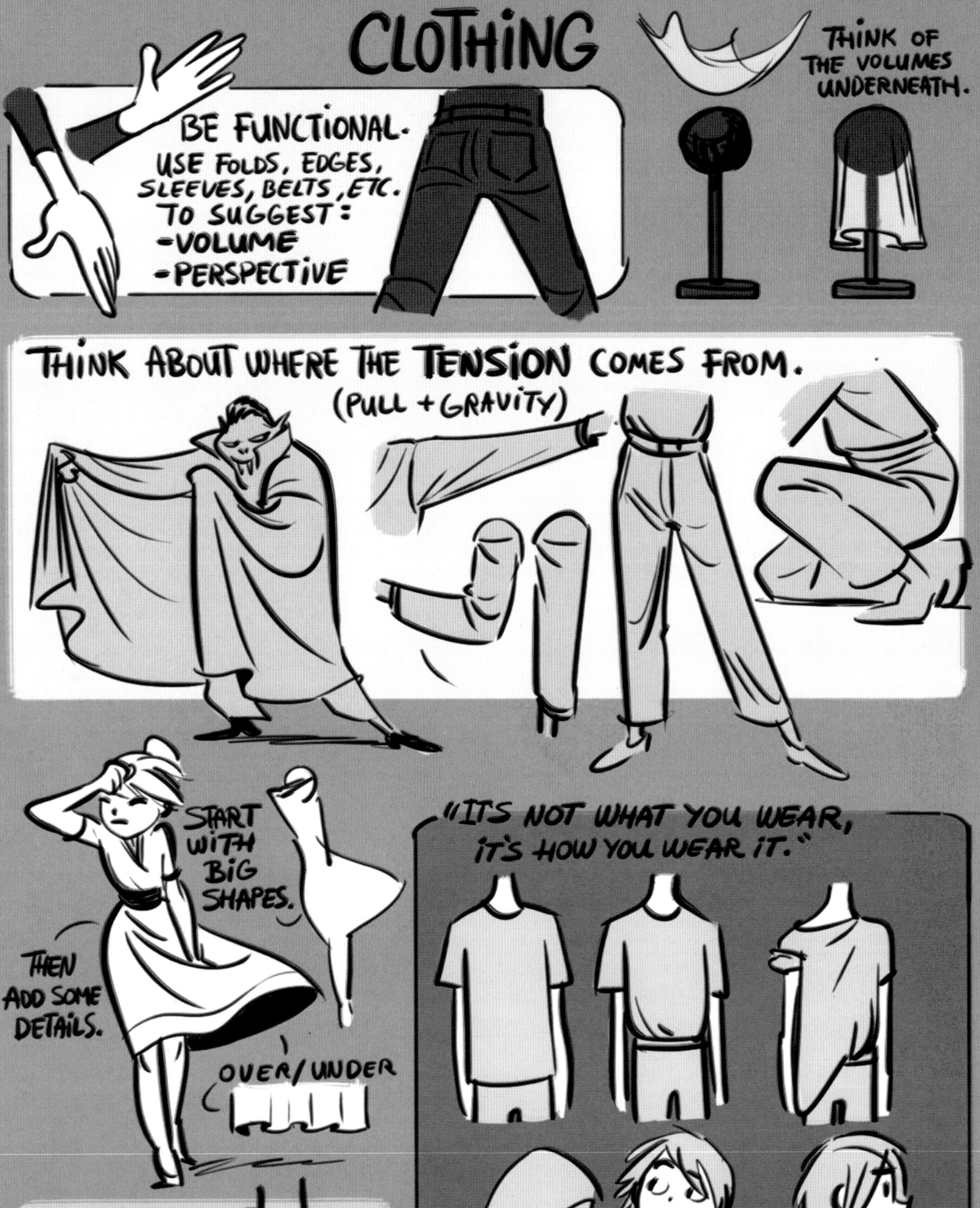

THINK ABOUT WHERE THE **TENSION** COMES FROM.
(PULL + GRAVITY)

START WITH BIG SHAPES.

THEN ADD SOME DETAILS.

OVER/UNDER

"IT'S NOT WHAT YOU WEAR, IT'S HOW YOU WEAR IT."

FIND YOUR OWN SHORTHANDS TO EVERYDAY ITEMS.

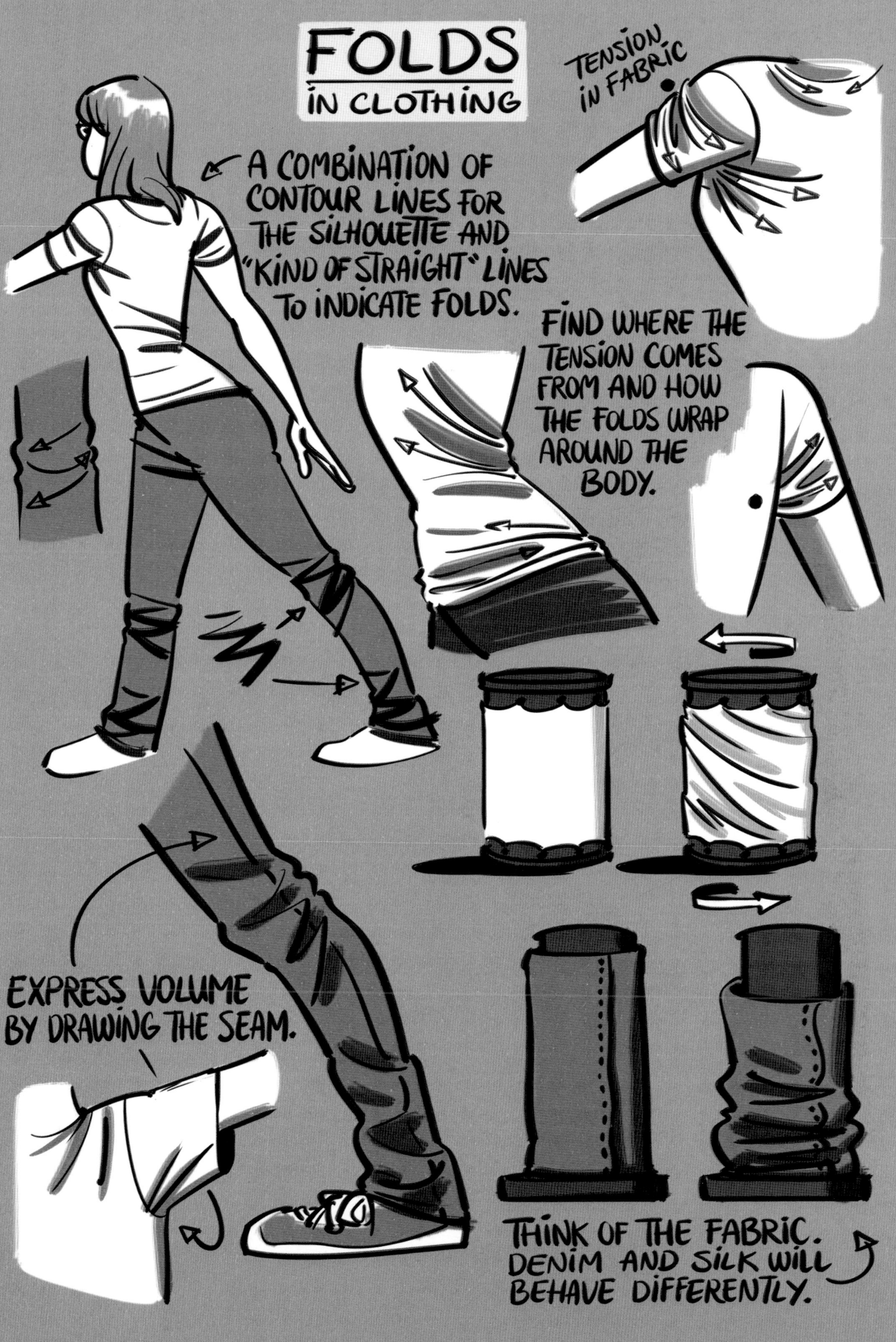
FOLDS
IN CLOTHING
TENSION IN FABRIC
A COMBINATION OF CONTOUR LINES FOR THE SILHOUETTE AND "KIND OF STRAIGHT" LINES TO INDICATE FOLDS.
FIND WHERE THE TENSION COMES FROM AND HOW THE FOLDS WRAP AROUND THE BODY.
EXPRESS VOLUME BY DRAWING THE SEAM.
THINK OF THE FABRIC. DENIM AND SILK WILL BEHAVE DIFFERENTLY.

Gouache Process

① Initial Sketch

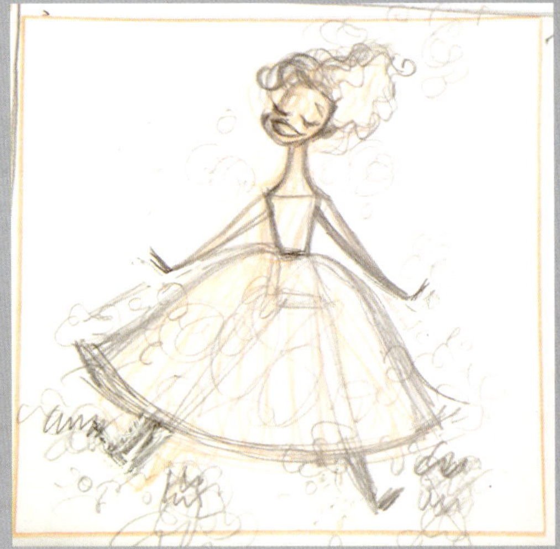

② Background color

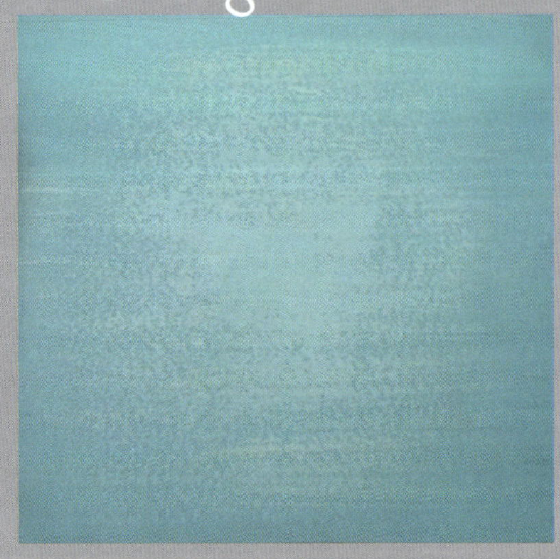

③ Transfer drawing

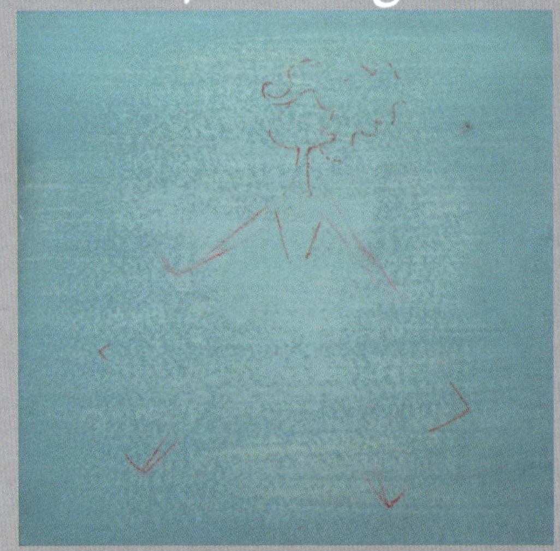

④ Base color

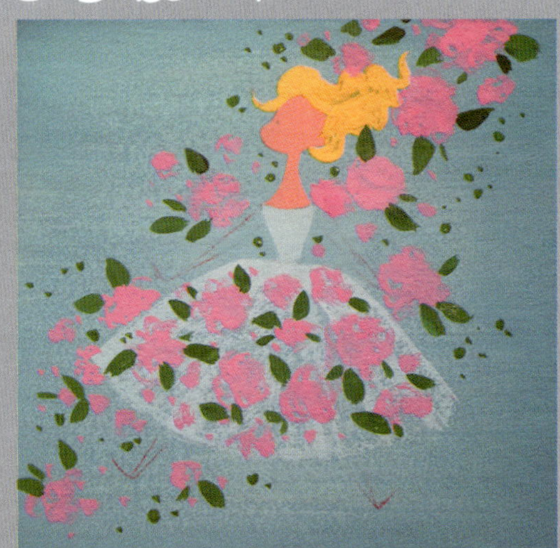

⑤ Add detail

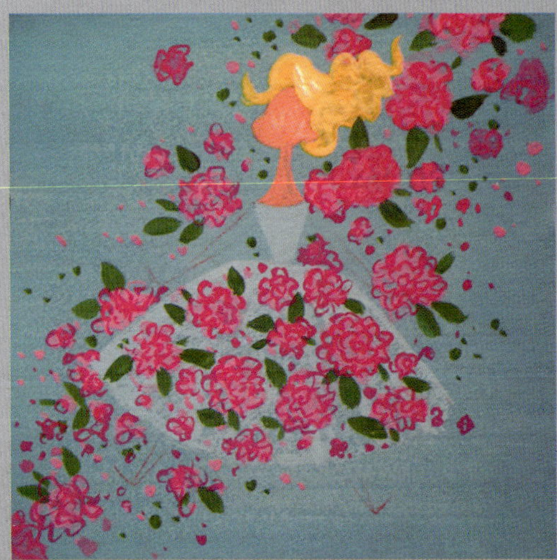

⑥ Finish painting

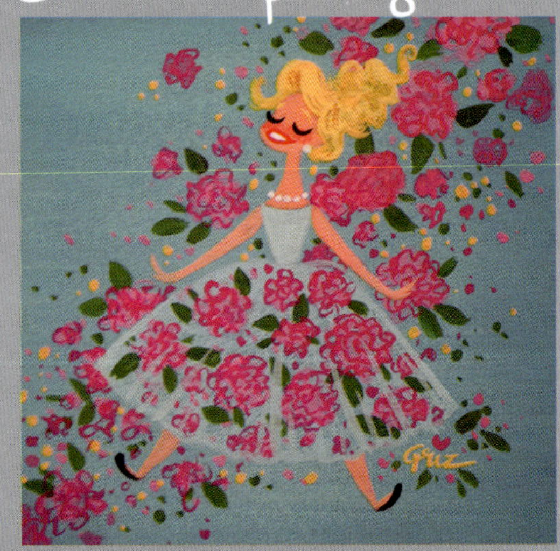

Glitter

① local color

② darker texture (on a separate layer)

③ lighter texture (on a separate layer)

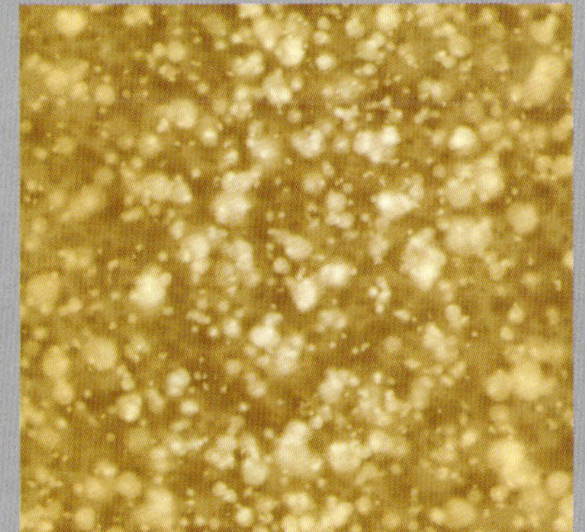

④ Color dodge the lighter texture

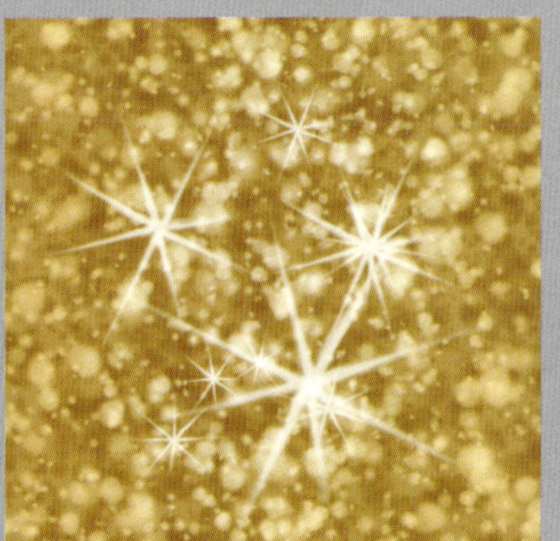

⑤ add stars

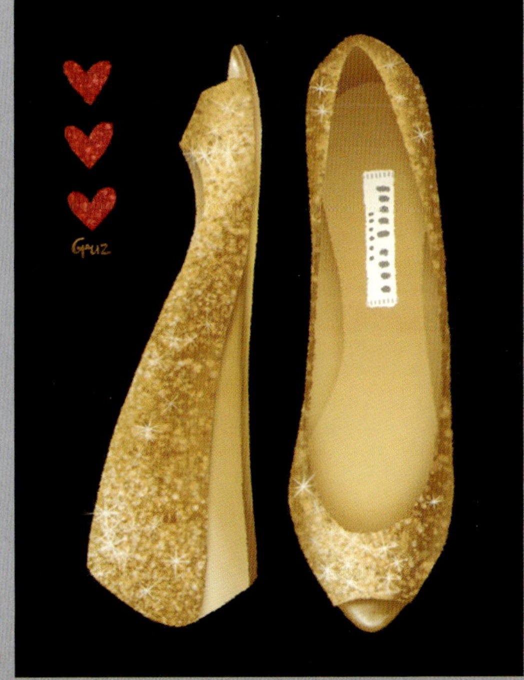

example →

LEG SUPPORT

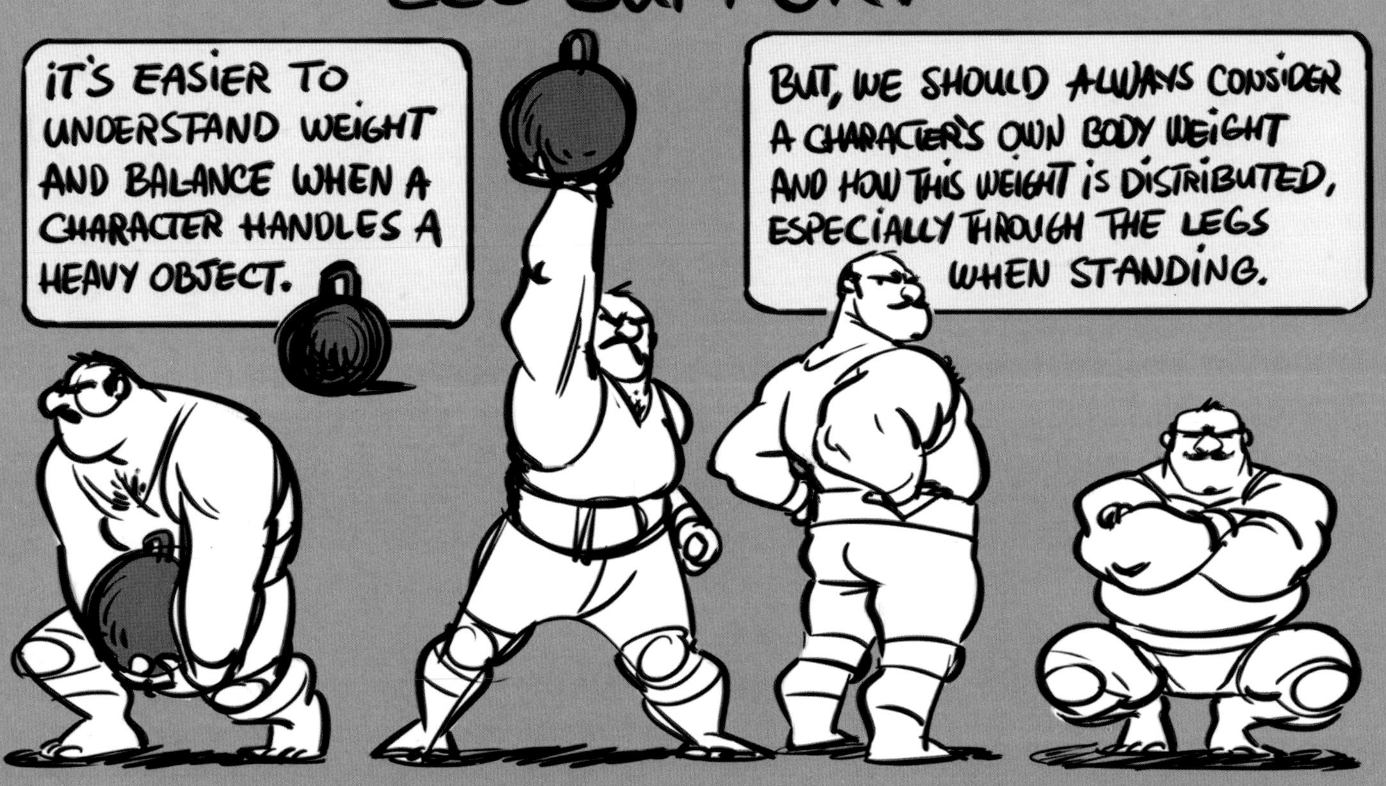

LEG STANCE IN GESTURE DRAWING

① -START WITH 2 LINES, FOR BOTH LEGS AND A GENERAL LINE OF ACTION.

② -SETUP FOOT POSITIONS WITH 2 SIMPLE LINES. (SOLES OF THE FEET)

③ -COMPLETE THE GESTURE WITH A SOLID "LEG FOUNDATION."

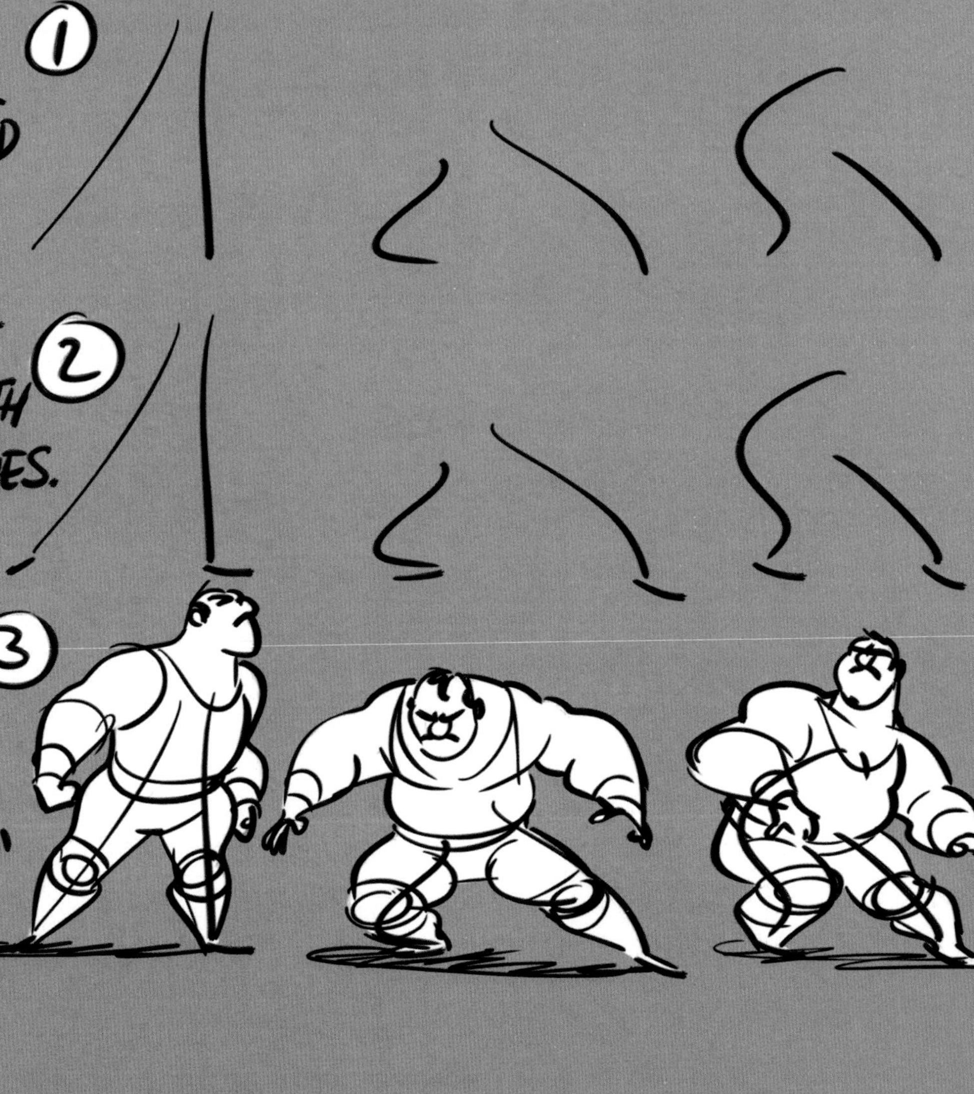

SHORTHANDS

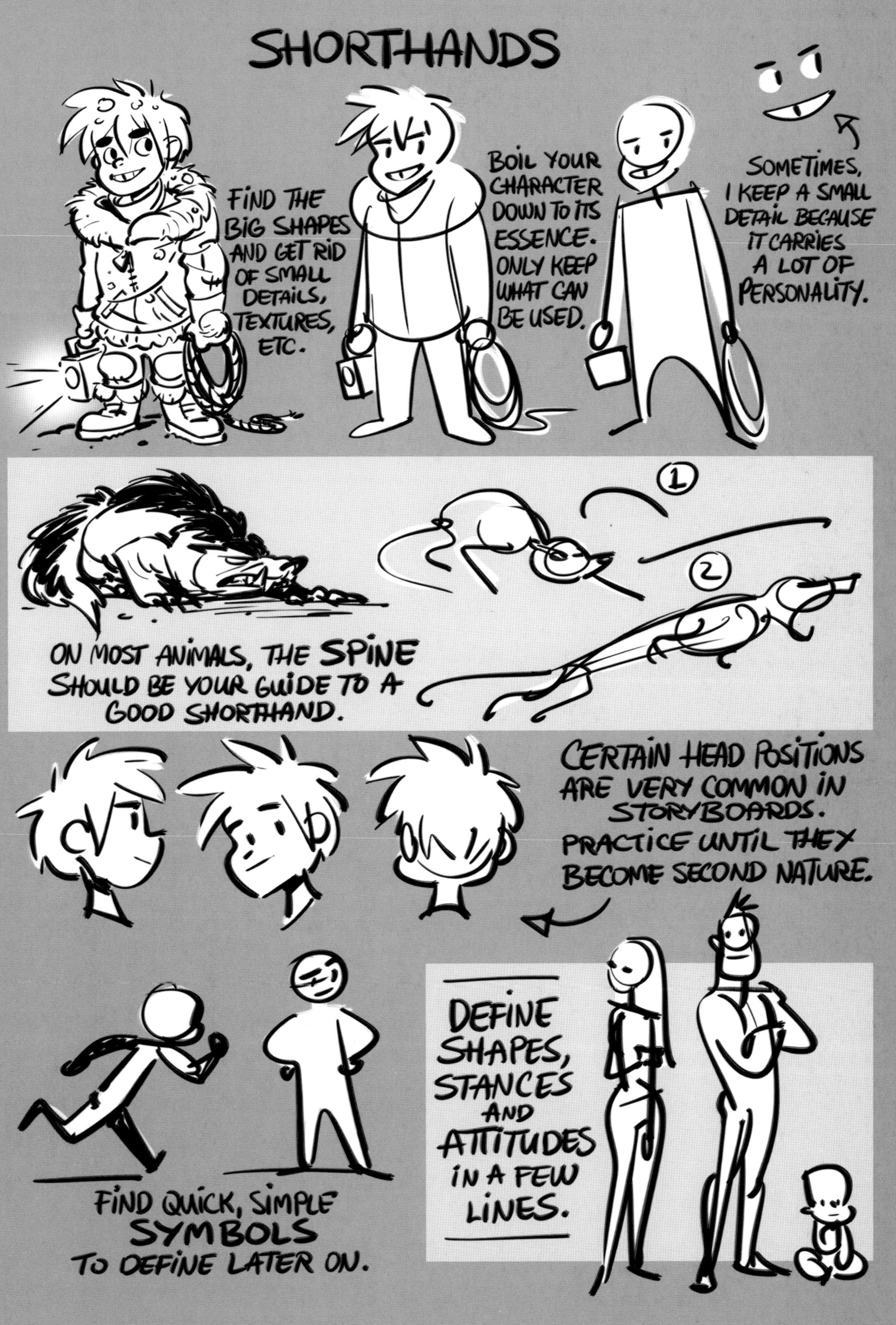
FIND THE BIG SHAPES AND GET RID OF SMALL DETAILS, TEXTURES, ETC.
BOIL YOUR CHARACTER DOWN TO ITS ESSENCE. ONLY KEEP WHAT CAN BE USED.
SOMETIMES, I KEEP A SMALL DETAIL BECAUSE IT CARRIES A LOT OF PERSONALITY.
1
2
ON MOST ANIMALS, THE SPINE SHOULD BE YOUR GUIDE TO A GOOD SHORTHAND.
CERTAIN HEAD POSITIONS ARE VERY COMMON IN STORYBOARDS. PRACTICE UNTIL THEY BECOME SECOND NATURE.
DEFINE SHAPES, STANCES AND ATTITUDES IN A FEW LINES.
FIND QUICK, SIMPLE SYMBOLS TO DEFINE LATER ON.

Basic Primitives -- SPHERE

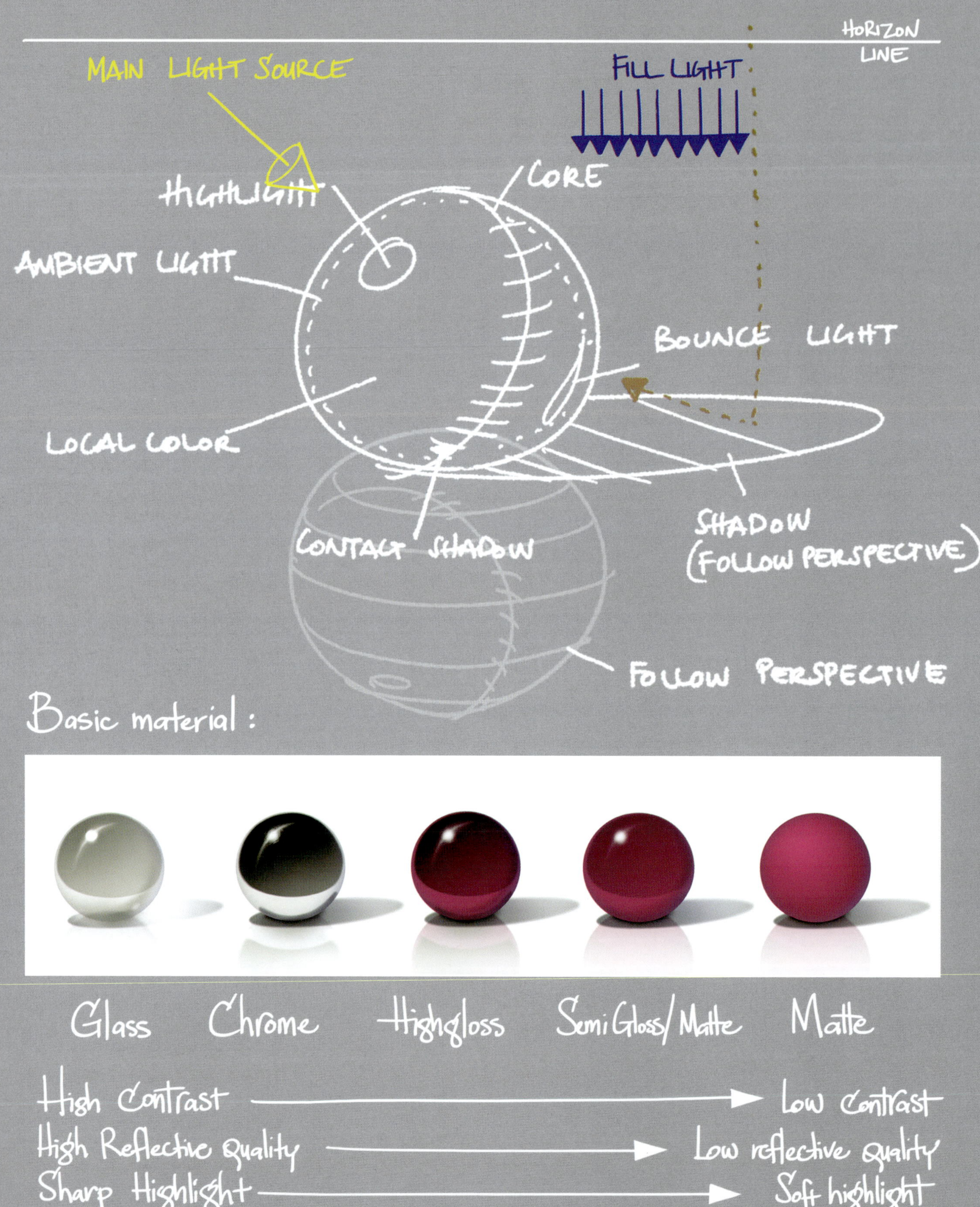

Basic Primitives -- CONE

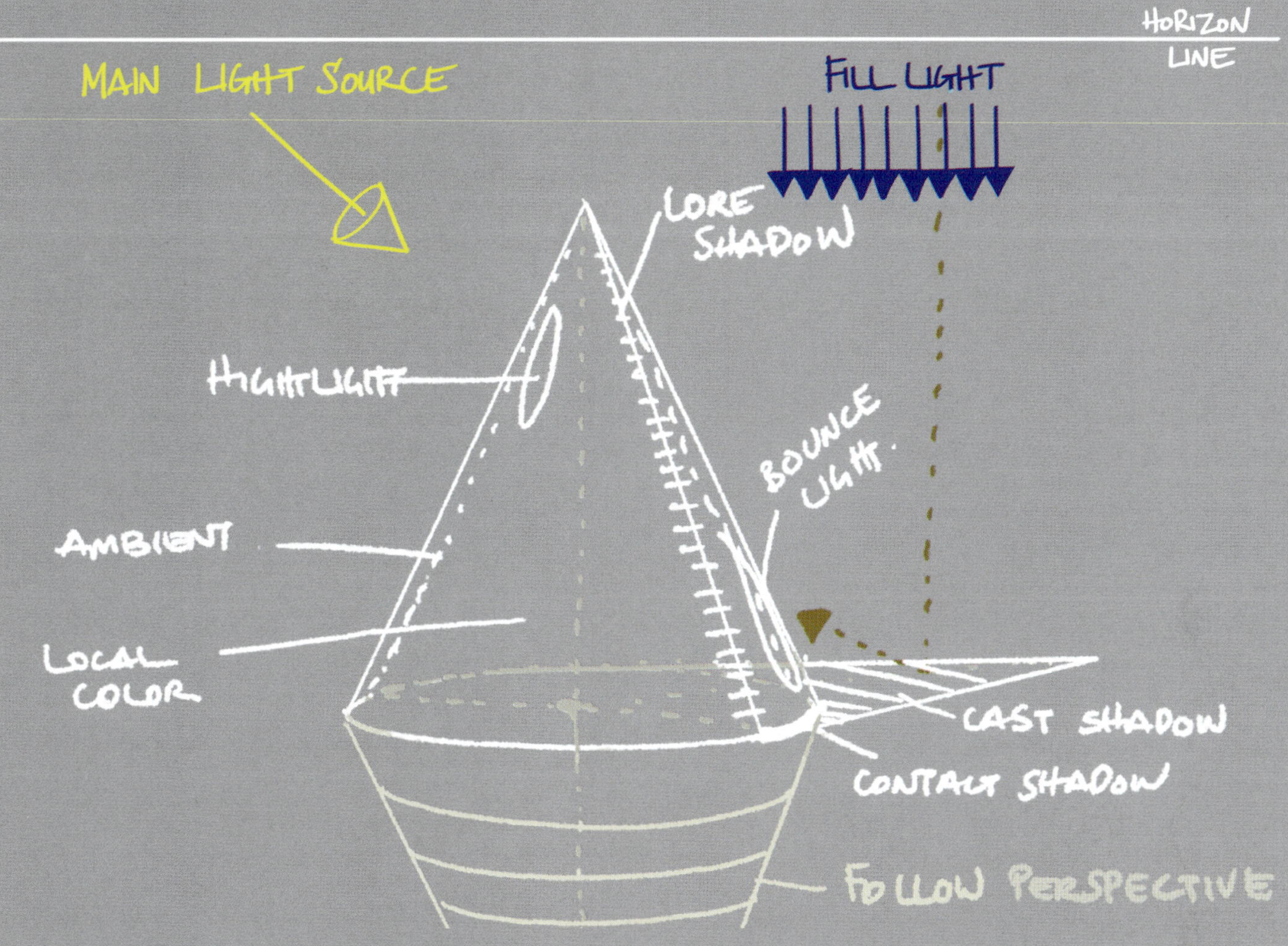

Basic material:

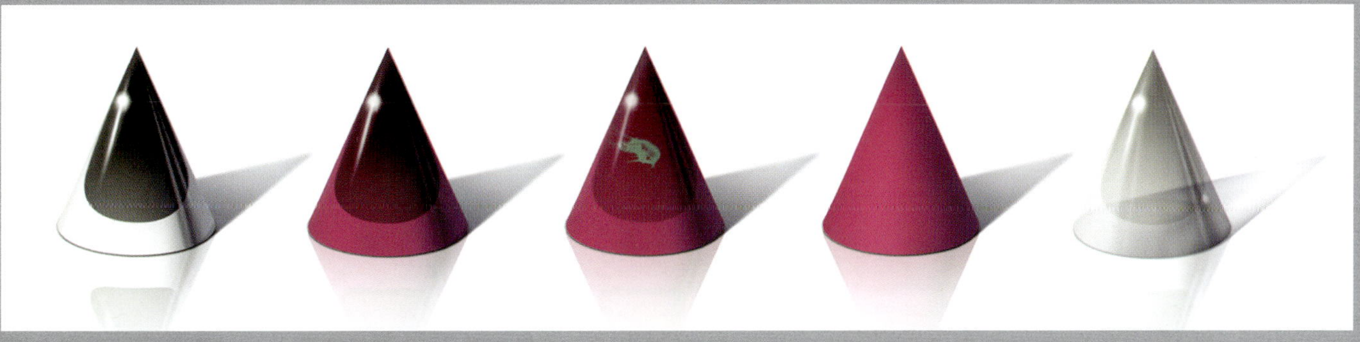

Glass Chrome Highgloss SemiGloss/Matte Matte

High Contrast → Low Contrast
High Reflective quality → Low reflective quality
Sharp Highlight → Soft highlight

Basic Primitives -- Cylinder

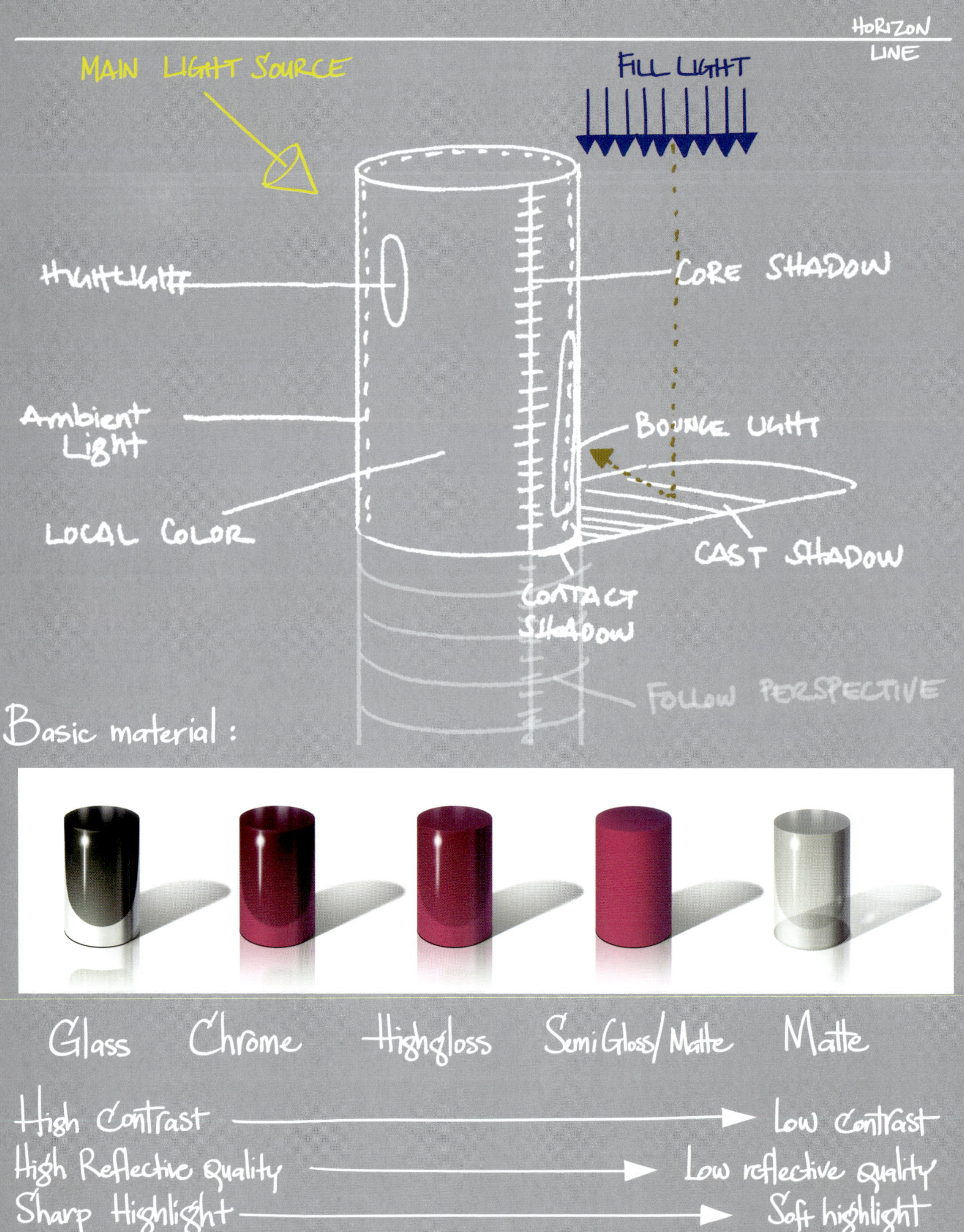

Glass Chrome Highgloss SemiGloss/Matte Matte

High Contrast → Low Contrast
High Reflective quality → Low reflective quality
Sharp Highlight → Soft highlight

Basic Primitives -- CUBE

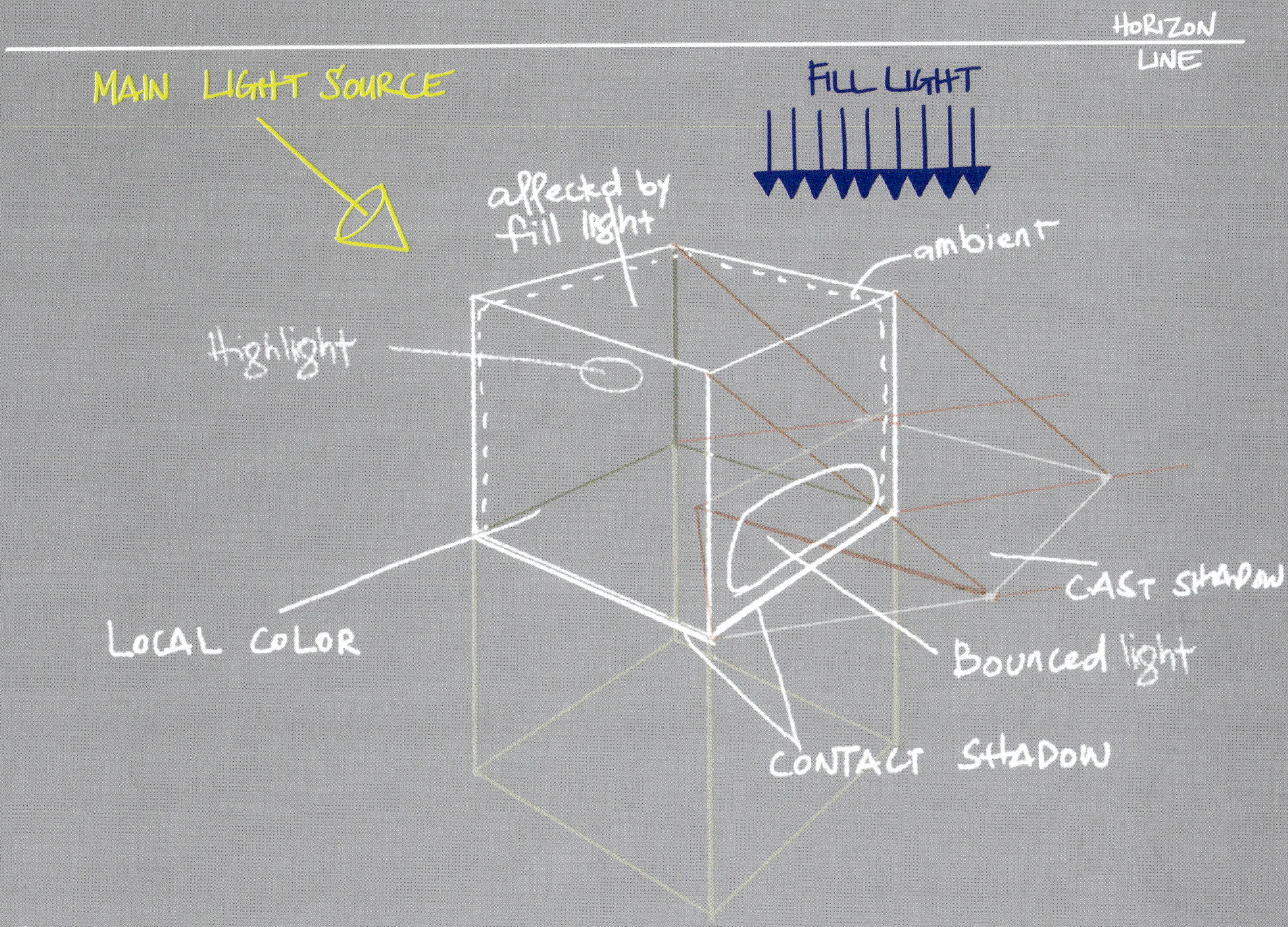

HORIZON LINE

MAIN LIGHT SOURCE

FILL LIGHT

affected by fill light

ambient

Highlight

CAST SHADOW

LOCAL COLOR

Bounced light

CONTACT SHADOW

Basic material :

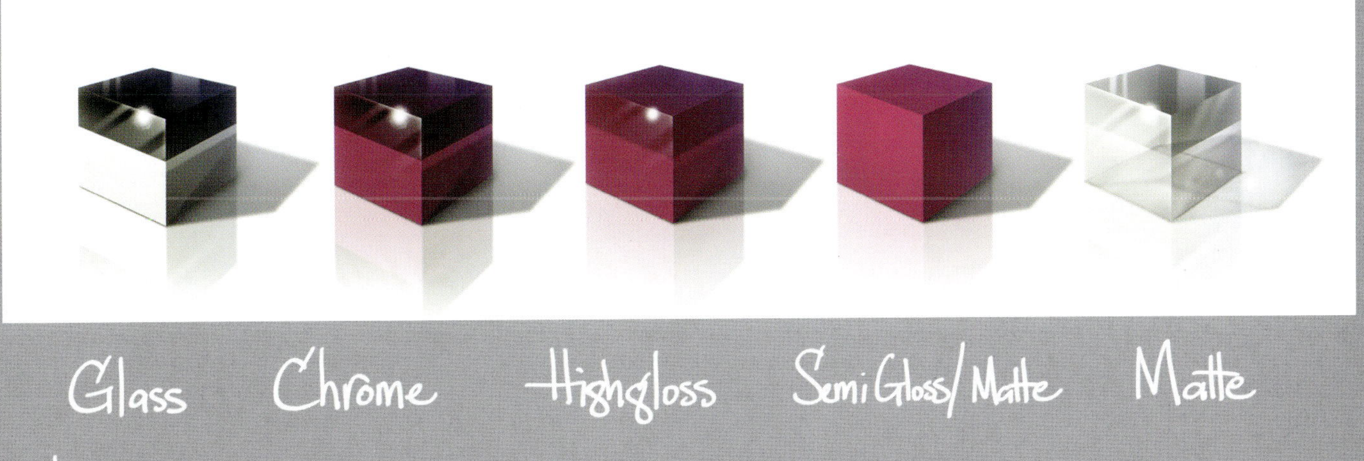

Glass Chrome Highgloss Semi Gloss/Matte Matte

High Contrast → Low Contrast

High Reflective quality → Low reflective quality

Sharp Highlight → Soft highlight

FACE PROFILE

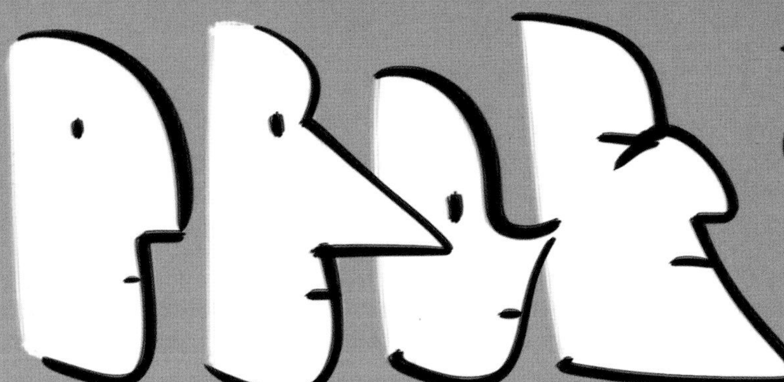

THE PROFILE OFFERS A TON OF VARIATIONS TO PLAY WITH. ANGLES/SIZES/PROPORTIONS OF BROW, NOSE, AND CHIN ARE A GREAT STARTING POINT.

TO WATCH FOR:

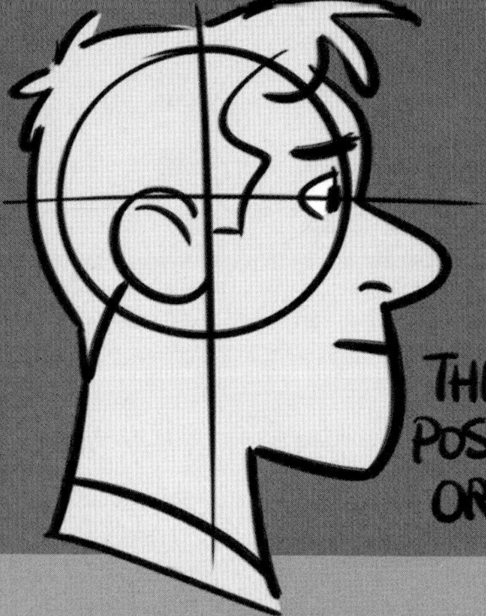

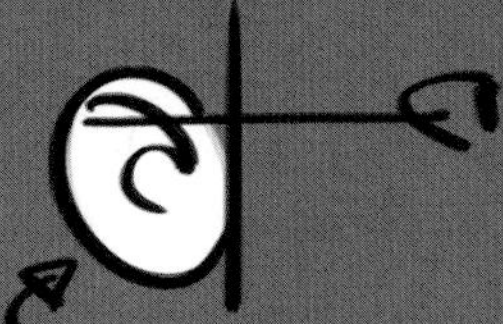

THE EAR IS OFTEN POSITIONED TOO HIGH OR TOO FAR BACK.

THE BACK OF THE HEAD IS OFTEN IGNORED.

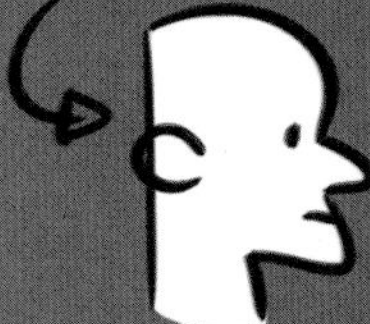

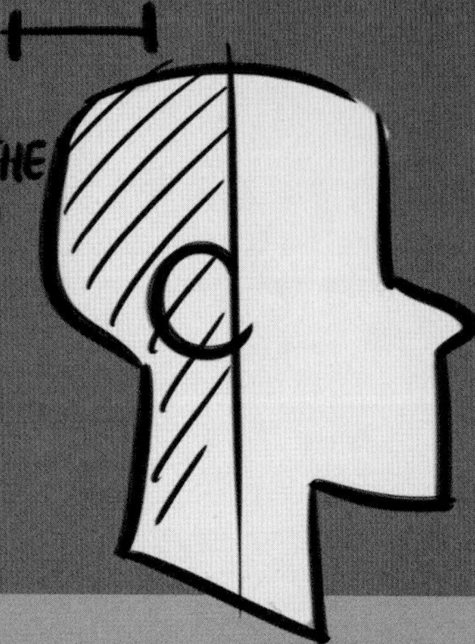

TO PLAY WITH:

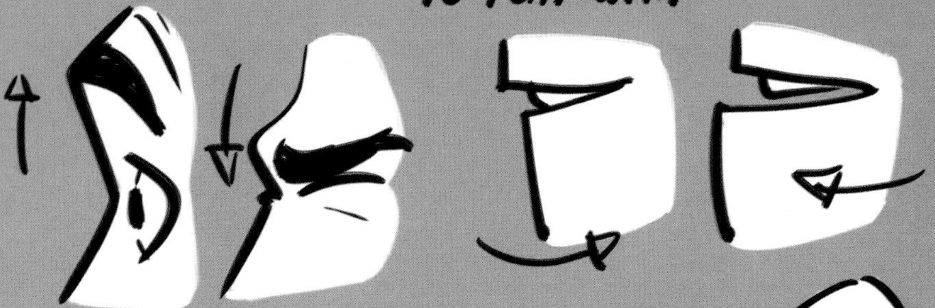

TYPES OF CHINS

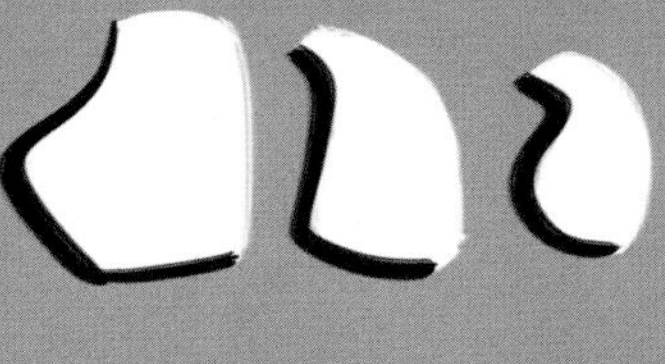

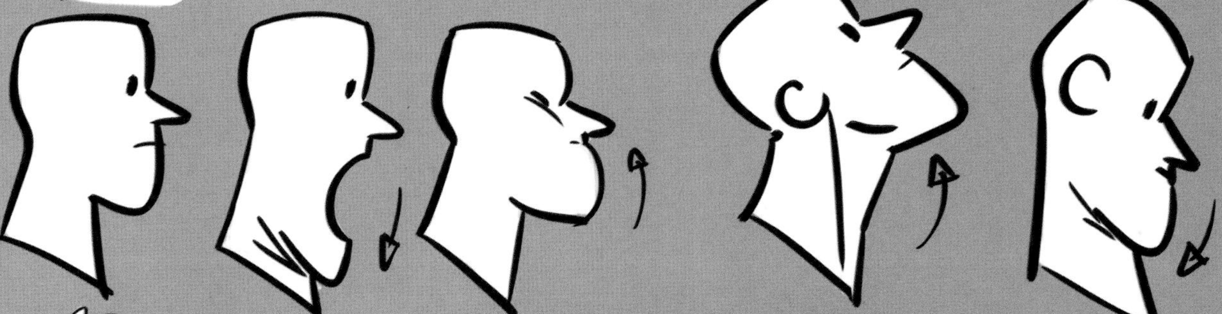

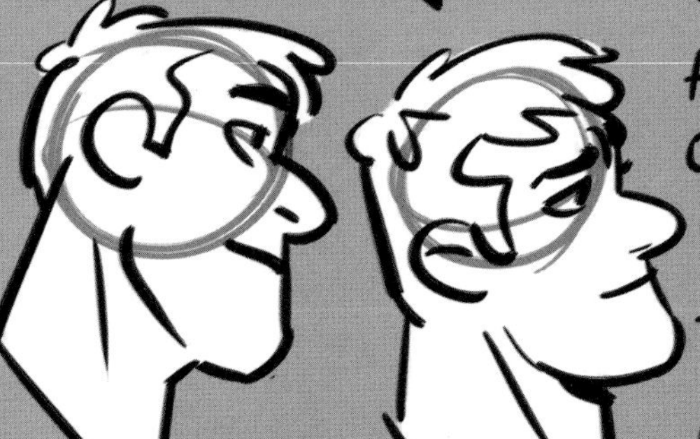

A SLIGHT TILT OF THE EYE LINE CAN ADD A LOT OF NUANCE TO A PROFILE.

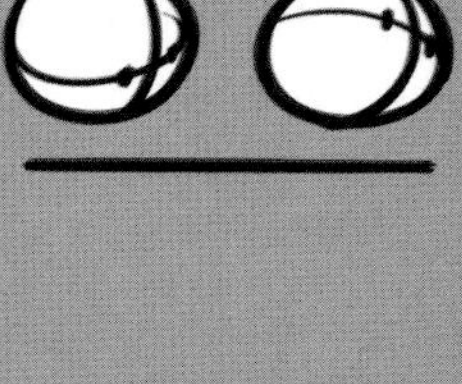

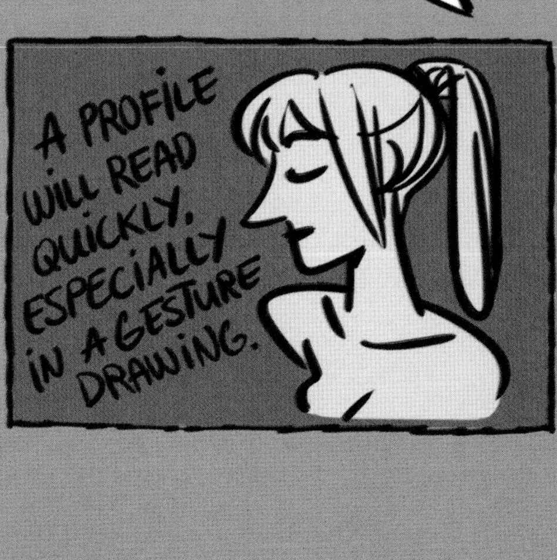

A PROFILE WILL READ QUICKLY. ESPECIALLY IN A GESTURE DRAWING.

ASYMMETRY IN FACIAL EXPRESSIONS

SYMMETRY EXPRESSES: BOREDOM, STABILITY, AUTHORITY, DETERMINATION, FEAR (SHOCK), ETC.

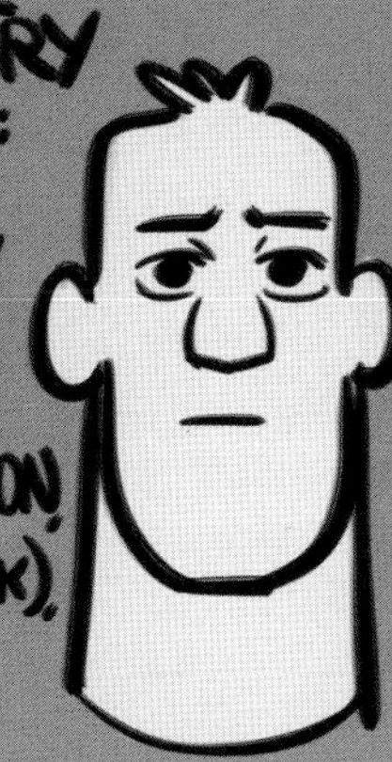

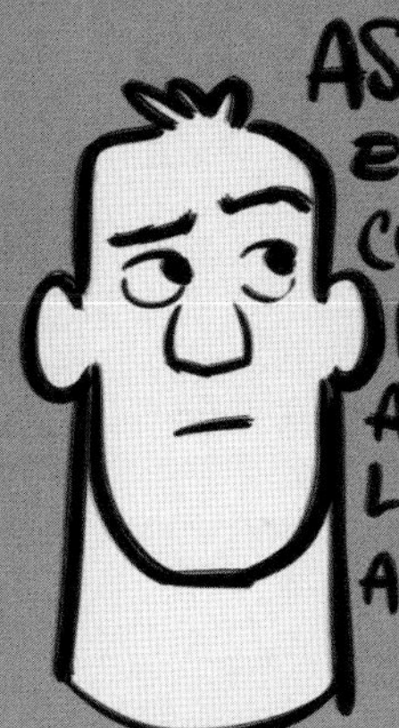

ASYMMETRY EXPRESSES: CURIOSITY, MOVEMENT, ANYTHING LOOKING FOR A RESOLUTION.

ADDING A TILT OF THE HEAD CAN ADD MORE NUANCE.

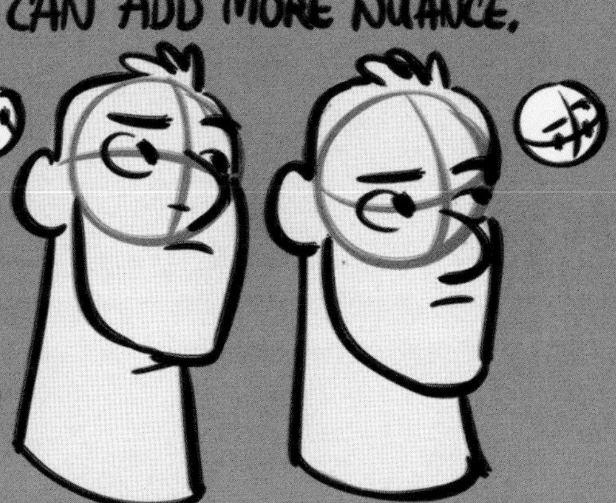

PUSH/PULL AREAS AROUND THE EYES (LIKE A MASK).

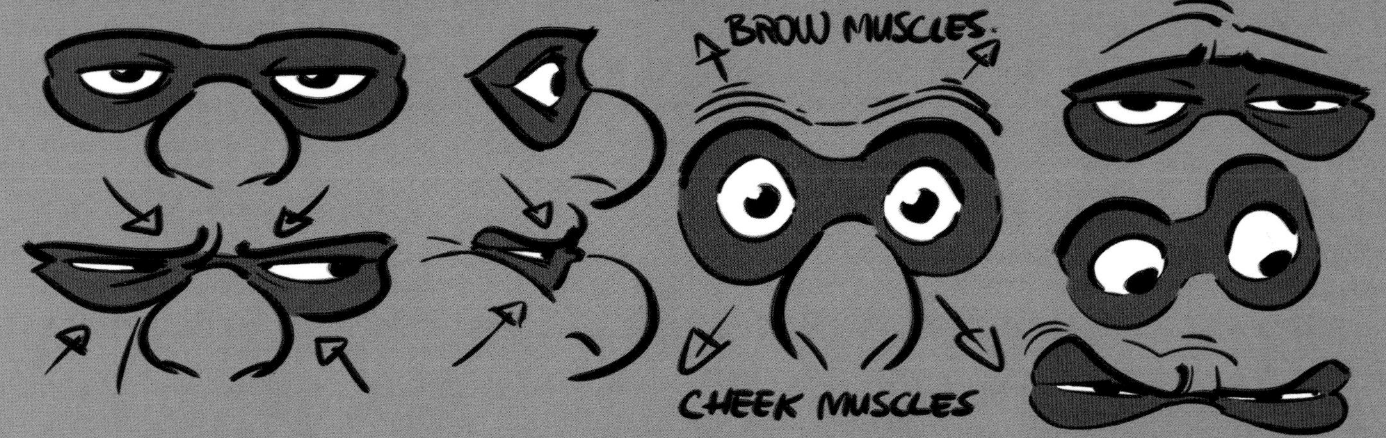

MOUTH: ALWAYS TRY TO FAVOR A SIDE (EVEN SLIGHTLY).

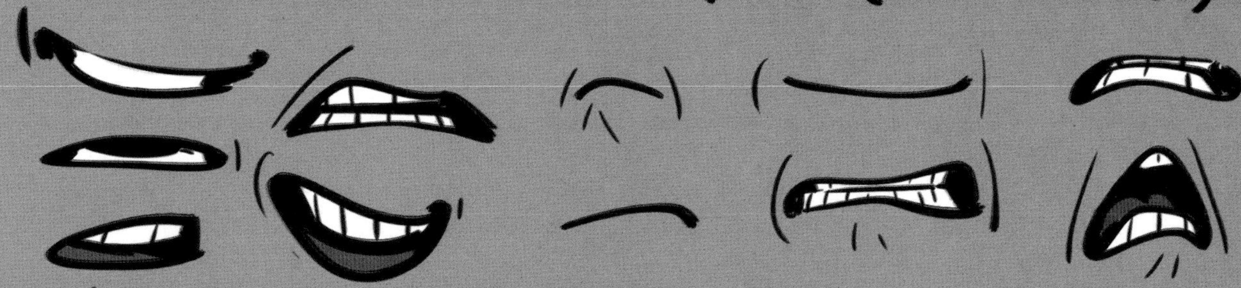

COMBINE AND HAVE FUN!

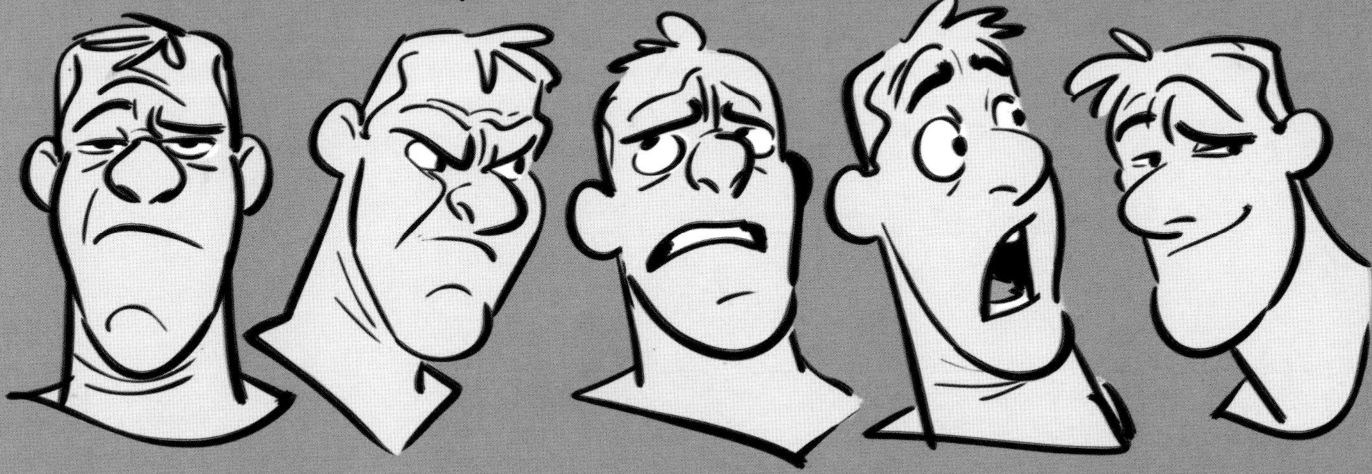

Exercise: Combine Primitives

Combine 4-6 primitives; must contain ALL basic primitives.
SPHERE, CONE, CYLINDER, CUBE

① Start w/ thumbnail

② Pick one & make sense of the lighting.

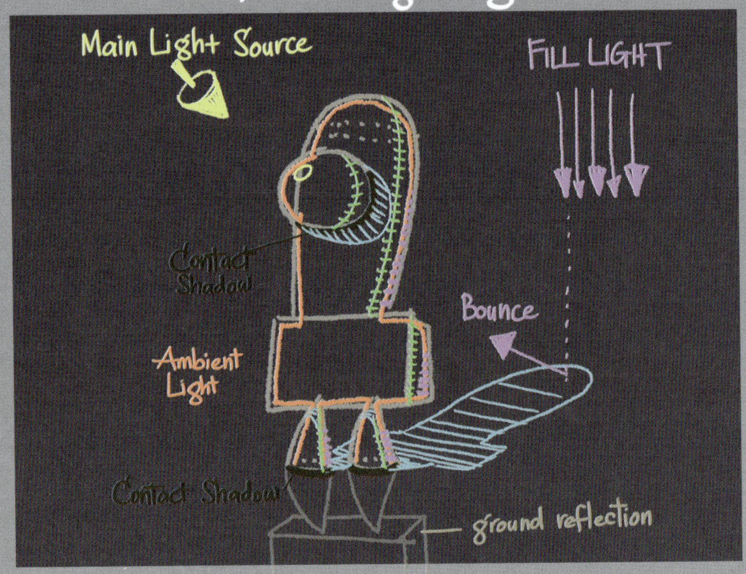

③ Paint basic value

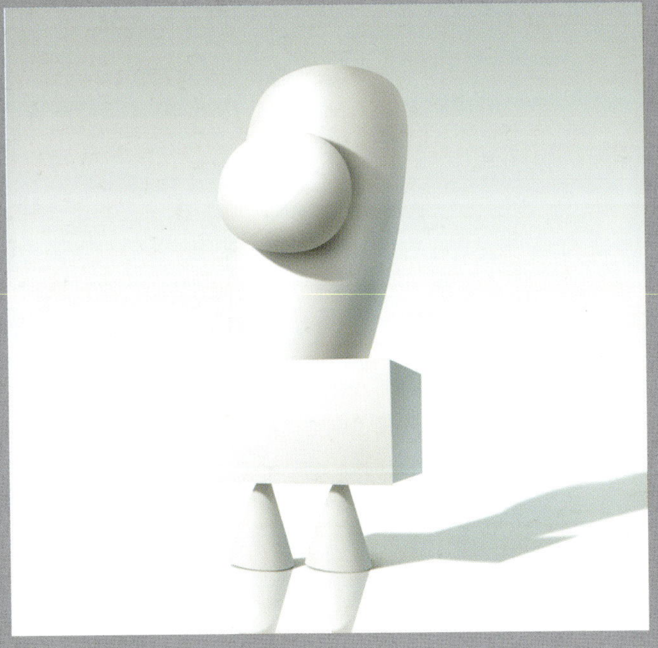

④ Add texture

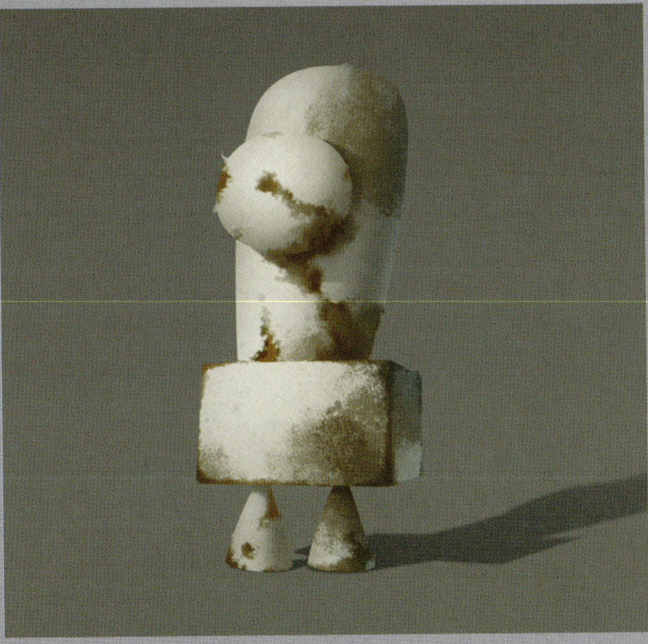

SHADOW

① CAST shadow -- shadow cast by an object or figure ➡ HARD
- will have the same shape as the object / figure
- indicates where the object is in the environment.
- follow light source & perspective

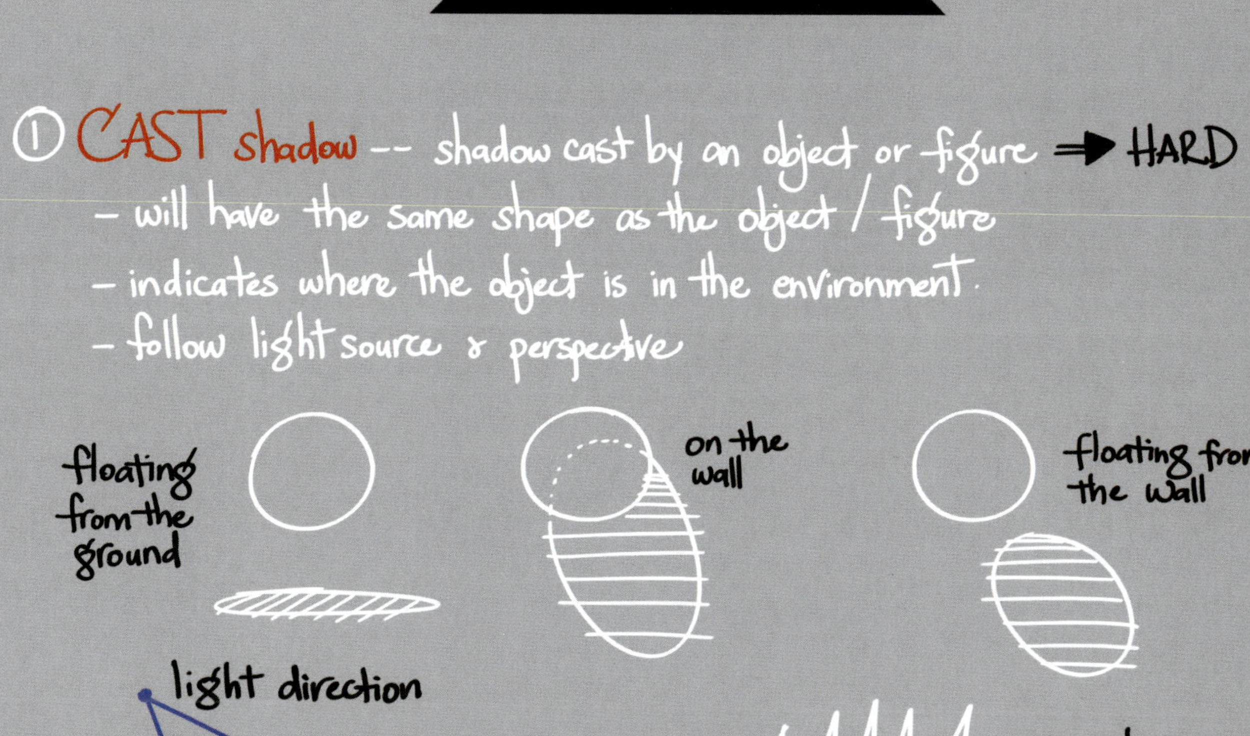

TIPS Cast shadow edge gets softer as it goes further from the object

② CORE shadow -- where light area turn into shadow area = SOFT
- a great way to indicate form

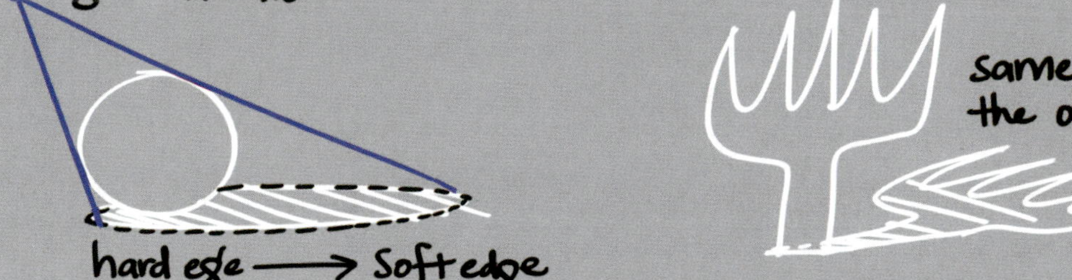
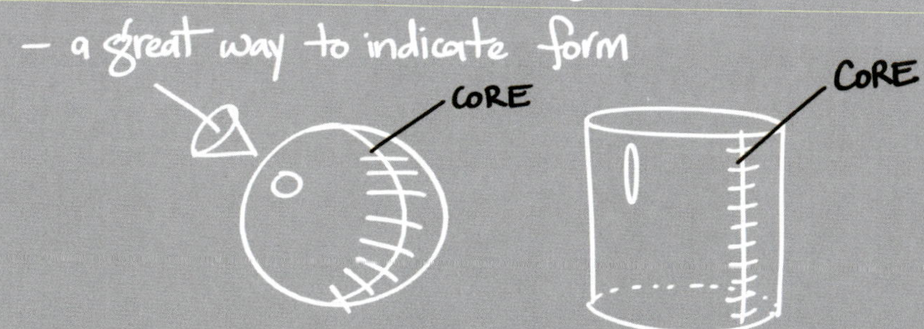

③ CONTACT shadow -- where 2 object touches
- the darkest part of the shadow

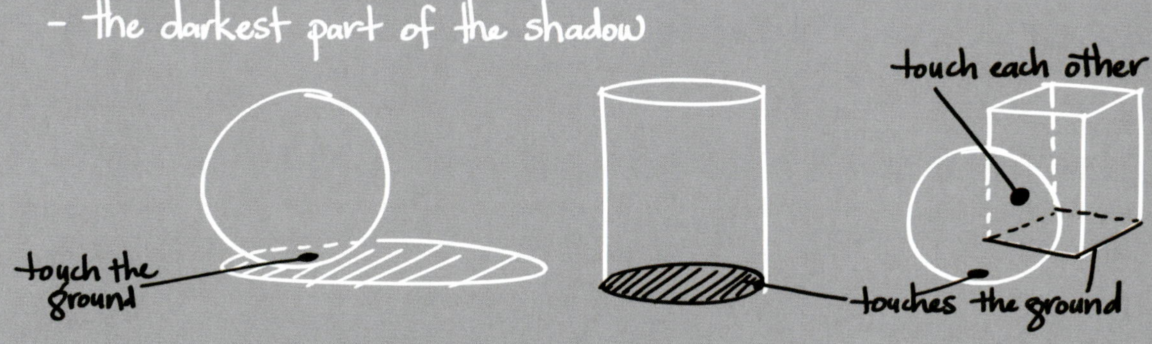

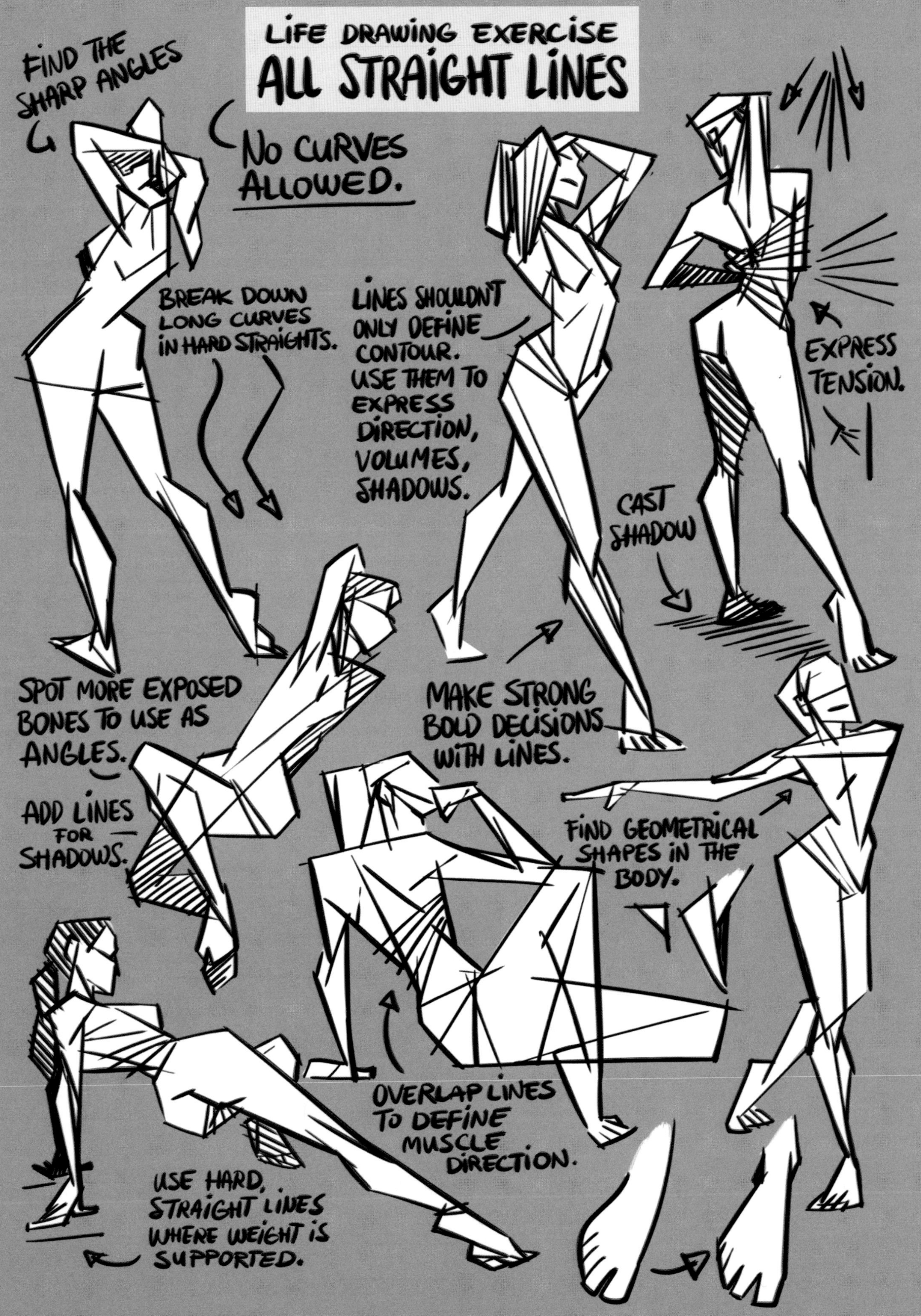
LIFE DRAWING EXERCISE
ALL STRAIGHT LINES
FIND THE SHARP ANGLES
NO CURVES ALLOWED.
BREAK DOWN LONG CURVES IN HARD STRAIGHTS.
LINES SHOULDN'T ONLY DEFINE CONTOUR. USE THEM TO EXPRESS DIRECTION, VOLUMES, SHADOWS.
EXPRESS TENSION.
CAST SHADOW
SPOT MORE EXPOSED BONES TO USE AS ANGLES.
MAKE STRONG BOLD DECISIONS WITH LINES.
ADD LINES FOR SHADOWS.
FIND GEOMETRICAL SHAPES IN THE BODY.
OVERLAP LINES TO DEFINE MUSCLE DIRECTION.
USE HARD, STRAIGHT LINES WHERE WEIGHT IS SUPPORTED.

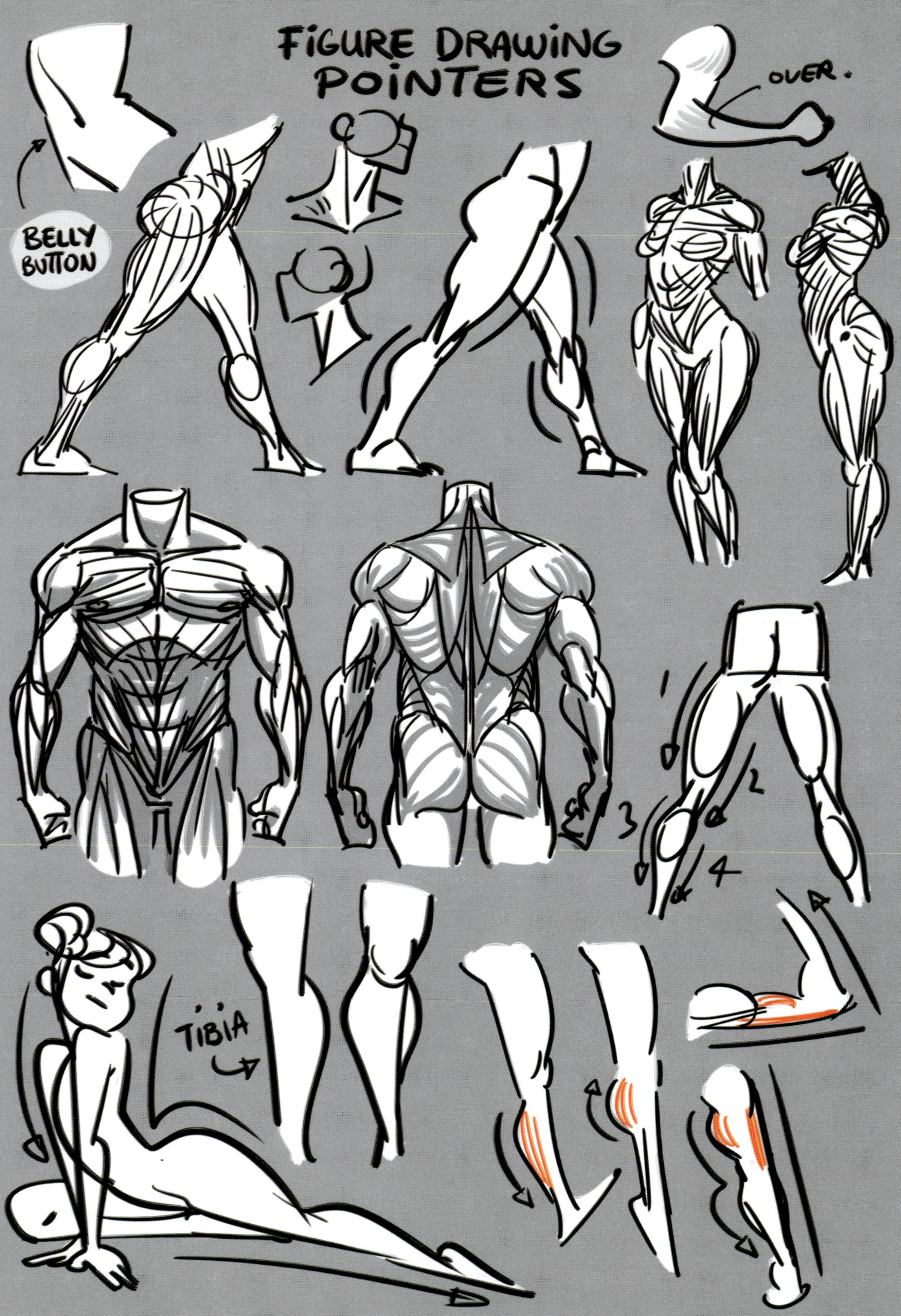
FIGURE DRAWING POINTERS
OVER.
BELLY BUTTON
1
2
3
4
TIBIA

Check your VALUE !!!

Value is the BLACK & WHITE image. This is another basic fundamental rule -- if your value reads, then your image will read, no matter how crazy your colors are.

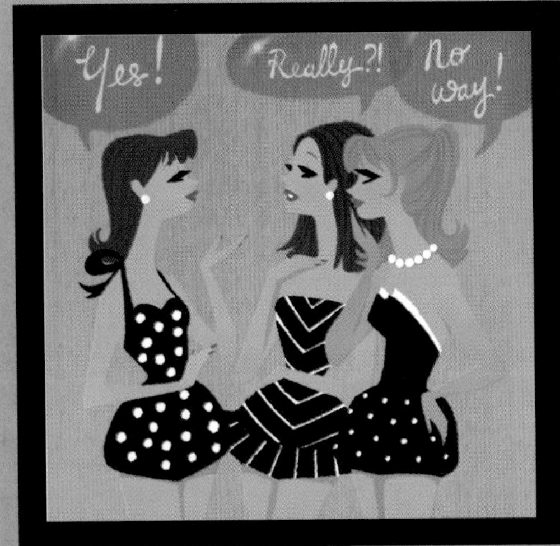

→ Contrast too Low.
No clean silhouette

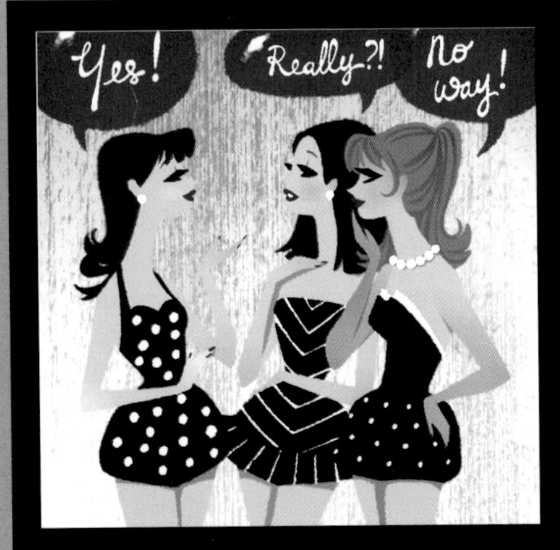

→ Very high contrast of value
Very spotty

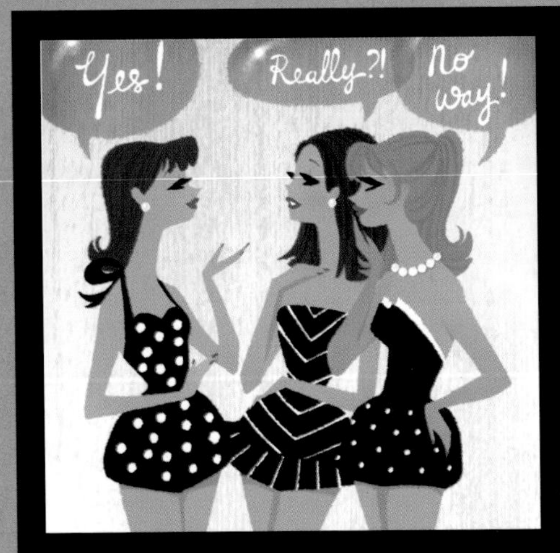

→ Better!
Good areas of dark & light contrast.
Clear silhouette.
Full range of value.

Color comp

Color comp or color thumbnails are different variations of what your final color would be.

Ex: I usually have an idea of the basic color combination that I want. Blue & orange.

① I would do different combination of the same hue, but changing the saturation and value of the hue.

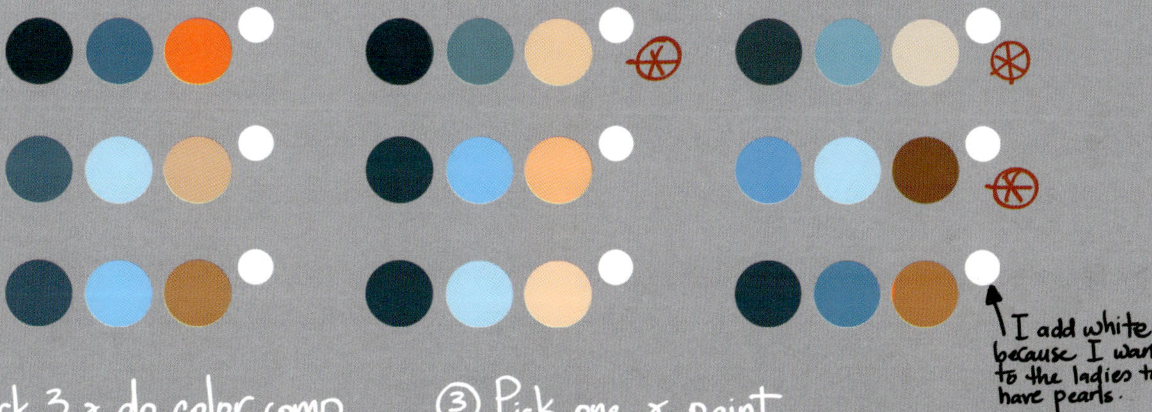

② Pick 3 & do color comp

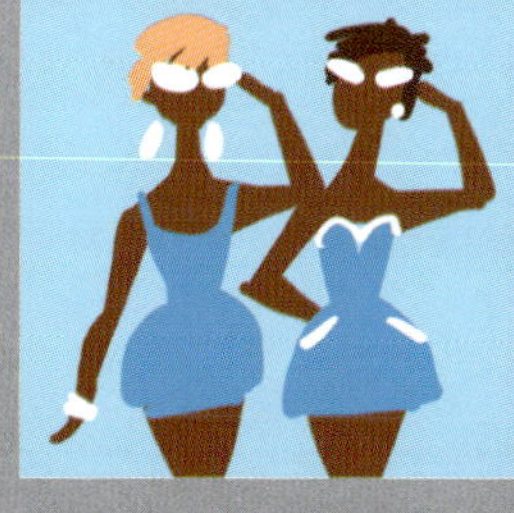

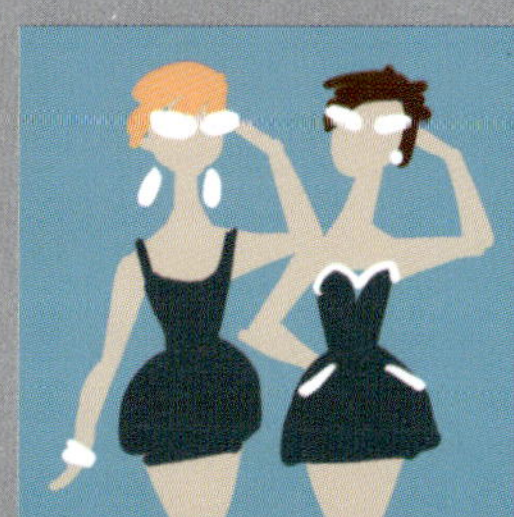

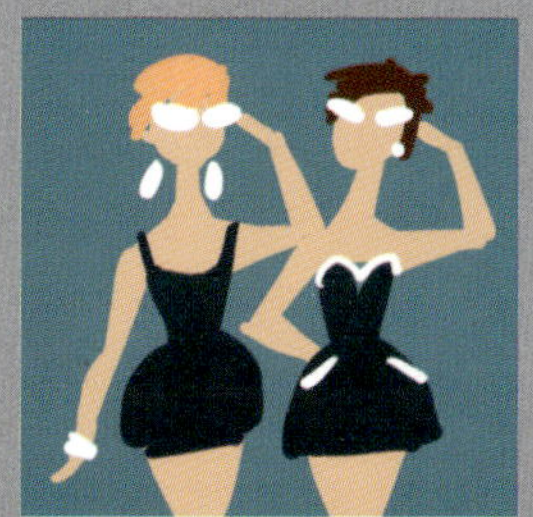

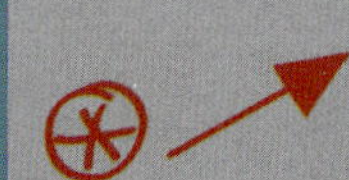

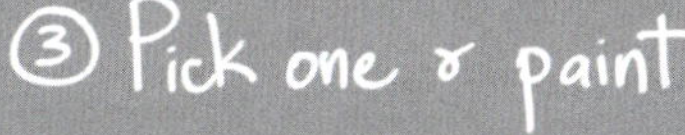

③ Pick one & paint

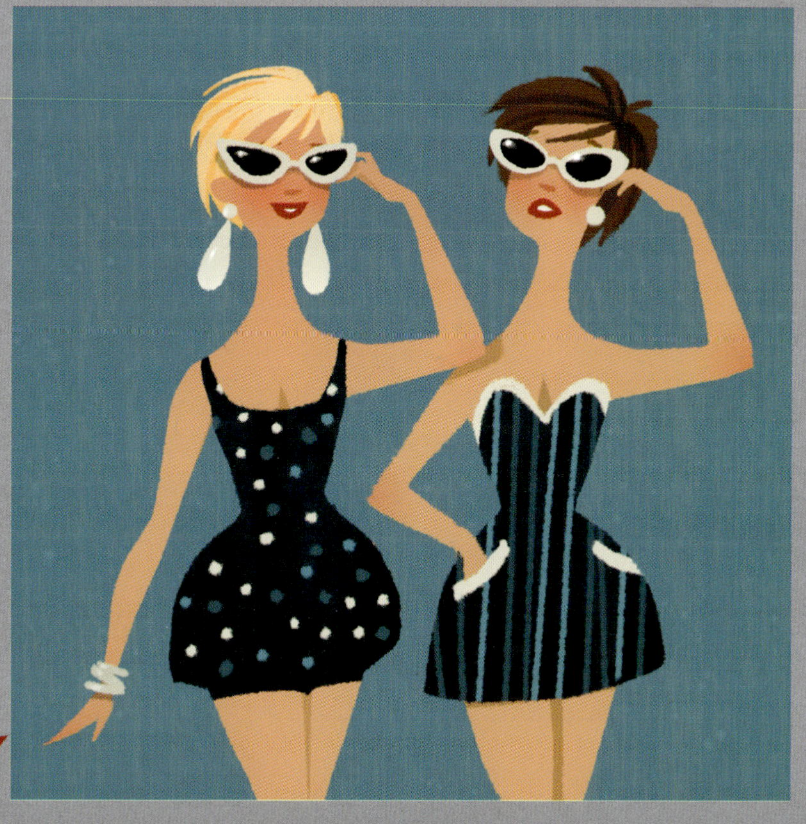

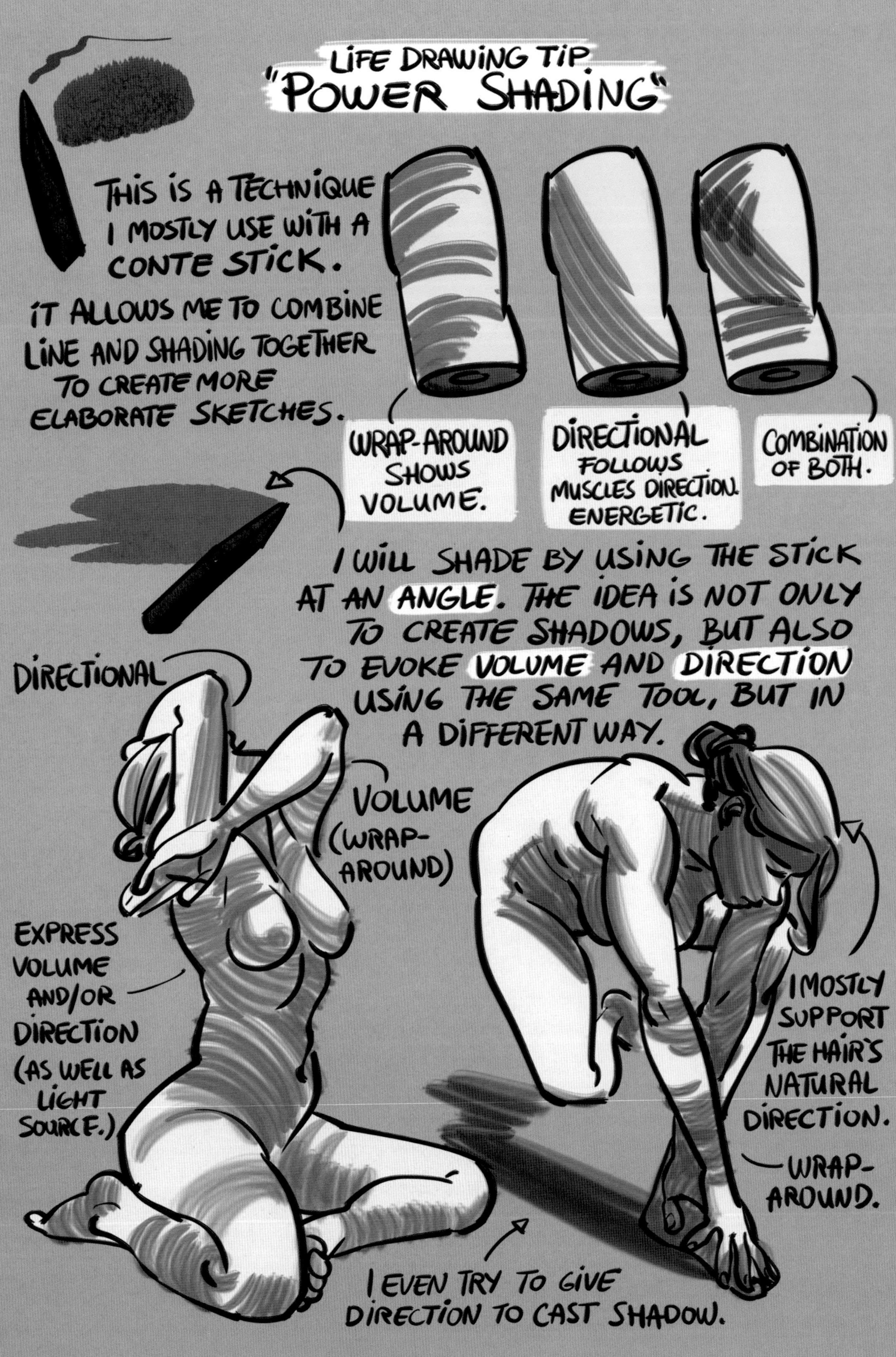
LIFE DRAWING TIP
"POWER SHADING"
THIS IS A TECHNIQUE I MOSTLY USE WITH A CONTE STICK.
IT ALLOWS ME TO COMBINE LINE AND SHADING TOGETHER TO CREATE MORE ELABORATE SKETCHES.
WRAP-AROUND SHOWS VOLUME.
DIRECTIONAL FOLLOWS MUSCLES DIRECTION. ENERGETIC.
COMBINATION OF BOTH.
I WILL SHADE BY USING THE STICK AT AN ANGLE. THE IDEA IS NOT ONLY TO CREATE SHADOWS, BUT ALSO TO EVOKE VOLUME AND DIRECTION USING THE SAME TOOL, BUT IN A DIFFERENT WAY.
DIRECTIONAL
VOLUME (WRAP-AROUND)
EXPRESS VOLUME AND/OR DIRECTION (AS WELL AS LIGHT SOURCE.)
I MOSTLY SUPPORT THE HAIR'S NATURAL DIRECTION.
WRAP-AROUND.
I EVEN TRY TO GIVE DIRECTION TO CAST SHADOW.

SIMPLE SHADOWS

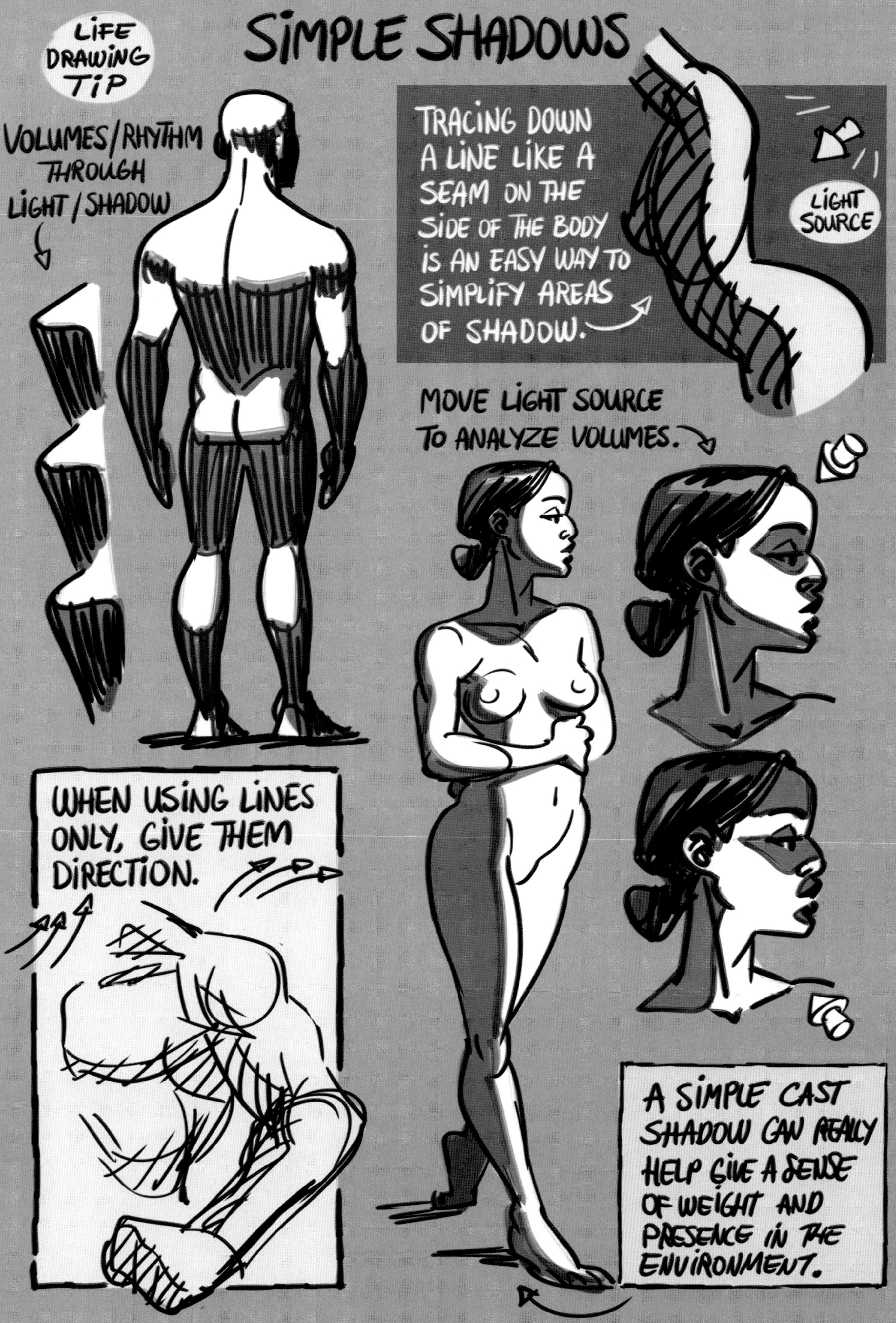

Thumbnails

Thumbnails are small sketches of ideas.

Ex: ① I usually do them very small & quick on the first pass.

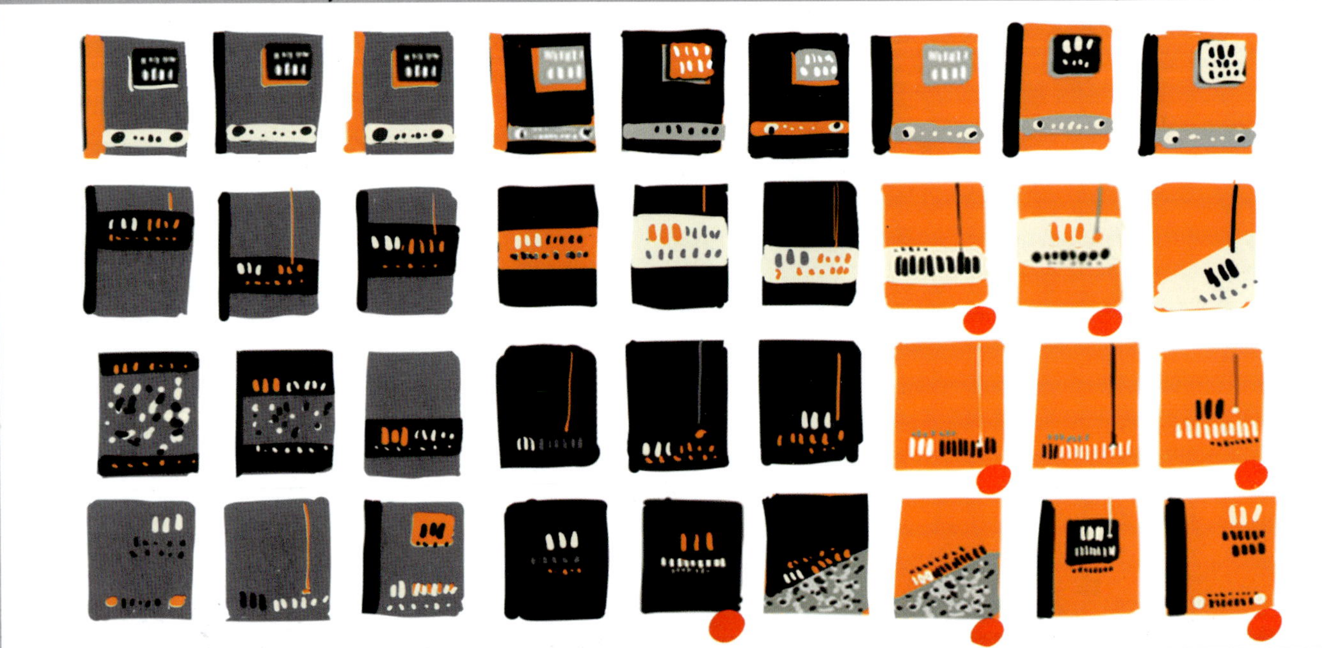

② Pick the ones that you like & do a clean version.

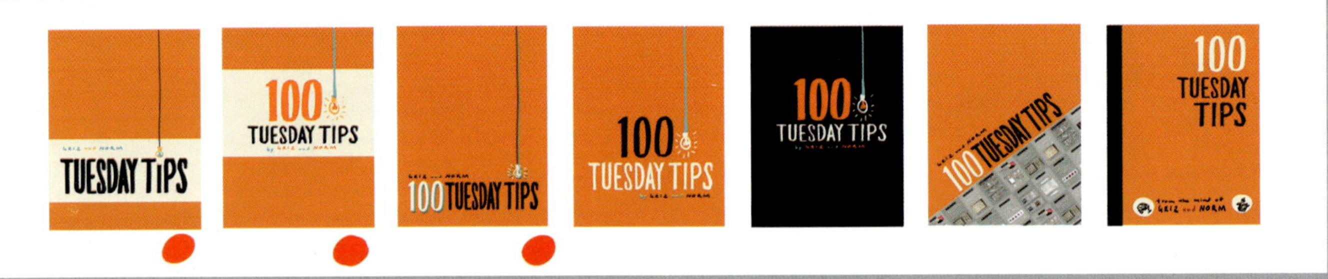

③ Pick 3 & do variations & see which one you like the most, then do your final.

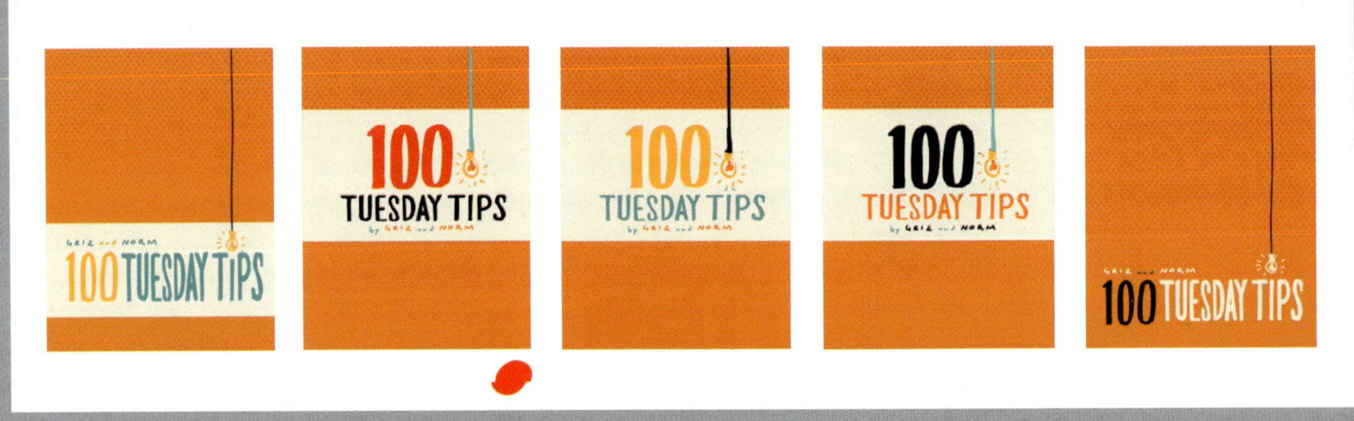

Printing Guide -- Business Card

For standard size -- 3.5" x 2"

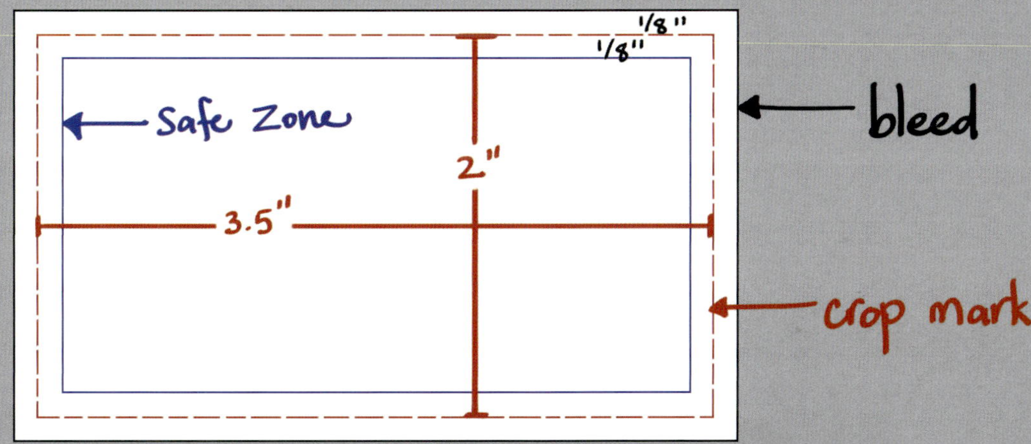

Bleed -- add 1/8" (or .125") all around ⟹ 3.75" x 2.25"
your image should extend to this line

Crop mark -- the final size ⟹ 3.5" x 2"

Safe zone -- all writing should only be inside the safe zone

What to put ⟹ Name
Website
Email
Phone #
Social media logo (optional)

⊛ Tips = your card orientation can be portrait or landscape, but make it consitent from the front & back design

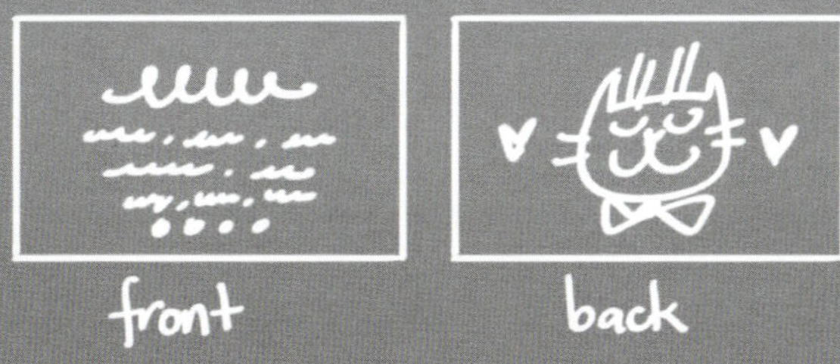

front back

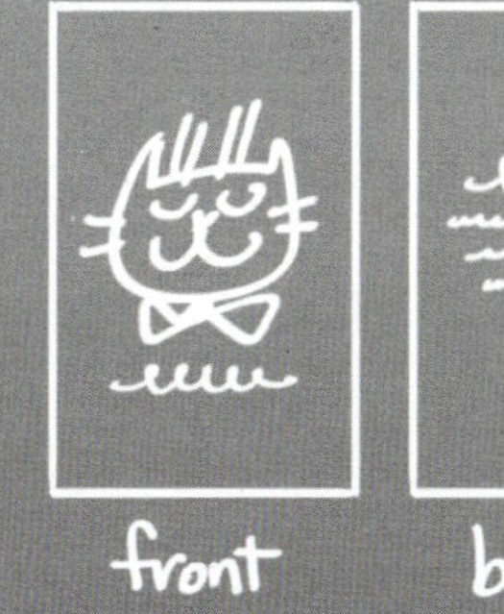

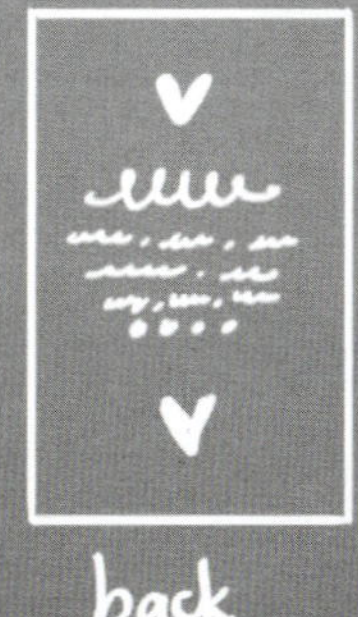

front back

BODY SHAPES

REPEATING A SIMILAR SHAPE WITHIN A MAIN BODY SHAPE IS A SIMPLE WAY TO UNIFY A BASIC CHARACTER DESIGN.

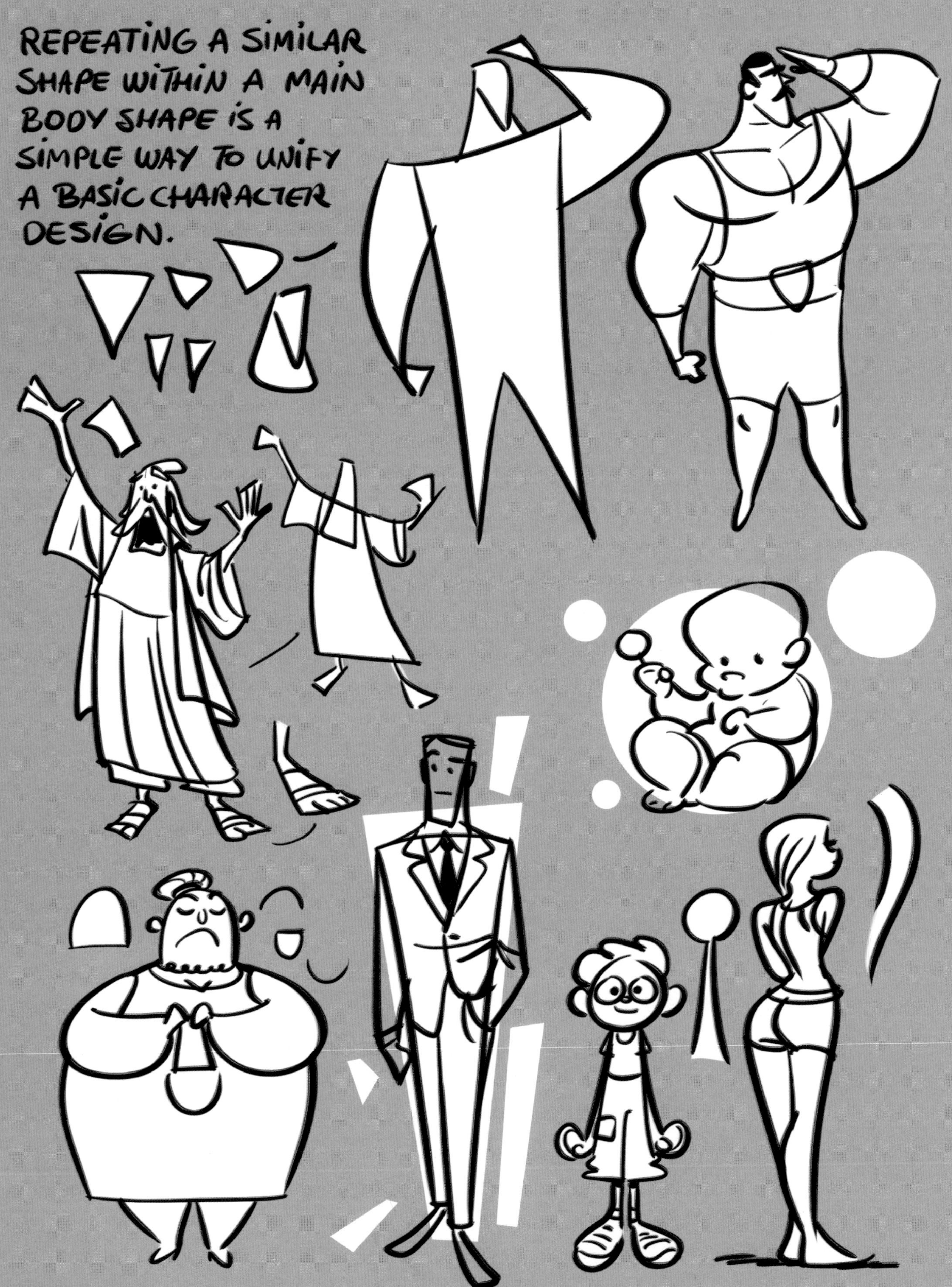

TEETH!

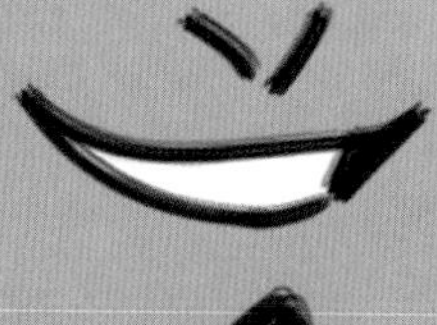
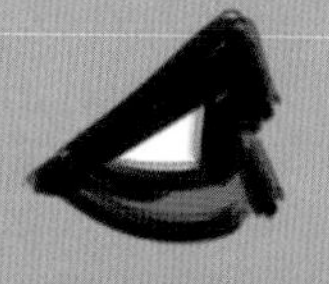

VERY OFTEN, YOU CAN GET AWAY WITH JUST FLASHING SOME WHITE.

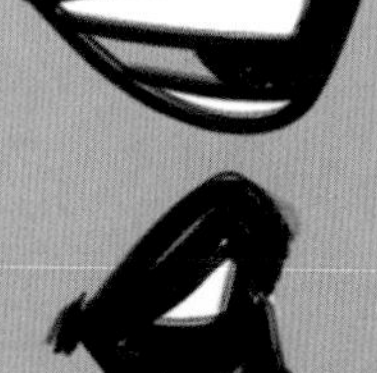
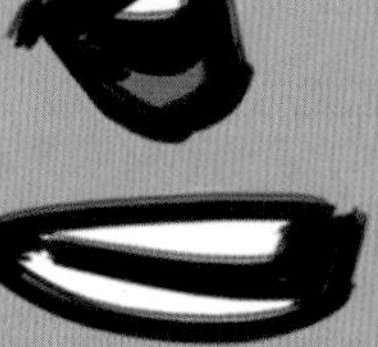

IT GETS SLIGHTLY TRICKIER WHEN THE MOUTH OPENS UP A LITTLE MORE.

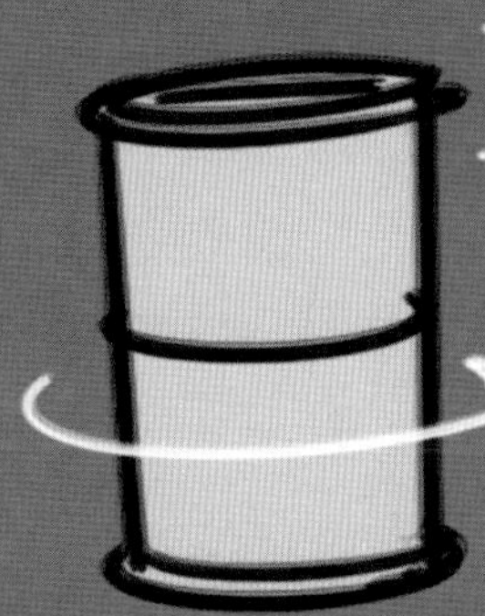

THINK OF THE ROWS OF TEETH AS VOLUMES.

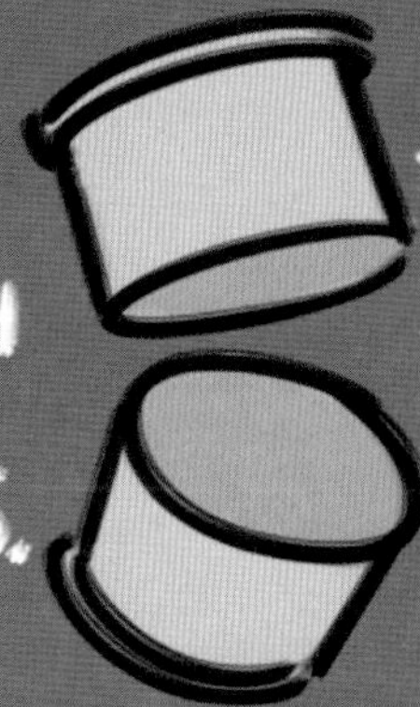

SIMILARLY, CONSIDER THE ANGLE YOU ARE DRAWING FROM.

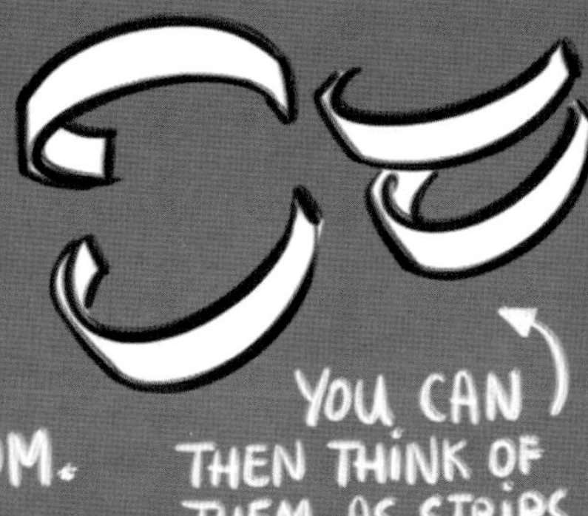

YOU CAN THEN THINK OF THEM AS STRIPS

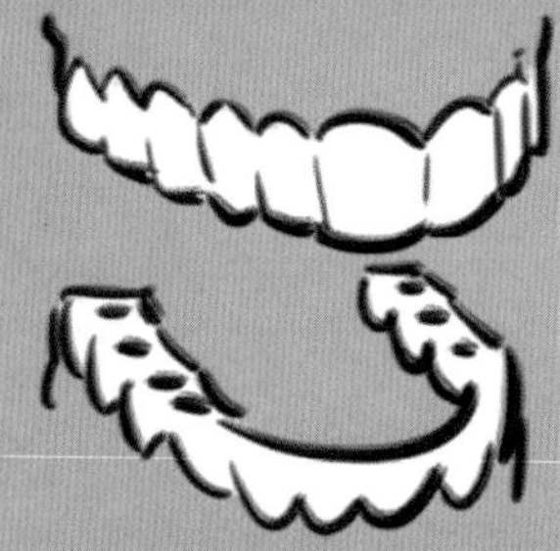

IT'S ALWAYS GOOD TO KNOW THE DIFFERENT SHAPES/VOLUMES OF TEETH.

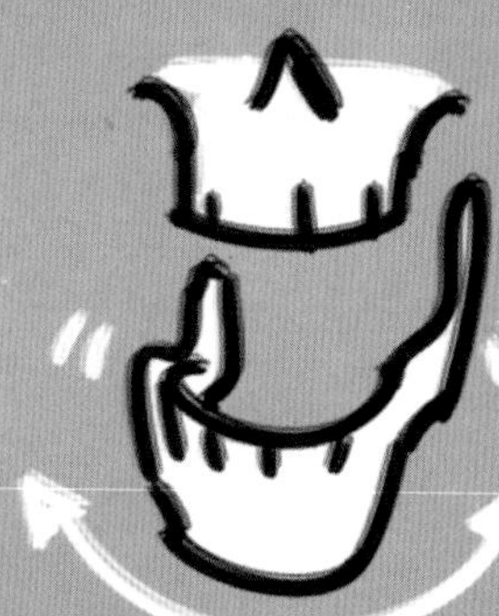

THE LOWER JAW CAN MOVE A LOT. ALWAYS THINK OF ITS POSITION.

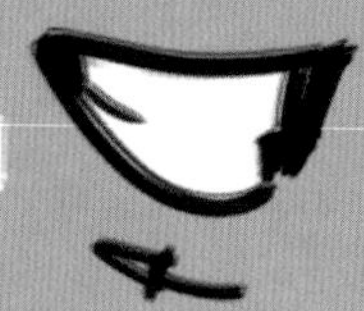
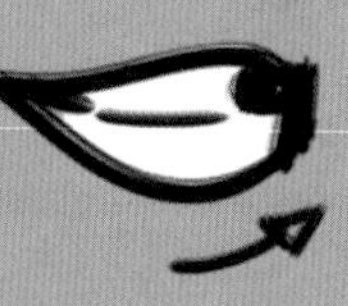

SLIGHT "IMPERFECTIONS" CAN ADD A LOT OF PERSONALITY TO A CHARACTER.

ONCE YOU KNOW THE BASICS, PLAY AROUND AND...

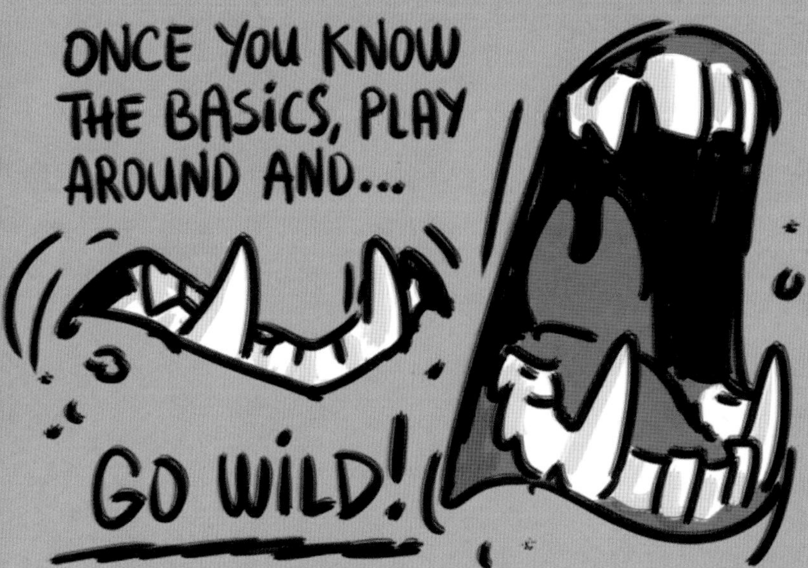

GO WILD!

Printing Guide -- Book Cover

1. CMYK color mode
2. Design it as a spread
3. Save it as a flattened file as jpg or tiff at 300 dpi, then convert it as PDF

⊛ Quick guide for soft cover perfect bound

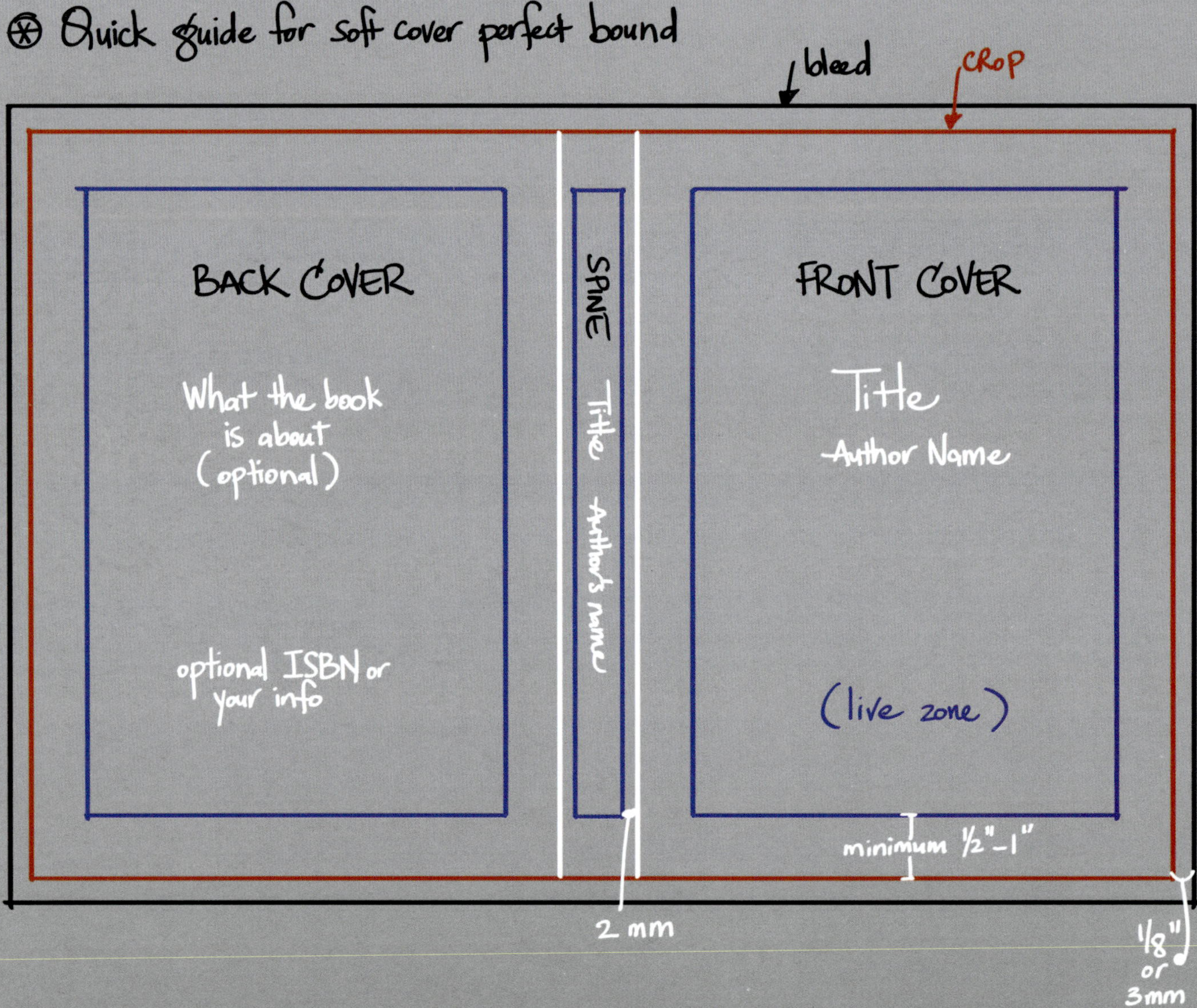

⊛ I.S.B.N -- International Standard Book Number
→ for self publishing book.

⊛ For portfolio -- include your name, website, email, phone, or social media icon.

Printing Guide -- Book (Inside pages)

① Convert your file to CMYK color mode

② Save each page as its own flattened file, as jpeg or tiff at 300 dpi

example : spread A

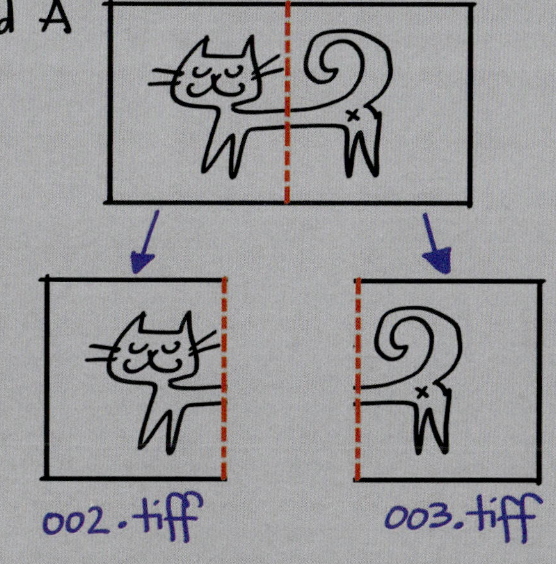

⊛ usually even # on the left & odd # on the right

⊛ number them in 2 digit for pages less than 99, or 3 digits for 100-999 pages; ...

③ Save as PDF.

Cropping GUIDE:

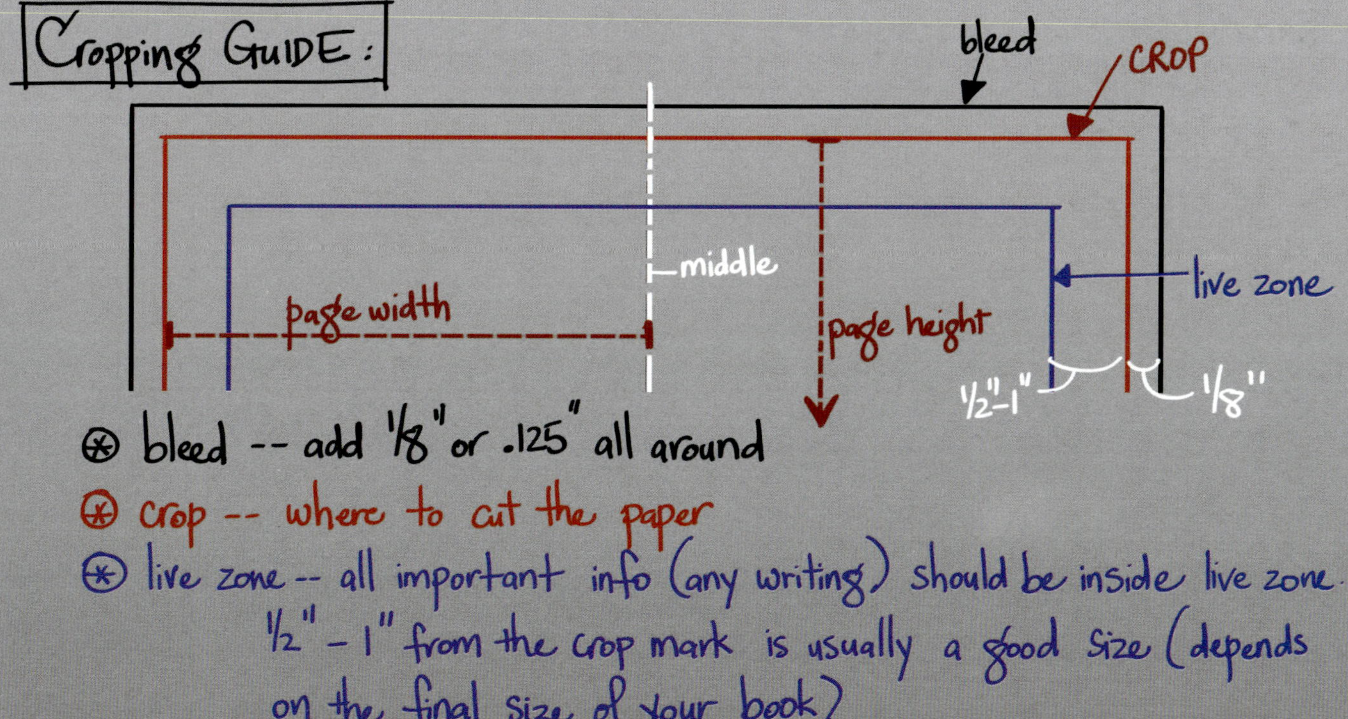

⊛ bleed -- add ⅛" or .125" all around

⊛ crop -- where to cut the paper

⊛ live zone -- all important info (any writing) should be inside live zone. ½" - 1" from the crop mark is usually a good size (depends on the final size of your book)

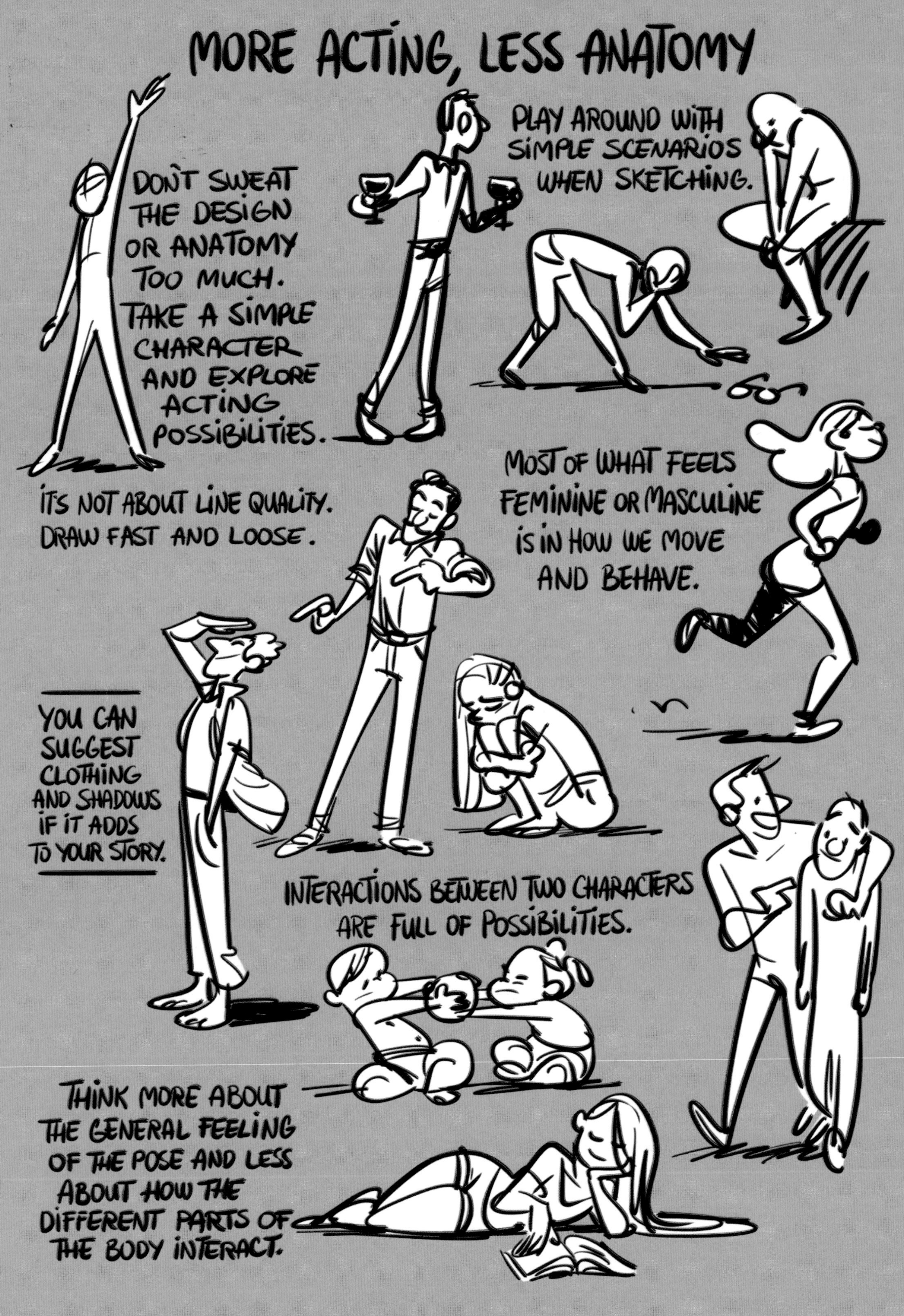
MORE ACTING, LESS ANATOMY
DON'T SWEAT THE DESIGN OR ANATOMY TOO MUCH. TAKE A SIMPLE CHARACTER AND EXPLORE ACTING POSSIBILITIES.
PLAY AROUND WITH SIMPLE SCENARIOS WHEN SKETCHING.
IT'S NOT ABOUT LINE QUALITY. DRAW FAST AND LOOSE.
MOST OF WHAT FEELS FEMININE OR MASCULINE IS IN HOW WE MOVE AND BEHAVE.
YOU CAN SUGGEST CLOTHING AND SHADOWS IF IT ADDS TO YOUR STORY.
INTERACTIONS BETWEEN TWO CHARACTERS ARE FULL OF POSSIBILITIES.
THINK MORE ABOUT THE GENERAL FEELING OF THE POSE AND LESS ABOUT HOW THE DIFFERENT PARTS OF THE BODY INTERACT.

WATCH YOUR BACK!

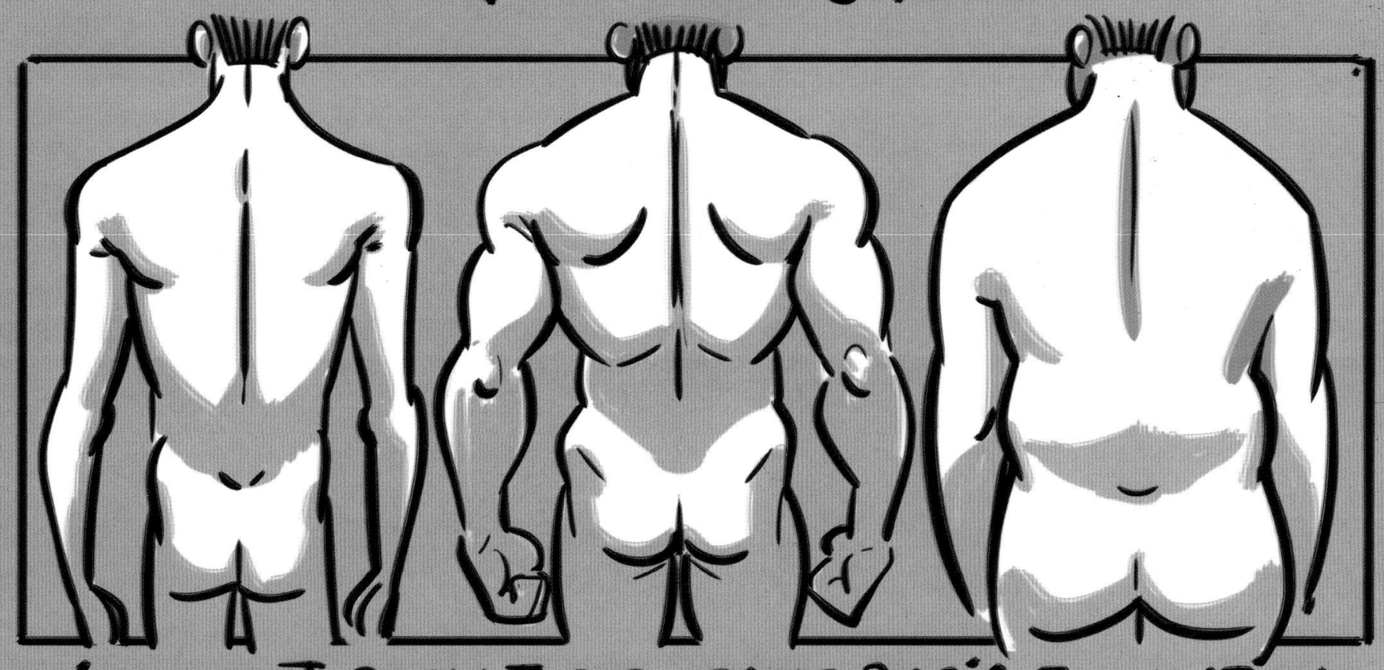

DIFFERENT BODY TYPES, SAME BASIC FOUNDATION.

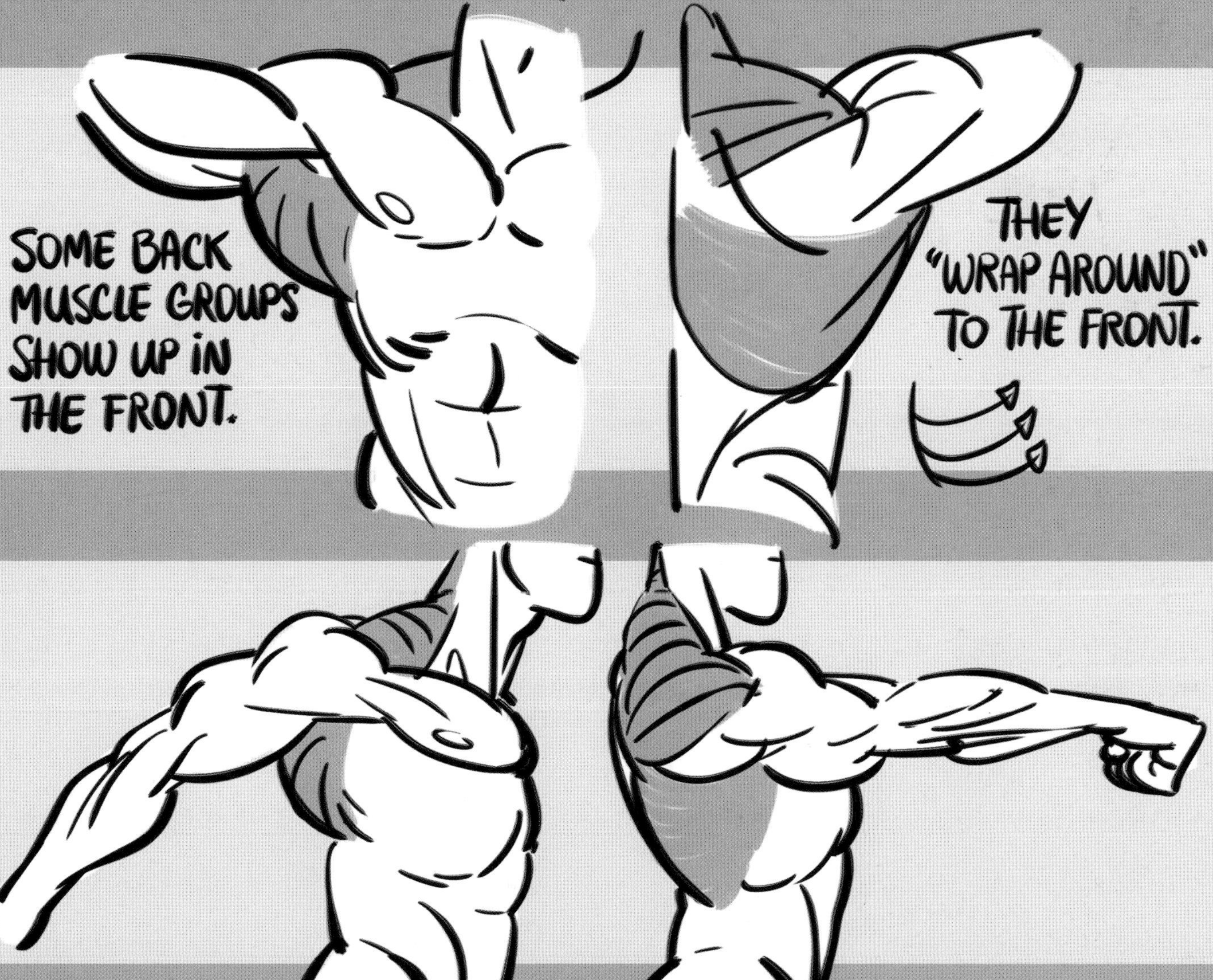

SOME BACK MUSCLE GROUPS SHOW UP IN THE FRONT.

THEY "WRAP AROUND" TO THE FRONT.

PORTFOLIO 101

① Know what you want in your finished book

decide on the # of pages

② Only put your BEST pieces in your book

BEST piece -- 1st page
2nd BEST -- LAST page
3rd BEST -- Middle

③ RHYTHM

make sure it tells a story

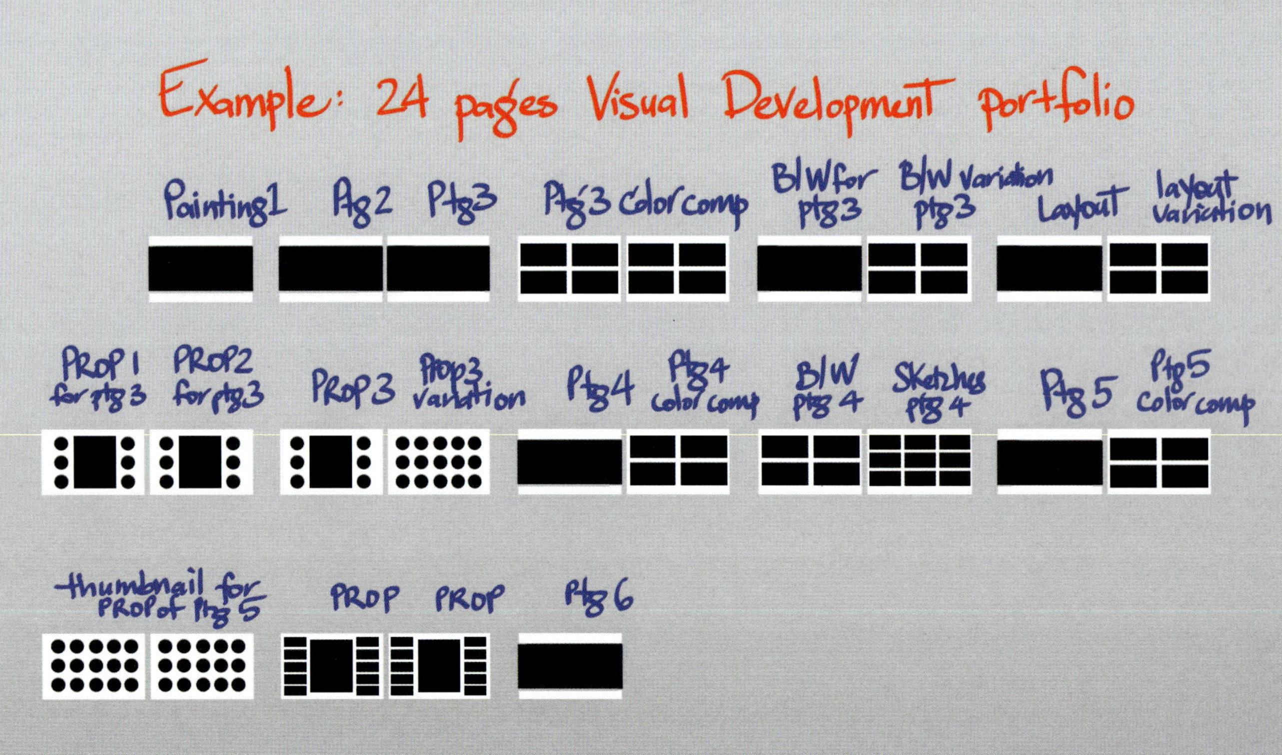